CULTURES OF COMMEMORATION
War Memorials, Ancient and Modern

PROCEEDINGS OF THE BRITISH ACADEMY · 160

CULTURES OF COMMEMORATION

War Memorials, Ancient and Modern

Edited by
POLLY LOW, GRAHAM OLIVER
& P. J. RHODES

Published for THE BRITISH ACADEMY

by OXFORD UNIVERSITY PRESS

Oxford University Press, Great Clarendon Street, Oxford OX2 6DP

Oxford New York
Auckland Cape Town Dar es Salaam Hong Kong Karachi
Kuala Lumpur Madrid Melbourne Mexico City Nairobi
New Delhi Shanghai Taipei Toronto

With offices in
Argentina Austria Brazil Chile Czech Republic France Greece
Guatemala Hungary Italy Japan Poland Portugal Singapore
South Korea Switzerland Thailand Turkey Ukraine Vietnam

Published in the United States
by Oxford University Press Inc., New York

© The British Academy 2012

Database right The British Academy (maker)

First published 2012

British Library Cataloguing in Publication Data
Data available

Library of Congress Cataloging in Publication Data
Data available

Typeset by New Leaf Design, Scarborough, North Yorkshire
Printed in Great Britain
on acid-free paper by
TJ International Ltd, Padstow, Cornwall

ISBN 978-0-19-726466-9
ISSN 0068-1202

Contents

Illustrations

Notes on Contributors

AVNER BEN-AMOS is Professor in the Jaime and Joan Constantiner School of Education, Tel Aviv University. His research interests include the history of education; late modern France and Israel; the formation of collective memory through rituals, monuments, and museums; and the teaching of history as a means to shape national identity. He is the author of *Funerals, Politics, and Memory in Modern France, 1789–1996* (2000).

ANGELOS CHANIOTIS is Professor of Ancient History and Classics in the School of Historical Studies, Institute for Advanced Study, Princeton. He is an expert in the social, cultural, religious, legal, and economic history of the Hellenistic world and the Roman East. The author of many books and articles (including *War in the Hellenistic World* [2005]), he works on a wide variety of topics: war, memory, identity, emotions, the communicative aspects of rituals, and strategies of persuasion in the ancient world.

ALISON COOLEY is a Reader in the Department of Classics and Ancient History at the University of Warwick. Her research focuses on Roman Italy and the early Principate in particular, and on the use of inscriptions in both ancient and modern times. She has published widely on Pompeii and Latin epigraphy, including a commentary on the *Res Gestae* (2009). Her next book is *The Cambridge Handbook to Latin Epigraphy* (2012).

STEFAN GOEBEL is Senior Lecturer in Modern British History at the University of Kent at Canterbury. His research focuses on the experience and memory of the two world wars and on urban history. His publications include *The Great War and Medieval Memory: War, Remembrance and Medievalism in Britain and Germany, 1914–1940* (2007) and, as co-editor, *Cities into Battlefields: Metropolitan Scenarios, Experiences and Commemorations of Total War* (2011). He is currently working on a comparative study of Coventry and Dresden in the aftermath of the Second World War.

POLLY LOW is Senior Lecturer in Ancient History at the University of Manchester. She has particular interests in interstate politics, imperialism, and the history of burial and commemoration within and beyond Athens. She is the author of *Interstate Relations in Classical Greece: Morality and Power* (2007).

GRAHAM OLIVER is Senior Lecturer in Ancient Greek Culture at the University of Liverpool. His research focuses on ancient Greek history, and in particular on political, economic, and social history, and on the classical tradition. He is the author of *War, Food and Politics in Early Hellenistic Athens* (2007) and is currently preparing a new *Handbook of Greek Epigraphy* for Cambridge University Press.

P. J. RHODES is Emeritus Professor in the Department of Classics and Ancient History at Durham University, and is a Fellow of the British Academy. He is a specialist in Greek history, with a particular interest in politics and political institutions. His most recent book is *Alcibiades* (2011).

LAWRENCE A. TRITLE is Professor of History at Loyola Marymount University, Los Angeles, California, and has taught at Loyola University Chicago and UCLA as visiting professor of history. A Vietnam combat veteran, he received his Ph.D. in history from the University of Chicago (1978) and is the author, editor, and co-editor of nine books on Greek history. His *New History of the Peloponnesian War* was published in 2009.

Abbreviations

Agora 17	*The Athenian Agora*, vol. 17: *Inscriptions: The Funerary Monuments.* Edited by D. W. Bradeen. Princeton: American School of Classical Studies at Athens. 1974.
CIL III	*Corpus Inscriptionum Latinarum*, vol. 3: *Inscriptiones Asiae, provinciarum Europae Graecarum, Illyrici Latinae.* Edited by T. Mommsen. Berlin: G. Reimer. 1873.
CIL V	*Corpus Inscriptionum Latinarum*, vol. 5: *Inscriptiones Galliae Cisalpinae Latinae.* Edited by T. Mommsen. 2 vols. Berlin: G. Reimer. 1872–77.
CIL VIII	*Corpus Inscriptionum Latinarum*, vol. 8: *Inscriptiones Africae Latinae.* Edited by T. Mommsen with G. Wilmanns. Berlin: G. Reimer. 1881.
CIL X	*Corpus Inscriptionum Latinarum*, vol. 10: *Inscriptiones Bruttiorum, Lucaniae, Campaniae, Siciliae, Sardiniae Latinae.* Edited by T. Mommsen. Berlin: G. Reimer. 1883.
CIL XI	*Corpus Inscriptionum Latinarum*, vol. 11: *Inscriptiones Aemiliae, Etruriae, Umbriae Latinae.* Edited by E. Bormann. 2 vols. Berlin: G. Reimer. 1888–1926.
F. Delphes III	*Fouilles de Delphes*, vol. 3: *Epigraphie.* Edited by E. Bourguet, G. Colin, G. Daux, et al. 6 vols. Paris: de Boccard. 1909–85
I. Metropolis	*Die Inschriften von Metropolis.* Edited by B. Dreyer and H. Engelmann. Bonn: Habelt. 2003–.
I. Milet	*Milet*, vol. 6: *Inschriften von Milet.* Edited by P. Hermann. Berlin: de Gruyter. 3 vols. 1997–2006.
I. Oropos	*Hoi epigraphies tou Oropou.* Edited by V. Petrakos. Athens: Archaiologike Hetaireia. 1997.
I. Priene	*Inschriften von Priene.* Edited by F. Hiller de Gaertringen. Berlin: G. Reimer. 1906.
IG i³	*Inscriptiones Graecae*, vol. 1, 3rd edn: *Inscriptiones Atticae Euclidis anno anteriores.* Edited by D. Lewis, with L. Jeffery and E. Erxleben. Berlin: de Gruyter. 3 vols. 1981–88.
IG ii²	*Inscriptiones Graecae*, vol. 2, 2nd edn: *Inscriptiones Atticae Euclidis anno posteriores.* Edited by J. Kirchner. 4 vols. Berlin: G. Reimer. 1913–40.

IG vii	*Inscriptiones Graecae*, vol. 7: *Inscriptiones Megaridis et Boeotiae*. Edited by W. Dittenberger. Berlin: G. Reimer. 1892.
IG ix.2	*Inscriptiones Graecae*, vol. 9, fasc. 2: *Inscriptiones Deli liberae*. Edited by F. Dürrbach. Berlin: G. Reimer. 1912.
IG xii.5	*Inscriptiones Graecae*, vol. 12, fasc. 5: *Inscriptiones Cycladum*. Edited by F. Hiller de Gaertringen. 2 vols. Berlin: G. Reimer. 1903–09.
IG xii.6	*Inscriptiones Graecae*, vol. 12, fasc. 6: *Inscriptiones Chii et Sami cum Corassiis Icariaque*. Part I. Edited by K. Hallof. Berlin: W. de Gruyter 2000. Part II. Edited by K. Hallof and A. P. Matthaiou. Berlin: W. de Gruyter 2003.
IGR	*Inscriptiones Graecae ad res Romanas pertinentes*. Edited by R. Cagnat. 3 vols. Paris: Leroux. 1906–27.
ILS	*Inscriptiones Latinae Selectae*. Edited by H. Dessau. 5 vols. Berlin: Weidmann. 1892–1916.
RIB I	*The Roman Inscriptions of Britain*, vol. 1: *Inscriptions on Stone*. Edited by R. G. Collingwood and R. P. Wright. Oxford: Clarendon Press. 1965.
SEG	*Supplementum Epigraphicum Graecum*.
Syll.[3]	*Sylloge Inscriptionum Graecarum*. Edited by W. Dittenberger. 3rd edn. 4 vols. Leipzig: Hirzel. 1915–24.

Preface

Our intention has been to study commemorative monuments for those killed in war, both in the classical past and in more recent times in parts of the world influenced by the classical tradition. We held a one-day symposium on the subject at the British Academy on 16 July 2004, and we now present in this volume revised versions of most of the papers read at that meeting (but, unfortunately, we were unable to obtain versions for publication of two of the papers read at the meeting).

This enterprise was originally planned by Polly Low and Graham Oliver, and I must begin by thanking them for inviting me to join them in it. We thank the British Academy for providing generous hospitality for the symposium (where we were helped particularly by Angela Pusey and Joanne Blore), and for agreeing to publish this volume and waiting patiently for it; and we thank all those who contributed to the symposium, by reading papers and by joining in discussion, and particularly those whose papers are published here. Polly Low and I thank Graham Oliver for putting the material together.

P. J. R.

Note

The contributions to this volume were substantially completed in early 2009, and reflect the state of scholarship at that point, although we have attempted to note any major subsequent developments, where relevant. We apologize (and should be held responsible) for any bibliographic omissions that might have resulted from the delayed appearance of this volume. PAL/GJO.

1

Comparing Cultures of Commemoration in Ancient and Modern Societies

POLLY LOW & GRAHAM OLIVER

SOME YEARS BEFORE this chapter was written, Trafalgar Square in central London was populated briefly by 300 'tombstones' each bearing the text, written in red capital letters, 'One person every minute killed by arms', the final three words larger than the previous two lines of text. The image was a striking one but all the more so because photographed among the tombstones was Doug Woollford.[1] His presence made the picture particularly publishable because Woollford wore the scarlet uniform, dressed with medals, of the Chelsea pensioner. It is difficult to assess just how successful this publicity event was for its organizers (Amnesty International and Oxfam).[2] Certainly the image that was manufactured that day in 2003 was a memorable one—for at least one person. But Trafalgar Square today reveals nothing to recall the event. This *lieu de mémoire*, or site of memory, will bear little trace of those temporary 'tombstones' in the future. But their image lives on, and the archivist will have the chance to dig up evidence of that day. But who will remember that day? How likely is it that the British public will be able to recall this event? Direct participants, the visitors who experienced the tombstones, may have a better chance of remembering. The former serviceman and protagonist of the photograph, who died at the end of 2008, may have found that the temporary tombstones and their message evoked personal memories. For many other viewers, however, the 'monuments' were not likely to have evoked personal memories of their own experiences of participation in war. In

---

[1] Photographer: Richard Pohle. The associated news story can be found at the time of writing at www.timesonline.co.uk/tol/news/uk/article1168149.ece (accessed 26 September 2011).
[2] The campaign's aim was to reduce the international trade of small arms. The campaign claims the support of more than 1 million people worldwide since its launch in 2003 (www.amnesty.org/en/campaigns/control-arms). D. Hillier and B. Wood, 'Shattered Lives: The Case for Tough International Arms Control', www.amnesty.org/en/library/info/ACT30/003/2003 (accessed 26 September 2011).

Proceedings of the British Academy, **160**, 1–11. © The British Academy 2012.

Britain, the living combatants who survived the First World War are now counted on the fingers of one hand. This is not true of the Second World War, but inevitably there will be a gradual reduction of this demographic cohort too. Many people will nevertheless be able to recall their own experiences of *acts of commemoration* either for the war dead or for other reasons when they reflect on the image of the tombstones and the photograph of the Chelsea pensioner standing among these 'monuments'. For commemoration is something that individuals share in and develop an awareness of. Although the experience of commemorative culture might be more acute if personal memories are evoked it is likely that all can engage at some level in most forms of commemoration.

The description of the event in London in 2003 introduces the theme to which this book is devoted: cultures of commemoration. For commemoration is crafted. There is an intentionality, or there are intentionalities, about acts of commemoration that are undeniable.[3] But unpacking the intent of commemorative acts or rituals, monuments, and spaces can be difficult. Can we identify the functions of commemoration? Can we assess whether commemoration served a need for the active participants or observers? Can we assess the impact of commemoration on its spectators or the audience? Do forms of commemoration take on their own lives: are monuments appropriated in ways not intended by those who conceived them? How do people develop rituals that perform their own acts of commemoration? The Trafalgar Square publicity event exploited public awareness of British commemorative cultures: the elements such as the choice of the location, the tombstones, and the presence of the Chelsea pensioner—a lucky coincidence for the photographer or part of a planned staging?—staged the commemorative event. Images and ideas can be transformed: the present produces new forms of viewing the past.

To interpret the Trafalgar Square scene we might need to remove the Chelsea pensioner from the frame temporarily. The organizers would have hoped that the choice of tombstones with their uniformity of design and text would remind us of those all-too-familiar slabs of inscribed Portland stone that appear in the cemeteries of the Commonwealth War Graves Commission (CWGC) commemorating the dead of the wars of the twentieth century. The tombstones representing the dead reinforced the association between firearms and death. Would the campaign have worked as well elsewhere? Its emotional impact might have been reduced. For the

---

[3] See now Gehrke's (2010) contribution to the publication of a conference exploring the presentation of the ancient Greek past, *Intentional History*.

image in Trafalgar Square that day depended on shared cultural under-standings that the 'tombstones' and their message would evoke. Although someone who had never seen a cemetery controlled by the CWGC would not have been oblivious to the obvious message, the impact would have been all the more significant for those who had visited such sites or were aware of their existence. The cemeteries for the twentieth-century war dead of other nations who participated in the world wars may differ from those operated by the Commonwealth War Graves Commission, but the sight of repeated ranks of tombstones was likely to have evoked compari-son with war cemeteries operated by other nations. We cannot determine how individuals would have reacted to the scene in Trafalgar Square but the event would have exploited what Hynes describes as our 'collective, *vicarious* memory'.[4] These memories might have tapped into our under-standing of images of war, but they would also have evoked if not memories of commemoration then at least ideas about commemorative culture.[5]

Cultures of commemoration can be formed in many ways, not all of them originating from a central authority. But it is a centralizing power that can often have the most considerable impact on such cultures. The presence in the public conscience today of the war cemetery is likely to be a prominent one. Many British schools offer trips for classes of teenagers to northern France and Belgium often as part of a history programme. Cinema exploits the experience of the visit to the battlefield cemetery. Perhaps one of the most successful films in recent years to have used this idea is *Saving Private Ryan* (1998, directed by Steven Spielberg). The film begins and closes with the return to Normandy of the eponymous American soldier. He owes his life to a group of soldiers who were given the dangerous mission to find and escort back from the combat zone the sole survivor of four brothers. The tombstone in the American cemetery belongs to the officer, Captain John H. Miller, who had led the recovery mission that saved Private Ryan. The telling of stories based on the monu-ments set up for the war dead provides the inspiration for Claude Duneton's *Le monument*, a novel that is based on the real war dead who are com-memorated in the Limousin village of Lagleygeolle. With the exception of the school trip, it would be hard to prove that the state has directly gener-ated the evocation of these commemorative cultures. However, there can

---

[4] Hynes 1999, 207.
[5] Winter 1995, p. v gathers some of the possible shapers of such ideas in the phrase 'Cultural codes and languages of mourning'.

be no doubt that the state has played its part in creating the context in which those cultures have developed.

'Choreographers of Commemoration'[6]

The commemoration of past wars and of their participants is now matched by the industrious attempts to invest in the memories of the dead, whether they be civilian or soldier, victims of civil war, genocide, or other conflicts. Commemoration of the dead is a familiar feature of contemporary societies worldwide. New memorials appear regularly. In San Salvador a monument lists the names of civilian victims murdered or 'disappeared' during the troubles in 1970 and 1980 and the civil war of 1981–82. For the families of the 25,000 dead civilians listed there is now a way of mourning their loss, but the monument does not pay homage to the soldiers and guerillas whose casualties amounted to a similar figure.[7] For those Salvadorans whose relatives' bodies were never recovered, the new monument may provide a focus for the act of mourning. But while such monuments certainly do act as a means for people to express their emotions, their very erection, their design, their conception rarely lack other forms of political purpose or symbolic message and meaning.[8] Emotion and politics go hand in hand, and commemoration can channel both: 'the past remains steadfastly alive for the political work of the present'.[9] But the idea that political agencies can shape the past in the present should not mislead us into thinking that the political has the exclusive capacity to shape commemorative culture. The important essay by Winter and Sivan on the ideas and theories lying behind the recent history of remembrance emphasizes that even in extreme forms of author-itarian government 'state agency does not control individual or group memory completely'.[10] This must be true: an individual's awareness of commemorative culture will be shaped by many factors not all of which need be the same for all people.[11]

In the last thirty years the academic study of memory, remembrance, and commemoration in history has flourished.[12] The discourse has moved

[6] The phrase is that of Winter and Sivan 1999, 38.
[7] *Le Monde*, 27 May 2004, 5.
[8] King 1998.
[9] Eng and Kazanjian 2003, 5.
[10] Winter and Sivan 1999, 29.
[11] See now Winter 2006, ch. 6 on social agency.
[12] Winter's (2006) 'memory boom'.

a considerable way from the rather restrictive view of collective memory that Halbwachs formulated in *Les cadres sociaux de la mémoire*, published in the early 1920s. This book argued that collective memory shaped the memories of individuals, and thus framed the ways in which people relate to the present.[13] Several decades later, Roger Bastide's greater emphasis on the function of individual memories in the shaping and maintenance of collective memory has influenced Winter and Sivan and, through their work, has affected this book too: 'The intermeshing of individual memories creates collective remembrance, feeds it, and maintains its continuity. It is through this remembrance that human societies develop consciousness as to their identity, as located in time.'[14]

Comparing Ancient and Modern:
Similarity, Analogy, and Difference

Time is the major concern in this comparative study of commemorative cultures. The volume owes a great deal to the important work that has been generated already by scholars such as Winter, Prost, Becker, and many others who have written about memory and remembrance. But while this volume acknowledges an enormous debt to these lively discussions, it seeks to give more stress to a feature that seems to have been neglected in the extensive work on commemorative culture. For this volume has grown out of a conference that gathered together historians of the recent past and the ancient past who shared a common interest in the production of remembrance. One of the great steps forward that Jay Winter's *Sites of Memory, Sites of Mourning* declared was to move away from the study of *mémoire* that was too tightly defined by national self-interest: 'interpretations of "modern memory" ... are rarely examined in a comparative perspective'.[15] Winter's approach in *Sites of Memory* is transnational, overtly comparative, and historically focused, being confined to the memory of the 1914–18 war. Our volume does not offer a narrowly historical focus on either the Great War or even the twentieth century. Instead it offers a comparative approach that does not confine

---

[13] Halbwachs 1925, 289: 'L'individu évoque ses souvenirs en s'aidant des cadres de la mémoire sociale. En d'autres termes les divers groups en lesquels se decompose la société sont capable a chaque instant de reconstruire leur passé.'

[14] Winter and Sivan 1999, 26.

[15] Winter 1995, 11. For a good critique of the study of remembrance in France, see S. Hazareesingh, 'Guard Dogs of Good Deeds', *Times Literary Supplement*, 21 March 2003, 12–13.

itself to the exploration of the recent past: it embraces the ancient world
in an attempt to stress the need to consider not only how remembrance in
ancient society is a useful counterpoint to modern cultures, but perhaps
more significantly to show that the distant past can be seen to have had
and indeed to have a lasting influence on commemorative practice in
modern times. The comparative approach allows the exploration of the
differences that the different societies have brought to their commemorative
practices.

This volume offers the reader an opportunity to view cultures of commemoration in a wider comparative perspective. It embraces the exploration of commemorative culture in two areas of historical study that are
often treated separately: ancient and modern history. This division may be
primarily an Anglo-Saxon phenomenon, the result in some cases of the
distance between ancient history and history in some university structures
in the United Kingdom. It is less evident in continental Europe, and
indeed, when one returns to some of the important French treatises on
memory, the ancient world often provides a starting point for thinking
about the treatment of the past over time.[16] It is perhaps not a coincidence that one of the most influential ancient historical works in this field
is a work of French scholarship: Nicole Loraux's *Invention of Athens* pioneered the study of the relationship between remembrance, collective
memory, and civic identity in fifth-century BCE Athens.[17] The treatment of
memory and 'collective remembrance' continues to flourish among historians of the Greek and Roman worlds.[18] Nevertheless, the dialogue
between ancient and modern is too often still either muted or marginal-
ized, and our aim here is to make that wider chronological perspective
central to our approach.[19] The idea that drives that aim—and therefore
lies behind this volume—is a simple one: to suggest that a sharper cross-
cultural understanding of commemoration can be achieved by stretching
the comparative approach not only across cultures but also across time.
Behind the contributions offered in this book is a shared appreciation of
the benefits of a long-term perspective.[20] The essays collected here show

[16] See, for example, Ricoeur 2000, who frequently turns to antiquity; see also Halbwachs 1925,
178–87 on collective religious memory; on the difficulties, see Le Goff 1988.
[17] Loraux 1981.
[18] For Greece, Wolpert 2002, Alcock 2002; for the Roman Empire, Gowing 2005; Flower 2006;
see now the series of conferences and associated publications, Benoist and Daguet-Gagey 2007;
2008; Benoist et al. 2009.
[19] Benoist et al. 2009 is an exception.
[20] Echoing the kind of approach seen, for example, in Ben-Amos's (2000, 380–9) comparative
survey of republican state funerals.

how the broadening of the chronological frame can allow ancient and modern historians to benefit from greater appreciation of both the material and the approaches found outside their immediate fields of expertise.

Our chapters provide a diachronic survey of commemorative practices in western culture, from fifth-century BCE Greece to the present day. Our coverage is inevitably incomplete, both geographically and chronologically, but our choice of case studies is not arbitrary. Three criteria in particular have shaped the content of the volume: we have aimed to include analyses of commemorative practice in the ancient and modern worlds where there is a rich body of material to make its interpretation more fruitful; we have taken our examples from a wide range of places, states, and political systems; but at the same time we have tried to focus on commemorative cultures that have enough in common to allow for meaningful and productive comparison.

This last criterion helps to explain a lacuna in our coverage which perhaps needs explanation: the fact that we move directly from Imperial Rome to Enlightenment France. This is a decision driven not by any belief in the unimportance of the commemorative practices of the intervening years, but rather by the fact that one of our interests is the exploration of the ways in which the commemorative habits that emerge in the ancient world are then consciously embraced and manipulated by more modern cultures. Such (re)appropriations of the ancient past become particularly apparent during and after the classical revival of the late eighteenth century, and are visible in various ways. Previous studies have concentrated on the ways in which more recent monuments have exploited (and sometimes rejected) the architectural legacy of antiquity,[21] and this theme also emerges in this volume, particularly in the essays by Ben-Amos (Chapter 5) and Goebel (Chapter 7). We are also, however, interested in other ways in which classical models are employed and reshaped in the modern world: in, for example, practices of the naming of the dead explored by Oliver (Chapter 6).

Similarities and overlaps between our case studies are not restricted to deliberate appropriations of this kind. A number of themes recur in this volume. Perhaps most obviously, the importance of the monuments themselves—their form, their location, and their relationship with their surroundings—is constantly emphasized. In both ancient and modern contexts, we see that the form of a commemorative monument is both

---

[21] Borg 1991.

driven by and productive of specific political, ideological, or cultural attitudes—in the minimalism of the Athenian monuments discussed by Low (Chapter 2), for example, or the iconography of the Trajanic victory monument analysed by Cooley (Chapter 4), or the loaded implications of a decision to turn to classicism rather than medievalism in the commemoration of the First World War, demonstrated in Goebel's study (Chapter 7).

Once created, these monuments take their place in a wider landscape, shaped both by existing monuments (a point exemplified particularly clearly in Cooley's study of the relationship between two of the Roman monuments at Adamclissi) and by the rituals that surround those monuments : it is the significance of these rituals, and the power that they have to transform the meanings of commemorative spaces, that forms a central part both of Chaniotis's analysis of Hellenistic commemorations (Chapter 3) and of Ben-Amos's study of the changing roles of the Panthéon and Arc de Triomphe in eighteenth- to twentieth-century France (Chapter 5).

Central to both of these analyses, too—and indeed to every chapter in this volume—is the question of the constituency (or, more often, constituencies) involved in both the creation and the further utilization of these commemorative monuments and rituals. As was noted above, attempts to fully comprehend processes of memory and commemoration must take account of both state and individual agency. The, often complex, interplay between individual and group, and between private and public, is visible throughout the studies included here, surfacing in a number of ways: the juxtaposition of private and public commemorative spaces argued for by Low (Chapter 2) in her account of the spatial arrangement of Athenian memorials, for example, or the private uses of collective memorials explored by both Chaniotis (Chapter 3) and Tritle (Chapter 8).

What also emerges strongly from the material discussed here, however, is the fact that the analysis of memorials and commemoration will often need to make space for a third type of agent: that is, 'subpolitical' (or sometimes extra-political) groups, who find in commemorative spaces and practices a venue for shaping their collective identity, or furthering their collective agenda. On occasion, this can be seen to be something deliberately planned for at the moment of a monument's creation: the memorials to specific, usually elite, groups even in the supposedly egalitarian context of Athenian commemoration, for example (discussed by Low, Chapter 2); or the ways in which arguments about appropriate (and inappropriate) commemorative acts become embedded in the rhetoric of the Roman civil wars (Cooley, Chapter 4); or, for a particularly rich and illuminating set of examples, the commemorative choices made by different communities in Britain and Germany in the aftermath of the First World War (Goebel, Chapter 7). But we also see how this co-option of commemoration by specific groups can be achieved through the reappropriation of existing monuments or commemorations: a particularly striking example emerges in Tritle's discussion of the ways in which the Vietnam Wall has been incorporated into rehabilitation programmes for veterans of that war, and of how that specific group's use of the monument intersects, and sometimes comes into conflict, with those pursuing other—educational or touristic—purposes (Chapter 8).

The cultures of commemoration that we explore in this volume do, therefore, share certain common themes. But an important function of comparative study is, of course, not only to highlight similarities but also to emphasize points of difference and discontinuity. In part, the various approaches and conclusions visible in this volume are conditioned by the different sorts of evidence available for the period(s) under consideration. For example, the personal, and especially emotional, aspect of commemoration—so important to Tritle's analysis of the Vietnam monument in Washington DC (Chapter 8)—is exceptionally hard to identify in our record of ancient commemoration. However, as Chaniotis in particular shows (Chapter 3), we would be making a serious mistake if we assumed that such factors did not also play a part in ancient commemoration of the war dead.

Other points of dissimilarity, however, are more real than apparent. One fundamental difference deserves special mention: namely, a marked divergence over the basic question of what sorts of events, and what sorts of people, are deemed worthy of commemoration. Hellenistic Greece, for example, was interested above all in commemorating its victories. The Romans—at some points in their history, at least—were, as Cooley demonstrates (Chapter 4), surprisingly willing to inscribe the memory of their most catastrophic defeats into their commemorative calendar. The Vietnam War offers another perspective on the commmoration of defeat (Chapter 8). The identification of these differences is of great importance, because it helps remind us of a central point. Alongside these cultures of commemoration—these records of the things that individuals, groups, and states invest monumental, religious, and emotional effort in endeavouring to remember—is an equally strong set of cultures of forgetting: of failing to record, or even deliberately suppressing, some aspects of the military past—embarrassing defeats, unheroic dead, inconvenient wars.[22] In this volume we have focused on the things that are remembered, but in doing so we hope we might also draw attention to those people and events which societies have sometimes chosen to forget.

Bibliography

Alcock, S. E. 2002. *Archaeologies of the Greek Past: Landscape, Monuments and Memories*. Cambridge: Cambridge University Press.

Ben-Amos, A. 2000. *Funerals, Politics, and Memory in Modern France 1789–1996*. Oxford: Oxford University Press.

Benoist, S. and A. Daguet-Gagey. eds. 2007. *Mémoire et histoire. Les procédures de condamnation dans l'Antiquité romaine*. Metz: Centre régional universitaire Lorrain d'Histoire site de Metz.

Benoist, S. and A. Daguet-Gagey. eds. 2008. *Un discours en images de la condamnation de mémoire*. Metz: Centre regional universitaire Lorrain d'Histoire site de Metz.

Benoist, S. and A. Daguet-Gagey. eds. 2009. *Mémoires partagées, mémoires disputés: écriture et réécriture de l'histoire*. Metz: Centre régional universitaire Lorrain d'Histoire site de Metz.

Borg, A. 1991. *War Memorials from Antiquity to the Present*. London: Leo Cooper.

Eng, D. L. and D. Kazanjian. eds. 2003. *Loss: The Politics of Mourning*. Berkeley: University of California Press.

Flower, H. 2006. *The Art of Forgetting: Disgrace and Oblivion in Roman Political Culture*. Chapel Hill, NC: The University of North Carolina Press.

Gehrke, H.-J. 2010. 'Representations of the Past in Greek Culture.' In *Intentional History: Spinning Time in Ancient Greece*, ed. L. Foxhall, H.-J. Gehrke, and N. Luraghi. Stuttgart: Franz Steiner, 15–34.

Gowing, A. M. 2005. *Empire and Memory: The Representation of the Roman Republic in Imperial Culture*. Cambridge: Cambridge University Press.

Halbwachs, M. 1925. *Les cadres sociaux de la mémoire*. Paris: Alcan.

Hynes, S. 1999. 'Personal Narratives and Commemoration.' In *War and Remembrance in the Twentieth Century*, ed. J. Winter and E. Sirvan. Cambridge: Cambridge University Press, 205–20.

King, A. 1998. *Memorials of the Great War in Britain: The Symbolism and Politics of Remembrance*. Oxford and New York: Berg.

Le Goff, J. 1988. *Histoire et mémoire*. Paris: Gallimard.

Loraux, N. 1981. *L'invention d'Athènes: histoire de l'oraison funèbre dans la cité classique*. Paris: Mouton (translated into English by A. Sheridan as *The Invention of Athens: The Funeral Oration in the Classical City*, Cambridge, MA: Harvard University Press, 1986).

Ricoeur, P. 2000. *La mémoire, l'histoire, l'oubli*. Paris: Seuil.

Schivelbusch, W. 2003. *The Culture of Defeat: On National Trauma, Mourning, and Recovery* (translated by J. Chase). London: Granta Books.

---

[22] Schivelbusch 2003.

Winter, J. M. 1995. *Sites of Memory, Sites of Mourning: The Great War in European Cultural History*. Cambridge: Cambridge University Press.

— 2006. *Remembering War: The Great War between Memory and History in the Twentieth Century*. New Haven, CT, and London: Yale University Press.

— and E. Sivan. eds. 1999. *War and Remembrance in the Twentieth Century*. Cambridge: Cambridge University Press.

Wolpert, A. 2002. *Remembering Defeat: Civil War and Civic Memory in Ancient Athens*. Cambridge: Cambridge University Press.

2

The Monuments to the War Dead in Classical Athens: Form, Contexts, Meanings

POLLY LOW

ATHENS WAS NOT THE ONLY GREEK CITY-state to place great importance on the provision of burial and commemoration for its war dead. Nor is it the only Greek city-state whose methods of burial and commemoration have been seen (by ancient and modern commentators) as being somehow emblematic of the political, social, or moral culture of the city.

Nevertheless, Athenian practice does deserve attention, both because it is the most richly attested among classical Greek examples, and because (partly as a result) it has exercised extensive influence on more recent commemorative cultures.[1] It should be emphasized, however, that the richness of evidence is only relative: much is still unclear, and one of the aims of this essay is to set out the parameters of what is known and unknown about the form and setting of the Athenian monuments to the war dead (the focus of the first and second sections), and (in the final part) about uses of and reactions to those monuments during the classical period.

A more general aim is to emphasize the complexity of the Athenian approach to the commemoration of the war dead. The ancient material, both archaeological and (especially) literary, can often encourage an interpretation that emphasizes a single, and usually state-dominated, explanation of the intention and effect of Athenian practice. I would suggest, however, that it is possible to acknowledge that simplifying imperative without feeling obliged to obey it. What I hope to do here is to look for some of the possible fluidity and instability that might underlie the commemorative practices of the classical Athenians.

---

[1] See Oliver, Chapter 6, this volume.

Proceedings of the British Academy, **160**, 13–39. © The British Academy 2012.

Form

The basic procedure by which the Athenians managed the burial and commemoration of their war dead is clear. Unlike some other Greek city-states (notably Sparta), Athens did not bury its dead immediately after, or at the site of, the battle in which they were killed. Instead, the cremated remains of the dead were brought back to Athens, where, at the end of the campaigning season, the city organized a collective burial and commemorative festival for all that year's casualties.[2]

The fullest account of these commemorative activities appears in Thucydides' narrative of the first year of the Peloponnesian War.[3] The historian describes how the dead were divided into ten groups according to their tribal affiliation,[4] a division which reflected both the political and military structures of the city.[5] (An eleventh group contained unidentified remains.) A two-day period provided an opportunity for relatives and friends to make their own offerings before the burial took place. The precise location of the burial is disputed (see further below), but it is clear that the tombs were located outside the north-west walls of the city, in an area known generally as the Kerameikos, and often referred to more specifically as the *demosion sema* (or 'public burial place').[6] The burial was followed by a speech, delivered by a notable orator (Pericles, in Thucydides' account), praising the glorious history, institutions, and characteristics of Athens and the Athenian citizens.[7]

Thucydides stops there, but other evidence shows that he has omitted some significant elements, not least the construction of a permanent

---

[2] For a survey of treatment of the war dead (in Athens and in other Greek cities), see Pritchett 1985, section II. Clairmont 1983 provides a catalogue (now slightly out of date) of all Athenian, and some non-Athenian, collective burials.

[3] Thucydides describes the funeral of 431 BCE (the end of the first year of the Peloponnesian War), but his account is clearly intended to provide a more general characterization of Athenian custom. Changes in the form of the funeral and monuments are discussed further below.

[4] *History of the Peloponnesian War* 2.34.

[5] The ten Athenian tribes were an artificial creation, intimately linked to the Cleisthenic democratic reforms, and also strongly associated with Athenian military organization: the tribe formed the basic structural unit of the Athenian hoplite forces (see Christ 2001; Graham, this volume, pp. 119–20).

[6] The term *demosion sema* is widely used in modern scholarship, although, as Patterson (2006a, 53–5 and 2006b, 27–31) points out, it is used in ancient sources only by Thucydides (at 2.34.5). Patterson suggests that the term does not refer to the public burials as a whole, but rather to the specific tomb being described by Thucydides, an explanation that would fit well with other evidence (discussed below) for the dispersed setting of the tombs.

[7] On the general characteristics of the funeral orations, see Ziolkowski 1981; on their role in inculcating Athenian democratic ideology, see especially Loraux 1986.

monument at the site of the grave.[8] These monuments can include various elements: sculpted relief, verse epigram, and, most prominently and most consistently, a list of names of the dead.[9] The lists vary in format and content, but share some common features. A main heading typically specifies the content of the list: 'these Athenians died' (Ἀθεναίον hοίδε ἀπέθανον), often with a reference to the battles or campaigns in which those losses were suffered. Lists of names follow, ordered (like the burial itself) according to the ten Athenian tribes. In other respects, however, the lists stand out for the minimal amount of information that they provide about the soldiers' lives or deaths. There are no details that might illuminate the dead man's background (the name of his father, or of his deme), still less any other personal information (details of age, individual qualities, etc.).

Considered as a whole, this method of burial and commemoration clearly represents, in many ways, the provision of an honour by the city to its war dead.[10] But it could also be see as a sort of imposition: the city takes over the burden (including, possibly not insignificantly for some Athenians, the financial burden) of burying and commemorating the dead;[11] but in doing so it also removes from the families and relatives of the dead at least some of the possibility for creating their own sites and symbols of memory and mourning.[12]

That interpretation has become a central part of the conventional picture of Athenian commemoration. Although, as has been seen, the family is allowed some place in the ceremonies surrounding the burial itself, it is there only by invitation. The focus of the ceremonies is the city of Athens: the city controls the shape of the commemoration; the city selects the orator who will provide the funeral speech; and the subject of

[8] The other striking omission from Thucydides' account is any reference to the funeral games (*Epitaphia*). For the (sparse) Classical evidence for these games, see Clairmont 1983, ch. 3; Prichett 1985, 106–24.

[9] The prominence of the lists in modern scholarship owes something to the relative richness of the surviving evidence, but this focus is not an exclusively modern phenomenon: Pausanias, *Description of Greece* 1.29.4 picks out the lists of names as the distinguishing feature of the monuments.

[10] For state burial as an honorific gesture, see Aristotle *Rhetoric* 1361a34–7, and as something particularly appropriate for the war dead, Plato *Republic* 468e–9b.

[11] On the average cost of burial in classical Athens, see Nielsen et al. 1989; Oliver 2000.

[12] Athenian citizens who died outside combat seem not to have received sculpted burial markers during the middle two quarters of the fifth century. It is unclear whether this is the result of legislation banning elaborate funerals in all cases save for the collective burial of the war dead, or whether wider (and not exclusively Athenian) social and cultural forces are responsible for the change in practice: for discussion, see Morris 1992, ch. 5; Morris 1993. On private commemoration of the war dead, see below p. 35.

that speech, in turn, concentrates not on the particular qualities of any individual—named individuals are notably absent from almost all examples of the speeches—but on the qualities of the city for which they died.[13] The shape of the monuments continues that universalizing theme. The epigrams and sculpted reliefs offer a generalized, and often idealized, depiction of conflict. This effacing of individuality is even more prominent on the casualty lists, where the identity of the dead soldier can seem to be entirely subordinated to that of the city. The absence of markers of personal status makes plausible—even persuasive—the claim that 'on these lists, fallen citizens had no status other than that of Athenians'.[14] The whole practice, in short, can come to look like a closed, self-contained system: this is commemoration of Athenians, by Athenians; it is interested in marking and sustaining a single, civic, identity and in excluding any details of status or individuality, or any other markers of affiliation to which the dead might, in other circumstances, have laid claim.

Closer examination of the monuments, however, and particularly of the casualty lists, suggests that this picture of the imposition of a uniform Athenian identity over all of the commemorated dead is at least partially misleading. Rather, the monuments acknowledge and commemorate individuals and groups both within and outside the Athenian citizen body, and also allow the dead to be distinguished by military function, social status, and possibly even ideological affiliation.

There is, first of all, clear evidence that this public burial and commemoration was not in fact restricted to Athenian citizens: both women and foreigners, as Thucydides notes (2.34.4) were able to observe and participate in various aspects of the funeral.[15] Less obvious in Thucydides' account, but demonstrable from the casualty lists, is the fact that non-Athenian casualties could be among those buried and commemorated by the city.[16]

In some instances, non-Athenian status is merely noted: outsiders can be labelled simply as χσένοι (*xenoi*, 'foreigners');[17] references elsewhere to 'barbarian archers' (τοχσόται βάρβαροι) are also likely to

---

[13] The conspicuous exception to this pattern is the funeral oration delivered by Hyperides in 322: see Ziolkowski 1981, 87–8.

[14] Loraux 1986, 23.

[15] Emphasized by Patterson 2006b, 26.

[16] There is also some literary evidence for this practice: Lysias' *Epitaphios* 66 (unusually) singles out the contribution made by (and burial given to) non-Athenians; Pausanias 1.29.7 notes with approval Athenian willingness to bury and commemorate slaves who had died for the city.

[17] *IG* i[3] 1180 (430s), 1184 (423), 1190 (*c*.411). It is possible that *xenoi* is being used here in a more technical sense, to mean 'resident alien' (or metic): see Bradeen 1969, 150.

record non-citizen contributions to Athenian military forces.[18] Other memorials provide a more specific identity to the non-Athenians they commemorate. A monument of the middle of the fifth century, for example (*IG* i³ 1150), includes among its eighty names a certain Deiodotus from the city of Keia (line 13). Allies appear in greater numbers on the casualty list for 464 (*IG* i³ 1144), which includes eight names under the heading [Βυζά]ντιο[ι] ('Byzantians': lines 119–27)), and at least two soldiers from Madytus, a city in the Chersonese (lines 34–8). Even more conspicuous recognition of an allied contribution to Athenian warfare can be seen in the monument that commemorates the Argives killed fighting alongside Athens at the battle of Tanagra in 458 (see Figure 2.1, *IG* i³ 1149; the monument is also mentioned by Pausanias, 1.29.8).[19]

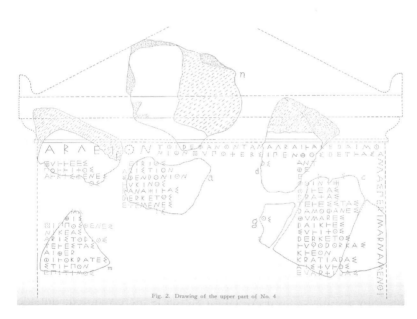

Figure 2.1   *IG* i³ 1149: list of Argive casualties from the battle of Tanagra (458). (Reconstruction from B. Merrit, 'Greek Inscriptions', *Hesperia*, 21 (1952), 354, fig. 2. Courtesy of the Trustees of the American School of Classical Studies in Athens)

---

[18] *IG* i³ 1172 (mid-fifth century), 1180 (430s), 1190 (*c.*411), 1192 (second half of the fifth century). A reference to 'barbarians' should, strictly, indicate non-Greeks, but it has been noted (Bradeen 1969, 149–50) that the names that follow these headings seem to be Greek; the label therefore possibly has a primarily military rather than ethnic connotation.

[19] Generally, on non-Athenians in the casualty lists, see Pope 1935, 75–80; Bradeen 1969, 149–51; Gauthier 1971, 60–5. Their presence is noted by Loraux 1986, 32–7, but (as pointed out by Patterson 2006b, 10) the implications of their inclusion have tended to be overlooked in subsequent studies of the public funeral.

The apparently Athenian-dominated practice of public burial and commemoration was not therefore reserved exclusively for citizens of Athens. This need not necessarily be thought of as a benign gesture. Non-Athenians are forced to conform to what is, arguably, a distinctively Athenian model of commemoration, a practice that might be seen as more imperialistic than inclusive. But a more positive reading is also possible, particularly in those cases where non-Athenians are given a more prominent position, and a more clearly defined identity than simply *xenoi*. In the Argive monument, for example, not only does the prominent label 'Of the Argives' (Ἀργε[ίον]) open the inscribed list, the document as a whole is written not in the alphabet of Athens, but that of Argos.[20] If the setting of the list seems overwhelmingly Athenian, its content is equally strikingly Argive, and the overall relationship between the two states suggested by the monument is more reciprocal than exploitative.[21]

It is similarly hard to predict exactly what effect the inclusion of foreigners in their city's casualty lists might have on Athenian viewers. In theory, the fact that so many outsiders were willing to fight alongside Athens (or that Athens was able to coerce such participation) could be seen as a sign of Athenian power and prestige. But it would also be possible for these foreign names to undermine a much more prominent theme in Athenian military and political discourse: the belief, that is, that the Athenians were self-sufficient, able to take on the rest of the world without the help of outsiders.[22]

The Athenian casualty lists do not, therefore, offer an uncomplicated picture of a military past that is an exclusively Athenian story. And similar complication of the straightforwardly 'Athenian' nature of those

---

[20] On the use of non-Attic script in Athenian public documents, see Buck 1913, who suggests (at 144) that the use of Argive script in this document implies that the Argives assumed complete responsibility for its construction. It is also possible, however, that the monument is an Athenian construction, using Argive forms as a concession to their allies (see Lalonde 1971, 192–3).

[21] For a comparable example, see *IG* i[3] 1164 (third quarter of the fifth century): a list of Lemnians which simultaneously demonstrates both the independent status of these soldiers (they receive a discrete monument, inscribed in the Ionic alphabet rather than the Attic script which would be usual on a list of this period) and their close ties to Athens (the Lemnian tribal names replicate those of the Athenian tribes, probably reflecting their origins as colonists or cleruchs of Athens: see Meiggs 1972, 424–5.)

[22] A particularly strong theme in Athenian characterizations of the Persian Wars (and notably in the reshaping of the story of the battle of Marathon to exclude the contribution made by non-Athenian contingents: see Walters 1981). That allies could make a contribution to Athenian strength is acknowledged, but the link is more often made in general terms of power and resource (see, for example, the Periclean assessment of Athenian imperial strength at Thucydides 2.13) than in terms of manpower.

included is also visible among the Athenian citizens listed. Although, as noted above, division into tribal groups is the dominant pattern of the lists, further subdivisions or even entirely different arrangements also appear, the result of which is to introduce military, socio-economic, or geographic distinctions within the supposedly egalitarian citizen group.

The most striking examples of such separation involve (probably not coincidentally) a socially and economically privileged group: the Athenian cavalry. A monument of the Peloponnesian War (probably to be dated to the 420s) lists thirty-one cavalrymen who were killed in engagements in Boiotia and northern Greece.[23] A less well-preserved monument of 395/4 (*IG* ii² 5222) seems also to have commemorated only the cavalry dead of that year's fighting.[24] It is unclear whether these monuments supplemented or complemented the 'official' lists for those years, and there is similar (and related) uncertainty as to whether they were erected by the *polis* or should be seen as pieces of independent commemoration by surviving members of the cavalry.[25] If the process of these monuments' creation remains obscure, however, their impact is more apparent: difference in life is perpetuated in death.

Other forms of separation are visible, albeit sometimes in less immediately obvious form, in other monuments too. Casualties are regularly divided according to the theatre, or even battle, in which they fell. The well-preserved list of the 440s (see Figure 2.2, *IG* i³ 1162) is a good example of such practice: those who died in northern Greece appear in one list (with headings in lines 1 and 49), casualties of 'other wars' (lines 41–2) are listed separately. A similar division has been suggested for the large monument for the fighting of 412: the (extensive) casualties of the Sicilian Expedition were listed, it is proposed, in the top half of the monument, while those from other operations were included on the lower part of each stele. In this case, the division between the two sets of casualties was emphasized by a horizontal dividing line (and, presumably less

---

[23] For the list, see Parlama and Stampolidis 2000, 396–9 (= *SEG* XLVIII 83).

[24] The monument is not fully preserved (only the upper frieze survives), but the heading reads: 'these cavalry died ...' (οἵδε ἱππέης ἀπέθανον). The likelihood that this monument commemorated only cavalry is increased by the existence of another monument for the same year (*IG* ii² 5221), which, although also incomplete, seems to have recorded a much larger number of casualties, from all ten tribes (for a reconstruction of this monument, see Brückner 1910, 244, fig. 6).

[25] The use of Ionic lettering in (part) of the fifth-century list might suggest that it was a private rather than state-produced text, but is not definitive proof (especially since Attic script appears elsewhere in the list). The findspots are similarly inconclusive: the fourth-century list was found close to several fragments of lists that are definitely 'public' (see further below); the fifth-century list was discovered near Kolonos, an area with strong connections to the cavalry, but in a secondary context (on the findspot and its implications, see Parlama and Stampolidis 2000, 397–8).

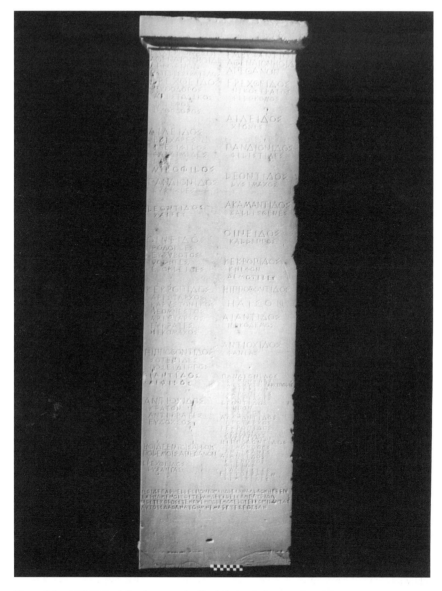

Figure 2.2 *IG* i³ 1162: Athenian casualty list (440s). (Athens, Epigraphic Museum. EM 10618)

intentionally, by the fact that the two sections were carved by different stone-cutters, each using rather different forms of the Attic alphabet).[26] It is possible that the unit in which a soldier (or sailor) had served would also be reflected in the lists: it has been argued that some of the names on *IG* i[3] 1190 (a list of the 410s) are those of sailors, arranged according to the crews in which they fought and died.[27] It has been suggested, too, that clusters of alphabetically ordered names within tribal listings on other monuments might also reflect the existence of smaller groups within the tribal structure (perhaps based on the demes, or on age classes).[28]

Such divisions and distinctions may well be entirely pragmatic in origin, reflecting simply the methods by which lists were assembled, and the practical problems of combining casualties from widespread locations in a single annual monument.[29] But it seems unlikely to be a coincidence that the list that shows some of the most diverse labelling of the dead comes from a period when Athenian citizen solidarity was just recovering from a dramatic collapse: the oligarchic revolution (and counter-revolution) of 411. This list, of around 409 (*IG* i[3] 1191), does follow the conventional division into tribes, but some of these dead (all from one tribe) are labelled explicitly as 'hoplites' (line 60). This is perhaps intended to distinguish them from the large number of naval casualties on the list: at least seventeen trierarchs appear on the monument (see Figure 2.3), and it therefore seems likely that many of the other casualties also served in the navy. But to make such a distinction, in the aftermath of a civil war in which divisions between naval and hoplite forces were a dominant theme, must be a loaded move.[30] The list also includes the unusual label ἄρχον τῶ ναυτικῶ ('leader of the fleet'; lines 105–10), which seems to be an ad hoc military rank, invented to cope with the duplications in command that resulted from the reunification of Athenian forces after the revolution: these

---

[26] On the letter forms of the inscription, see Tsirigoti-Drakotou 2000, 94–8. The dividing line appears after line 32. On the date and overall form of the monument, see below, pp. 25–6.

[27] Suggested by Clairmont 1983, 196. Trierarchs (ship commanders) appear at lines 3 and 42: if all the names from lines 4 to 41 served on a single ship, this would represent a casualty rate of slightly less than 25 per cent of the crew—a high, but not impossible, figure (on casualties in triremes, see Strauss 2000a; generally on Athenian treatment of naval dead, Strauss 2000b).

[28] Smith 1919, 358.

[29] For example, the cramped layout of the second set of casualties in *IG* i[3] 1162 implies that details of their death reached Athens only at a late stage in the year, when the size of monument required had already been fixed. Conversely, the extensive blank spaces on *IG* i[3] 1191 might suggest that fewer names were reported than had originally been anticipated (Clairmont 1983, 194).

[30] On the date and format of the list, see Bradeen 1964, 43–55. The fact that the hoplite label is adopted by only one tribe implies that individual units had some flexibility in the form in which they arranged for their dead to be listed.

Figure 2.3   Fragment of *IG* i³ 1191 (c.409) listing several trierarchs among the casualties. (Agora I 1659a. Photograph courtesy of American School of Classical Studies at Athens: Agora Excavations)

commanders were those who had led the democratic forces based on Samos, and who had retained their commands even after the end of the war.[31] This list as a whole might seem, therefore, to demonstrate renewed Athenian unity after the political upheavals of the previous years—its heading reassuringly reads, as usual, 'these Athenians died …' ([hοίδε] Ἀθ[εν]αῖ|[οι ἀπ]έ[θανον …)—but its contents indicate that the practical and ideological splits created by the civil war lingered on.

[31] Bradeen 1964, 49–50.

The fact that the Athenians did not make more of an effort, here or elsewhere, to remove such anomalies, or to impose the sort of absolute uniformity visible on other (particularly more recent) forms of war memorial might suggest that absolute egalitarianism in death was not, in fact, as central to the Athenian practice of commemoration as has sometimes been alleged. It is not, it turns out, strictly true that the only identity available to those listed here is that of Athenian citizen. Athenian citizenship is not a prerequisite for inclusion on these lists; nor is it the only factor that determines their appearance and arrangement. Difference and distinction may not leap out from these lists, but are there for those who choose to look closely at them.

Contexts

But were these lists ever subjected to such close scrutiny by their classical audiences? It is not easy to offer a direct answer to this question. The indirect answer requires a slight shift of methodological focus: a move away from thinking about the monuments as war memorials, part of the diachronic history of the commemoration of war, and towards placing them in the context of the classical Athenian epigraphic and monumental landscape. How accessible were these memorials, in terms of legibility and location? How prominent a position did they occupy in the landscape of the city? And how, if at all, did contemporary Athenians interact with the monuments, as sites either of collective memory or private mourning?

Reconstructing a context for the monuments to the war dead is not an entirely straightforward task. The fullest description of the layout of this part of the city comes from the second-century CE travel guide of Pausanias. It is from Pausanias, above all, that the picture emerges of the public burials located in a distinctive area of the city, an area in which the individual monuments combined to form 'a monumental military history of Athens'.[32] Pausanias introduces this section of his guide by saying that he is about to describe 'a *mnema* for all the Athenians whose fate it has been to fall in battle, whether at sea or on land, except such of them as fought at Marathon' (ἔστι δὲ καὶ πᾶσι μνῆμα Ἀθηναίοις ὁπόσοις ἀποθανεῖν συνέπεσεν ἔν τε ναυμαχίαις καὶ ἐν μάχαις πεζαῖς πλὴν ὅσοι Μαραθῶνι αὐτῶν ἠγωνίσαντο) (1.29.4). The Loeb edition translates *mnema* as 'a monument'; other readers too have been inclined to take Pausanias'

---

[32] Curtius 1891, 120.

Polly Low

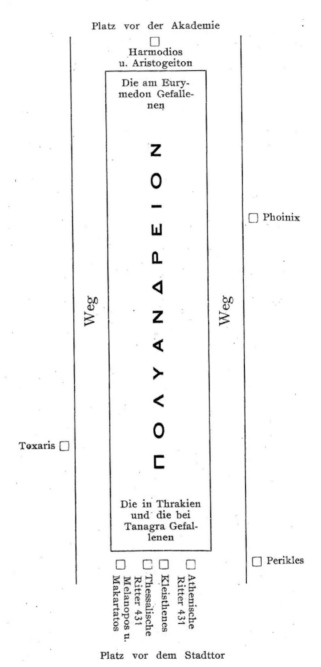

Figure 2.4 Hypothetical reconstruction of the 'demosion sema'. (A. Brückner, 'Kerameikos-Studien.' *Mitteilungen des Deutschen Archäologischen Instituts, Athenische Abteilung* 35 [1910] 188)

singular here quite literally, and to imagine this area as being basically a unified, single monument. The plan of the area drawn up by Brückner at the start of the twentieth century is perhaps the most extreme example of this interpretation (see Figure 2.4).[33] Vestiges of his model persist in more recent works: according to Nicole Loraux, 'only one thing is sure: the *demosion sema* comprised continuous rows of tombs forming a unity'.[34]

There is, however, a danger of placing too much weight on the Pausanian interpretation of the area of the public burials. Even if Pausanias gives an accurate description of the appearance of this area at the time of his visit,[35] it would certainly be unsafe to assume that he reports absolutely everything that he sees, or that it is possible to use his description to recreate with total certainty the area through which he walks.[36] It is also clear that both the monuments themselves and the area in which they stood underwent considerable changes between the fifth century BCE and the second century CE. Demosthenes is alleged to have destroyed public tombs in his efforts to increase Athens' defences against Philip II in the 330s;[37] and the area was heavily damaged in attacks on the city by Philip V of Macedon (200 BCE) and Sulla (86 BCE).[38] In addition, silt deposits caused by regular flooding entirely obscured some monuments and resulted in the narrowing of one of the major roads through the area.[39]

Classical literary sources offer strikingly little information about the appearance of the area and its monuments, but epigraphic material is more useful. The physical remains of the lists, although they are usually fragmentary and incomplete, can be used to reconstruct the (diverse) appearance of some of the monuments. At one end of the spectrum is the fairly small, self-contained version, such as the list of the 440s (Figure 2.2, *IG* i[3] 1162): this (complete) stele is 168cm high and less than half a metre wide, contains fifty-nine names arranged in two columns, and includes a

[33] Brückner 1910, 188.

[34] Loraux 1986, 351, n. 39.

[35] Pritchett 1998, 38–60 offers a strong defence of Pausanias' accuracy.

[36] The point can be demonstrated by comparing pre-excavation plans of the Athenian Agora, drawn up from Pausanias' account, with later versions based on the results of excavation. In the former, most of the right buildings are shown, but not necessarily in the right order: see, for example, Curtius 1868, plate 4.

[37] Aeschines 3.236: Aeschines' allegations may be exaggerated, but are not implausible. Lycurgus (1.43) also refers to destruction of tombs in this period, and extensive rebuilding of the city walls in this area is also attested, see Tsirigoti-Drakotou 2000, 87–92.

[38] Livy 31.24 and Plutarch *Sulla* 14.3 respectively. For other relevant literary testimonials, see Pritchett 1998, 11–25.

[39] Stroszeck 2003, 76. Further changes in the topography of the area from the classical to Roman periods are briefly discussed by Siewert 1999.

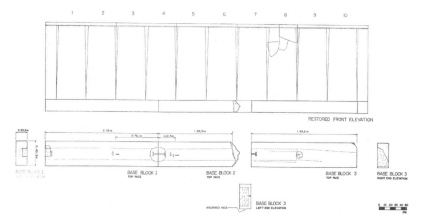

RESTORED FRONT ELEVATION

BASE BLOCK 1
TOP FACE

BASE BLOCK 2
TOP FACE

BASE BLOCK 3
TOP FACE

BASE BLOCK 3
RIGHT END ELEVATION

BASE BLOCK 3
LEFT END ELEVATION

Figure 2.5 *IG* i³ 1163: Athenian epigrams and casualty lists (440s or 420s). (Reconstruction from D. Bradeen 'Athenian casualty lists.' *Hesperia* 33 [1964] 26, fig. 1. Courtesy of the Trustees of the American School of Classical Studies in Athens)

four-line verse epigram. At the other extreme, another monument of uncertain date (see Figure 2.5, *IG* i³ 1163) is reconstructed as having consisted of five slabs (each approximately 1m x 1m), topped by a frieze and standing on a large base, inscribed with an epigram; the total monument would have had space for around 850 names.[40] Further variations are also possible. *IG* i³ 1147, for example (Figure 2.6, probably to be dated to the 450s), is a single slab, which seems to have been free standing. However, since it contains the names of only one tribe, it seems likely that it stood near to nine other similar lists, creating an overall monument that must have been on a similar scale to, but quite different in appearance from, *IG* i³ 1163.[41] Although, therefore, the corpus of these monuments is far from complete,[42] it is possible to see how much variation there is within it: the differences perceived in the detailed presentation of content are carried through into overall appearance. In contrast to (for example) modern British military gravestones (or even, in fact, classical Spartan military gravestones), there is little sign of a 'house style' for these Athenian monuments.

[40] The reconstruction is proposed by Bradeen 1964, 23–9. Tsirigoti-Drakotou (2000, 99–111) suggests that the recently discovered late fifth-century casualty list formed part of the same monument. Bradeen proposed a date in the 440s for the list, but Tsirigoti-Drakotou suggests that the monument is the one seen by Pausanias (1.29.11), recording the casualties of 412, from Sicily, Euboea, Chios, and Asia.

[41] *IG* i³ 1147bis has been identified as a second stele from the same monument, and associated (tentatively) with the tribe Aegeis (Koumanoudis 1984, 197).

[42] Approximately fifty casualty lists survive (the fragmentary state of most remains makes it hard to reach a definitive figure). Lewis 2000–03 provides a good survey of the current state of (and gaps in) knowledge of this material.

Figure 2.6   *IG* i³ 1147: casualty list of the tribe Erechtheis (450s). (Musée du Louvre MA863; © RMN / Hervé Lewandowski)

If a diachronic element is added, the impression of diversity becomes stronger. The first attested casualty list in central Athens is usually dated to 464 BCE (*IG* i³ 1144), but literary and epigraphic sources suggest that collective monuments to the war dead existed before the Persian Wars.[43] The monuments of the middle two quarters of the fifth century seem to have been undecorated, but document reliefs become more common (though still not at all widespread) towards the end of the fifth and start of the fourth centuries.[44] And since the latest safely dated list commemorates the dead of 395/4 (*IG* ii² 5221),[45] it seems likely that lists either stopped being included in monuments, or that they underwent some change in format which makes their fragmentary remains harder to identify. It has been tentatively suggested, for example, that fourth-century lists might have started to include patronymics or other information, a change in style that would make them look very similar to, and liable to identification as, other sorts of lists of names (lists of magistrates, for example).[46]

The remains of the inscribed lists suggest, therefore, that there was much more diversity between the monuments than Pausanias' reference to singular *mnema* might immediately suggest. Nor, I would suggest, did unity emerge from the arrangement of the different memorials within a defined, controlled space.

Such a claim can be made only tentatively. The precise arrangement of the various memorials is still imperfectly understood: none of the extensive

---

[43] Pausanias (1.29.7) reports seeing a monument to a pre-Persian Wars conflict with Aegina; Thucydides' comments (at 2.34.5) on the exceptional decision to bury the dead of Marathon at the site of the battle (rather than in Athens) also imply that repatriation of the dead was a normal Athenian custom by the start of the fifth century. Clairmont 1983, 87–8 suggests that *IG* i³ 1033 might be a (mid-sixth-century) casualty list, while Matthaiou 1988, 2003 argues that the epigrams for the Persian Wars (*IG* i³ 503/4) formed part of a cenotaph to the Marathon war dead, located in the same area as the collective burials. Steinhauer's (2004–09) publication of a recently discovered casualty list for the dead of the battle of Marathon reveals both that the Athenian practice of creating these lists extends back at least as far as 490, and that the lists were not confined to monuments within the city: as noted above, the dead of Marathon were buried at the site of the battle, and Steinhauer convincingly suggests that this list would have formed part of a monument located at Marathon itself. Lougovaya 2004, 113–25 surveys the evidence, usefully emphasizing the probability that the ceremonies would have evolved over an extended period rather than being created from scratch at a single moment.

[44] Generally on the uses of iconography in Athenian war memorials, see Stupperich 1994.

[45] The latest securely dated list is *IG* ii² 5221, of 395/5, although two other apparently fourth-century fragments do exist: *Agora* 17.24 (= *SEG* XXI 825) and *Agora* 17.25 (both dated by letter-forms: Bradeen 1964, 55–8 suggests that the former could be the casualty list for the battle of Chaeroneia (338); Lewis 2000–03, 14–15 is sceptical).

[46] Suggested by Dow 1983, 98; further comments in Lewis 2000–03, 14–17. Such change is apparent in other aspects of the ceremony too: the funeral games become much more prominent in the Hellenistic period (see briefly Pritchett 1998, 36–7).

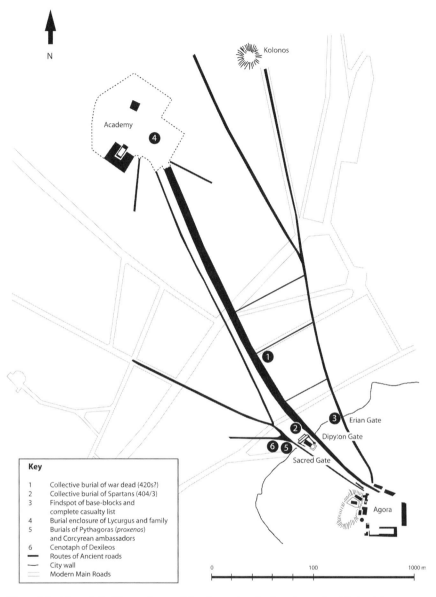

Figure 2.7   Map of the Kerameikos and Academy, showing locations of public burials.

epigraphic fragments of the casualty lists can definitively be said to have been found *in situ*,[47] and archaeological exploration of this part of the city is still incomplete. Nevertheless, it is possible to develop some impression of the distribution of monuments in this area (see Figure 2.7). Pausanias' narrative shows that he left Athens by the Dipylon Gate before starting his walk among the monuments, and many have therefore argued that all the burials were located somewhere along the road from the Dipylon to the Academy.[48] Unambiguous proof for this hypothesis was, however, lacking,[49] until, in the late 1990s, rescue excavations at a site about 500m north-west of the Dipylon revealed a series of well-constructed burial enclosures—whether these are four or five distinct burials or sections of a single monument is uncertain—together with about 90kg of human bone; and a range of funerary deposits.[50] The site has been plausibly identified as a collective burial of Athenian war dead, dating to the third quarter of the fifth century. Although no traces of ancient road were found in this excavation, it is clear (from segments of the road that have been found nearby) that these structures were located by or very close to the Dipylon–Academy road.[51]

However, although other material connected with the public burials has been found along the course of this same road,[52] it is important to acknowledge that another substantial cluster of material is focused around a different road, one coming from the so-called 'Erian' Gate (north-east of the Dipylon). Three large base blocks, probably to be associated with the large monument discussed above (*IG* i³ 1163), were found in this area,

[47] On the findspots of the casualty lists, see Alipheri 1992–98, 2000–03.

[48] Influential examples of this view include Travlos 1971, 299–301; Camp 2001, 263. For further discussion of conventional views of the topography and location of the *demosion sema*, see Patterson 2006a, 52–6. For a detailed and authoritative study of the topography of the *demosion sema,* analysing findspots of inscriptions as well as the archaeological evidence, see now Arrington 2010 (whose work unfortunately appeared at too late a stage for me to respond to in detail in what follows).

[49] One collective tomb was known to be located on this road (just outside the Dipylon Gate): the tomb of the Spartans killed in the fighting surrounding the democratic counter-revolution of 403 (see Willemsen 1977, with the brief report on the preliminary results of recent re-excavation in *Archaeological Reports* 49, 8). But there is no agreement on whether these Spartans would have been buried inside the *demosion sema* or deliberately placed outside it—that is, whether this tomb should act as evidence for where the *demosion sema* was located (see, for example, Stupperich 1977, 26–31), or as proof of where it could not have been located (Clairmont 1983, 44).

[50] Preliminary results of the excavation appear in Stoupa 1997.

[51] On the route of this road, see Costaki 2006, 142.

[52] Particularly significant are *IG* i³ 1162 (one of the few complete stelae extant, dated to the 440s), one (large) fragment of *IG* i³ 503/4 (fragment C, inscribed with epigrams for the Persian War dead), and *IG* ii² 5222 (part of the monument to the cavalry dead of 395/4: see above). For a brief discussion, see Matthaiou 2003, 198–9.

as was a complete stele associated with that monument. Although both the blocks and the casualty list were found in a secondary context (built into a Roman wall) their size, weight, and good condition of preservation make it unlikely that they would have been moved very far from their original location.[53] Certainty is impossible, but that at least some of the monuments to the war dead were located along this road (which could also be used, albeit more indirectly, to reach the Academy) cannot be ruled out.[54]

This small collection of material can usefully be supplemented by reference to the, rather better, evidence for state-funded burials of individuals. This form of public burial, offered as an honour by the city to prominent politicians (and others), has a strong spatial connection with the public, collective burial of war dead. Pausanias' account of this part of the city mentions the public burials of (among others) the fifth-century statesmen Pericles (1.29.3) and Cleisthenes (1.29.6), the successful general Conon and his son Timotheus (1.29.15), and the fourth-century politician Lycurgus (1.29.15). This last tomb, which appears to have been seen by Pausanias at the very end of his walk, has now persuasively been identified with a burial enclosure by the edge of the Academy, at the far end of the road leading from the Dipylon Gate.[55]

The discovery of Lycurgus' burial enclosure is useful, not only because it offers an unusually precise triangulation point for Pausanias' account, but because it forces the recognition of another crucial factor about this area of the city: namely the mixture of public and private burials that characterized the use of space here. Lycurgus was given a public burial, meaning that the city agreed to pay for the costs of his grave monument, and probably undertook responsibility for the design and construction of his grave.[56] But the structure by the Academy is the grave enclosure of

---

[53] Ritchie 1985, 773–7 advocates this view.

[54] Costaki 2006, 142 (and fig. 86) shows that at least three cross-streets joined the Dipylon and Erian roads quite close to the city, while a subsequent branch in the road from the Erian Gate led towards the Academy. It is possible, therefore, that Pausanias' route took him along one or more of these branch roads, rather than directly down the main Dipylon–Academy street.

[55] On the discovery and identification of the burial enclosure, see Matthaiou 1987, and on its relationship to the road, Costaki 2006, 557–8 (Catalogue Number X.4). Other archaeologically attested public burials (all of non-Athenians) are located closer to the Sacred Gate (e.g. Pythagoras, *proxenos* of Selymbria, *IG* i³ 1154; Corcyrean ambassadors Thersander and Simylos, *IG* ii² 5224).

[56] For Lycurgus' public burial, see [Plutarch] *Mor.* 852A. The best evidence for the procedure of giving public burial to a private individual comes in the decree voting public burial for Zeno, as reported by Diogenes Laertius 7.11: five men are to be appointed to oversee the construction of the tomb. That such burials became the responsibility of the family once they had been constructed is implied by the story of Chabrias' wastrel son, who attempted to make money by selling off the stones from his father's public burial monument (Athenaeus 4.165ef).

Lycurgus' whole family (including members to whom public burial was, as far as we know, never granted). That is, a burial area that was initially public soon evolved into something private. This is perhaps an unusually clear example of the potential for the fusion of public and private space, but it is repeated in a less stark form all over this part of the city. The picture is still incomplete, deriving largely from scattered rescue excavations rather than methodical exploration, but enough can be seen to make it clear that this area is rich in individual and family burials, dating from the Archaic to the Roman periods (and beyond).[57]

The pattern of burial in this area of the city of Athens does not, therefore, look all that dissimilar to that found in other parts of the city, and the place in which the war dead were buried and commemorated starts to look much less like the coherent island of commemoration imagined by Brückner, and much more like a dispersed space, possibly lying alongside more than one road, and very probably extending over at least 1.5 kilometres from the city walls. This space is marked, it is true, by burials of high quality and of eminent figures, but it is not exclusively (or perhaps even primarily) associated with the burials of the Athenian war dead.

Meanings

How, though, does such a conclusion help in approaching the question —asked at the start of the previous section—of the connection between the nature of this space and the ways in which Athenians might have engaged with the commemorative monuments located there?

In principle, the monuments to the war dead seem to have been some of the most accessible public inscriptions in Athens. The majority of their content should have been comprehensible even to those whose literacy was limited,[58] while unlike other public documents (many treaties, for example) they were not enclosed inside a sacred precinct but were constantly available to be seen and read by anyone walking past. Moreover, the open, dispersed nature of this space makes it more likely that people

---

[57] Compare Clairmont 1983, 44 (who reaches a similar conclusion on the use of space in this area, but argues nevertheless that 'the whole area ... was charged with heroic sacrality'). The results of the various rescue excavations in this area are usefully catalogued by Costaki 2006 (see, for example, 142, n.94 for references to catalogue entries relevant to the road from the Dipylon: of forty-three excavations along the route of the road, nineteen produced evidence of burials; in at least six of these sites, some or all of the burials were classical in date). On the misleading effect of labelling Athenian burial grounds 'cemeteries', see Patterson 2006b, 11–21.

[58] On the legibility of lists, see Thomas 1989, 64–6.

would have walked past regularly: a visit to this area of the city did not have to be prompted by a particular commemorative festival, or even a specific desire to visit an individual monument.[59]

It is, however, difficult to assess how far that theoretical accessibility was exploited in practice. Certainly, at the time when the public funeral and associated rituals took place, this area must have become one of the most politically (and emotionally) charged spaces in Athens.[60] It cannot be a coincidence that of the few references in classical sources to monuments in this part of the city the majority come, precisely, in a funeral oration: Lysias, in his speech for the dead of the Corinthian War, uses a pre-existing burial—that of the dead Spartans[61]—to support his argument for the unfailing heroism of the Athenians, while Plato's *Menexenus* repeatedly asserts its connection to the place in which it was being delivered by its references to the dead of previous wars who surround the speaker and his audience.[62]

But such appeals to the monuments to the war dead are not an inevitable part even of the funeral orations, and evidence for the formal incorporation of the existing monuments being formally embedded in subsequent commemorative activities appears only in the Hellenistic period.[63] If the monuments to the war dead played a similarly prominent role in the classical *Epitaphia*, then this has left no trace in either literary or epigraphic sources.[64] And those sources are almost as silent about the uses made of these monuments during the rest of the year, when this area of the city was no longer dominated by the commemorative festivals

---

[59] The activities attested for this area of the city—ranging from prostitution to religious ceremonies—are discussed by Stroszeck 2003, 78–9.

[60] These ceremonies most probably took place in the winter, at the end of the campaigning season. It is unclear whether they were held every year: Loraux 1986, 37–9 suggests that some aspects of the ceremony (the funeral games, for example) were held annually, even if no casualties had been suffered that year; Pritchett 1998, 29–35 argues that celebration of the ceremonies could have been more intermittent.

[61] See note 49 above.

[62] References to the dead who 'lie here' (ἐνθάδε κεῖνται) appear at 242d (Archidamian War); 242e (Deceleian War); 243c (the Arginusae dead do *not* lie here—a loaded point, since it was their lack of burial, according to Diodorus (13.101.1–2), that provoked the Athenians to execute the generals who had commanded at that battle); 246a (the dead currently being buried).

[63] *IG* ii² 1006 (dated to 122/1) contains a list of activities to be undertaken by the ephebes, including participation at the *Epitaphia*, and a 'race in armour from the *polyandreion*' (line 24); for further examples, see also Chaniotis, pp. 50–1, this volume.

[64] Clairmont 1983, 17 argues that similar activities already took place in the classical period, but see Chaniotis 2005, 237–40 for a strong argument for placing the inscription firmly in a Hellenistic cultural, political, and military context.

and rituals, and occupied with the collective, politicized acts of commemoration and mourning that those festivals entailed.

It can be tempting to speculate that the absence of the political allows space for the entry of the personal—for the sort of close, private, engagement with these monuments, as sites of mourning rather than (or as well as) sites of commemoration which has been identified for many modern war memorials.[65] It has already been seen that the public funeral itself is an appropriate venue for mourning by the family of the dead, and acknowledgement that that lamentation will form a part of the activities of these days is a recurring theme of the extant funeral orations.[66] Subsequent private visits to the collective tombs seem, in theory, to be likely. Regular visits to ancestral tombs played an important part in Athenian burial practice (whether on specific anniversaries of birth or death, or in the context of civic festivals such as the *Genesia*), and it is plausible that these activities could be transposed to the sites of collective burials.[67]

Firm evidence, however, is hard to locate. Literary sources maintain their almost total silence on the subject of the collective graves, and those mentions that do appear tend to be very general. Lycurgus' *Against Leocrates* (142), for example, attempts to shame the coward Leocrates by describing how, in slinking away from the battlefield and back to Athens, 'he felt no shame before the epitaphs engraved on the memorials, but thought it necessary to stroll shamelessly before the eyes of those mourning their loss'.[68] Material evidence is slightly more forthcoming: it has been argued that a number of Athenian white-ground lekythoi and loutrophoroi might depict the public tombs and, more importantly, show individuals mourning at those tombs. But even if the identification of these scenes is correct, the context in which such visits took place (or in which the vessels depicting these visits would have been used) remains unclear.[69]

---

[65] Including memorials that are similar in format to the Athenian casualty lists: a notable example is the Vietnam Memorial in Washington DC (discussed by Tritle 2000, ch. 9; Tatum 2003, ch. 1; Tritle, pp. 166–77, this volume). Generally on war memorials as sites of private mourning, see Winter 1995.

[66] Ziolkowski 1981, ch. 8.

[67] Garland 2001, ch. 7.

[68] οὗτος οὐδὲ τὰ ἐλεγεῖα τὰ ἐπιγεγραμμένα τοῖς μνημείοις ἐπανιὼν εἰς τὴν πόλιν ἠδέσθη, ἀλλ' οὕτως ἀναιδῶς ἐν τοῖς ὀφθαλμοῖς τῶν πενθησάντων τὰς ἐκείνων συμφορὰς ἡγεῖται δεῖν ἀναστρέφεσθαι.

[69] No figures are preserved on the clearest example of the representation of a casualty list (Immerwahr 1990, no. 674: a small fragment which seems to show stelae inscribed with the characteristic geographical headings). Other vases have clearer representations of mourning by one or two figures, but it is less clear in these cases that the tombs at which they are standing are those of the war dead. For discussion (favouring a connection with the public tombs), see Clairmont 1983, 74–85; see also Oakley 2004, 29, 181–2, 192, 202, 224.

There is also some evidence suggesting that the preferred private response to the practice of collective burial was to construct an entirely separate site of mourning by building a cenotaph for the dead soldier. The monument of the cavalryman Dexileos (*IG* ii[2] 6217), situated outside the Sacred Gate, not far from the general area of the public burials, is the most famous example of this phenomenon, and also the only case in which it can conclusively be shown that this private memorial exists in addition to a collective monument.[70] It seems unlikely, however, that the response of Dexileos' family was unique. Literary evidence suggests that private commemoration, and even private burial, of the war dead was a possibility in some circumstances.[71] It is tempting to suspect, too (although impossible to prove), that at least some of the many late fifth- and fourth-century private gravestones with representations of soldiers (and particularly those with representations of combat) should be associated with men who died in battle.[72]

In this case, too, I would suggest that there is unlikely to be a single answer, or a single model, for private mourning of the war dead, and that individual responses would have been influenced by many variables. Wealth must have been an issue in determining how many families were able to afford to construct an alternative monument. So too must geographical location: a family living in the deme Kerameis, in whose territory the public graves were located, would surely have a different relationship with these monuments than a family from, for example, Sounion (at the very southern end of Attica), let alone one from Lemnos or Argos. The fact that this area was not marked out by prominent boundaries or by a consistent appearance would only enhance the possibility of diverse responses to and uses of the monuments located in it.

---

[70] Dexileos also appears on the cavalry monument for the fighting of 395/4 (*IG* ii[2] 5222; see above), but is not named on the preserved portion of the general monument for that year (*IG* ii[2] 5221). His cenotaph subsequently becomes the focus of a family burial enclosure (see, briefly, Garland 1982, A1)

[71] Lysias 32.21 mentions the construction of a *mnema* for a soldier killed at Ephesus; Isaeus 9.4 describes the private repatriation and burial of an Athenian killed on campaign at Mytilene.

[72] On depictions of soldiers on private funerary monuments, see Stupperich 1977, 139–99; Bergemann 1997, 63–4, 79–80. Clairmont 1983, 70–1 suggests that the trierarch Lykeas and Chairedemos commemorated on the (private) gravestone *IG* i[3] 1314 might be identical with the men of the same name who appear on the casualty lists *IG* i[3] 1190 (line 42) and 1191 (line 250) respectively.

Conclusion

A claim that an ancient practice has an indeterminate form or indefinable meaning can sometimes be a thinly disguised confession that the state of the evidence simply does not allow modern commentators to identify things that would have been perfectly clear, and eminently well defined, to contemporary participants and observers. It is certainly the case that our current state of knowledge of the Athenians' treatment of their war dead, and particularly of Athenian responses to it, is still flawed. Many details of practice are unknown—the date at which the custom originated, and at which it died out; the timing and frequency of the commemorative festivals; the precise location of almost all the monuments—and it is very hard, too, to get a concrete sense of the role that the monuments might have played in the lives of classical Athenians.

Nevertheless, the claim to complexity which has repeatedly been made in this chapter does rest on something more than the imperfection of the evidence. Both literary sources and, to a much greater extent, material evidence show that Athenian commemoration was not so monologic, monovalent a practice as it can sometimes appear to be. Rather than being uniform in nature, exclusively public in use, and dominated by a single (Athenian, civic, even democratic) identity, the Athenian monuments to the war dead reflect—at a detailed level and at a larger one—some of the idiosyncrasies of the society in which those dead had lived, or on whose behalf they fought: a society, that is, in which the boundaries between public and private, citizen and outsider, are less solid than is sometimes imagined; and in which the nature and significance of the place in which they are buried is not rigidly determined, but open to repeated, multiple reinterpretations.

Bibliography

Alipheri, S. 1992–98. 'Τὰ διεσπαρμένα μνημεῖα ὡς πηγὲς γιὰ τὴν καταστροφὴ τοῦ Δημοσίου Σήματος.' *Horos* 10–12, 183–203.

——— 2000–03. 'Οἱ περιπέτειες τῶν λίθων καὶ τῶν ἀπόψεων.' *Horos* 14–16, 373–9.

Arrington, N. 2010. 'Topographic Semantics: The Location of the Athenian Public Cemetery and its Significance for the Nascent Democracy.' *Hesperia* 79, 499–539.

Bergemann, J. 1997. *Demos und Thanatos: Untersuchungen zum Wertsystem der Polis im Spiegel der attischen Grabreliefs des 4. Jahrhunderts v. Chr. und zur Funktion der gleichzeitigen Grabbauten.* Munich: Biering & Brinkmann.

Bradeen, D. W. 1964. 'Athenian Casualty Lists.' *Hesperia* 33, 16–62.

—— 1969. 'The Athenian Casualty Lists.' *Classical Quarterly* 19, 145–59.

Brückner, A. 1910. 'Kerameikos-Studien.' *Mitteilungen des Deutschen Archäologischen Instituts, Athenische Abteilung* 35, 183–234.

Buck, C. D. 1913. 'The Interstate Use of the Greek Dialects.' *Classical Philology* 8, 133–59.

Camp, J. M. 2001. *The Archaeology of Athens*. New Haven, CT: Yale University Press.

Chaniotis, A. 2005. *War in the Hellenistic World: A Social and Cultural History*. Malden, MA: Blackwell Publishing.

Christ, M. R. 2001. 'Conscription of Hoplites in Classical Athens.' *Classical Quarterly* 51, 398–422.

Clairmont, C. W. 1983. *Patrios Nomos: Public Burial in Athens during the Fifth and Fourth Centuries B.C.: The Archaeological, Epigraphic-literary, and Historical Evidence*. 2 vols. Oxford: B.A.R.

Costaki, L. 2006. 'The intra muros Road System of Ancient Athens.' Ph.D. dissertation, University of Toronto.

Curtius, E. 1868. *Erläuternder Text der sieben Karten zur Topographie von Athen mit Lithographirten beilagen und holzschnitten*. Gotha: J. Perthes.

—— 1891. *Die Stadtgeschichte von Athen*. Berlin: Weidmannsche Buchhandlung.

Dow, S. 1983. 'Catalogi generis incerti. *IG* ii^2 2364–2489: A Check-list.' *Ancient World* 8, 95–106.

Garland, R. 1982. 'A First Catalogue of Attic Peribolos Tombs.' *Annual of the British School at Athens* 77, 125–76.

—— 2001. *The Greek Way of Death*. Bristol: Bristol Classical Press.

Gauthier, P. 1971. 'Les ξένοι dans les textes Athéniens de la seconde moitié du Ve siècle av. J.-C.' *Revue des Etudes Grecques* 84, 44–79.

Immerwahr, H. R. 1990. *Attic Script: A Survey*. Oxford: Clarendon Press.

Koumanoudis, S. 1984. Ἐμ πολέμωι.' *Horos* 2, 189–201.

Lalonde, G. V. 1971. 'The Publication and Transmission of Greek Diplomatic Documents.' Ph.D. dissertation, University of Washington.

Lewis, D. M. 2000–03. 'Κατάλογοι θανόντων ἐν πολέμωι.' *Horos* 14–16, 9–17.

Loraux, N. 1986. *The Invention of Athens: The Funeral Oration in the Classical City*. Cambridge, MA: Harvard University Press.

Lougovaya, J. 2004. 'An Historical Study of Athenian Verse Epitaphs from the Sixth through the Fourth Centuries B.C.' Ph.D. dissertation, University of Toronto.

Matthaiou, A. 1987. Ἡρίον Λυκούργου Λυκόφρονος Βουτάδου.' *Horos* 5, 31–44.

—— 1988. Νέος λίθος τοῦ μνημείου μὲ τὰ ἐπιγράμματα γιὰ τοὺς Περσικοὺς πολέμους.' *Horos* 6, 118–22.

—— 2003. Ἀθηναίοισι τεταγμένοισι ἐν τεμένεϊ Ἡρακλέος (Hdt. 6.108.11).' In *Herodotus and his World*, ed. P. Derow and R. Parker. Oxford: Oxford University Press, 190–202.

Meiggs, R. 1972. *The Athenian Empire*. Oxford: Clarendon Press.

Morris, I. 1992. *Death-ritual and Social Structure in Classical Antiquity*. Cambridge: Cambridge University Press.

—— 1993. 'Everyman's Grave.' In *Athenian Identity and Civic Ideology*, ed. A. L. Boegehold and A. C. Scafuro. Baltimore, MD: Johns Hopkins University Press, 67–101.

Nielsen, T. H., L. Bjertrup, M. H. Hansen, L. Rubinstein, and T. Vestergaard. 1989. 'Athenian Grave Monuments and Social Class.' *Greek, Roman and Byzantine Studies* 30, 411–20.

Oakley, J. H. 2004. *Picturing Death in Classical Athens: the Evidence of the White Lekythoi*. Cambridge: Cambridge University Press.

Oliver, G. J. 2000. 'Athenian Funerary Monuments: Style, Grandeur, Cost.' In *The Epigraphy of Death: Studies in the History and Society of Greece and Rome*, ed. G. J. Oliver. Liverpool: Liverpool University Press, 59–80.

Parlama, L. and N. C. Stampolidis. 2000. *Athens, the City beneath the City: Antiquities from the Metropolitan Railway Excavations*. Athens: Kapon Editions.

Patterson, C. B. 2006a. '"Citizen Cemeteries" in Classical Athens?' *Classical Quarterly* 56, 48–56.

—— 2006b. 'The Place and Practice of Burial in Sophocles' Athens.' In *Antigone's Answer: Essays on Death, Burial, Family and State in Classical Athens*, ed. C. B. Patterson. Lubbock, TX: Texas Tech University Press, 9–48.

Pope, H. 1935. *Non-Athenians in Attic Inscriptions*. New York: Cosmos.

Pritchett, W. K. 1985. *The Greek State at War*. Part 4. Berkeley, LA, and London: University of California Press.

—— 1998. *Pausanias Periegetes*. Amsterdam: J. C. Gieben.

Ritchie, C. E., Jr. 1985. 'The Athenian Boundary Stones of Public Domain.' Ph.D. dissertation, University of Colorado at Boulder.

Siewert, P. 1999. 'Literarische und epigrapische Testimonien über "Kerameikos" und "Kerameis".' *Mitteilungen des Deutschen Archäologischen Instituts, Athenische Abteilung* 114, 1–8.

Smith, G. 1919. 'Athenian Casualty Lists.' *Classical Philology* 14, 351–64.

Steinhauer, G. 2004–09. 'Στήλη πεσόντων τῆς Ἐρεχθηίδος.' *Horos* 17–21, 679–92.

Stoupa, C. 1997. 'Ὁδός Σαλαμίνος 35.' *Archaeologikon Deltion* Chr B1, 52–6.

Strauss, B. S. 2000a. 'Democracy, Kimon, and the Evolution of Athenian Naval Tactics in the Fifth Century BC.' In *Polis & Politics: Studies in Ancient Greek History Presented to Mogens Herman Hansen on his 60th Birthday, August 20, 2000*, ed. P. Flensted-Jensen, T. H. Nielsen, and L. Rubinstein. Copenhagen: Museum Tusculanum Press, 315–26.

—— 2000b. 'Perspectives on the Death of Fifth-century Athenian Seamen.' In *War and Violence in Ancient Greece*, ed. H. van Wees. London: Duckworth and the Classical Press of Wales, 261–83.

Stroszeck, J. 2003. 'Ὅρος Κεραμεικοῦ: Zu den Grenzsteinen des Kerameikos in Athen.' *Polis* 1, 53–83.

Stupperich, R. 1977. 'Staatsbegräbnis und Privatgrabmal im Klassischen Athen.' Ph.D. dissertation, Münster.

—— 1994. 'The Iconography of Athenian State Burials in the Classical Period.' In *The Archaeology of Athens and Attica under the Democracy*, ed. W. D. E. Coulson, O. Palagia, T. L. Shear Jr, H. A. Shapiro, and F. J. Frost. Oxford: Oxbow, 93–103.

Tatum, J. 2003. *The Mourner's Song: War and Remembrance from The Iliad to Vietnam*. Chicago: University of Chicago Press.

Thomas, R. 1989. *Oral Tradition and Written Record in Classical Athens*. Cambridge: Cambridge University Press.

Travlos, J. 1971. *Pictorial Dictionary of Ancient Athens*. London: Thames & Hudson.

Tritle, L. A. 2000. *From Melos to My Lai: War and Survival*. London: Routledge.

Tsirigoti-Drakotou, I. 2000. 'Νέα στήλη πεσόντων από το Δημόσιον Σήμα. Μια πρώτη παρουσίαση.' *Archaeologikon Deltion* 55 A, 87–111.

Walters, K. R. 1981. '"We Fought Alone at Marathon": Historical Falsification in the Attic Funeral Oration.' *Rheinisches Museum* 124, 203–11.

Willemsen, F. 1977. 'Zu den Lakedämoniergräbern im Kerameikos.' *Mitteilungen des Deutschen Archäologischen Instituts, Athenische Abteilung* 92, 117–57.

Winter, J. M. 1995. *Sites of Memory, Sites of Mourning: The Great War in European Cultural History*. Cambridge: Cambridge University Press.

Ziolkowski, J. E. 1981. *Thucydides and the Tradition of Funeral Speeches at Athens*. New York: Arno Press.

3

The Ritualized Commemoration of War in the Hellenistic City: Memory, Identity, Emotion

ANGELOS CHANIOTIS

War Memorials: Beyond the Physical Objects

IN A VERY PROMINENT LOCATION IN MESSENE, opposite the *bouleuterion* (the seat of the council), a Hellenistic peribolos was found, the burial ground of six men and four women.[1] Their names were written on an epistyle, probably in the second century BCE. This is a very unusual find indeed. Burial within the city wall is a privilege reserved to city founders, benefactors, and saviours. The gymnasium was often used for such burials of distinguished individuals, also in Messene.[2] The excavator, Petros Themelis, has plausibly argued that this honour was given to persons who were killed in a war, possibly in street fights during an attack in the late third century (214 or 201 BCE).[3] More names were added in the next centuries (another six women and eight men), until the second century CE.

This monument is one of many categories of monuments and physical objects commemorating wars in Hellenistic cities and in the countryside: *polyandreia* (common graves of the war dead) and cenotaphs of warriors killed in battles both in the remote past—for example at Marathon and Plataia, and the Milesians killed in the period of colonization[4]—and in recent wars; individual graves of fallen soldiers; statues of warriors and generals—for example the statue of Eugnotos, a general of Akraiphia who committed suicide when his troops were defeated by Demetrios

---

[1] *SEG* XLV 320; XLVI 428; L 403; LI 494; Themelis 2000, 96–102; Themelis 2001, 206–7; cf. Schörner 2007, 235–7.

[2] Chiricat 2005. For Messene, see Themelis 2000, 96–102 and 2001, 199–201 (*SEG* XLVII 406; LI 493); Schörner 2007, 245–7; Fröhlich 2008, 210–19.

[3] For an alternative (persons killed during a civil war), see Fröhlich 2008, 204–8.

[4] *I. Milet* 732; Merkelbach and Stauber 1998, 124–5, no. 01/20/08.

Proceedings of the British Academy, **160**, 41–62. © The British Academy 2012.

Poliorketes (291 BCE), and the memorial for Apollonios, the commander of the troops of Metropolis during the Aristonikos War (133 BCE), and his fallen soldiers in the market place of Metropolis;[5] dedications of war booty and war monuments in sanctuaries; images on coins; and trophies at the sites of battles.[6] An Athenian decree concerning the restoration of sanctuaries in Attica continually refers to war memorials and shows the visibility of the physical commemoration of wars in late Hellenistic or early imperial Athens:

> where the trophy of Themistokles against the Persians is as well as the common tomb of those who were killed in the battle; ... where they sacrificed during the war against the Megarians for the island; ... the sanctuary of Athena Herkane, founded by Themistokles before the sea-battle at Salamis ... .[7]

We approach these monuments visually, reading the inscriptions that often accompany them, or looking at the representations (the dying Gauls, the Nike of Samothrace, etc.) and the architectural remains. The monument of Messene gives us, however, a good opportunity to consider also some more elusive aspects of war memorials and commemoration of war, which are the subject of this chapter.

The monument of Messene reminds us that women's share in war was far more complex than that of mourners of husbands, fathers, brothers, and children.[8] It reminds us that the stage of war was not only the battlefield, but also the city—besieged, attacked, raided. It reminds us that for a large part of the population the traumatic experience of war was not only viewing the dead bodies of male relatives being brought back for burial, or the notification that a beloved person had been buried abroad, but also watching battles from the city walls, actively participating in the defence of the city, experiencing a clear and present danger, fearing for one's own life and freedom and that of relatives, and seeing the destruction of property. We get a feeling of this anxiety when we read, for instance, Diodorus' description of how the Rhodians watched the fleet of Demetrios Poliorketes approaching their city in 305 BCE (20.83.2):

---

[5] Eugnotos: Ma 2005 (cf. *SEG* LVI 553); Apollonios: *I. Metropolis* 1, lines 45–8.

[6] For some examples and a bibliography, see Chaniotis 2005a, 233–40.

[7] *IG* ii² 1035; *SEG* XXVI 121 lines 33–5: [ἀκρωτήριο]ν ἐφ' οὗ κεῖται τὸ Θ[εμισ]τ[οκ]λέους τρ[όπαι]ον κατὰ Περσῶν καὶ τὸ πολυανδρεῖον τῶν [ἐν τῆι μάχηι τευλετησάντων· ...]ένοις καὶ προθυσαμένο[ις] ἐν τῶι πρὸς Μ[εγαρέας] πρὸ τῆς νήσου πολέμωι· line 45: [ἱερὸν Ἀθηνᾶς Ἑρκάνης, ὃ ἱδρύσατο Θεμιστοκλῆς πρὸ τῆς περὶ Σαλαμῖνα ναυμαχίας.

[8] On women's participation in war, see Loman 2004; Chaniotis 2005a, 104–14.

The soldiers of the Rhodians occupied the walls awaiting the approach of the enemy fleet, while the old men and the women watched from their houses, as the city is built like a theatre; and all of them terrified at the size of the fleet and at the bright light reflected by the shining weapons were in great agony.

We cannot fully understand the function of war memorials in the Hellenistic world, if we associate wars only with men and battlefields. It would be an unfounded generalization to claim that in the Hellenistic period war was a universal experience, but it was certainly an experience that any individual could have personally, whether man or woman, adult or child, city-dweller or farmer, free or slave, citizen or foreigner.

Petros Themelis dates the funerary peribolos in Messene to the early second century, considering the possibility that its first occupants, killed in the late third century, were buried there some time after their death. Of course, there is no way to prove this, but we may be confident that this place was the stage of rituals—certainly so during the burial, possibly also later, for example on the anniversary of each individual's death. We cannot fully understand the function of war memorials without considering the rituals for which the memorials served as a stage. Unfortunately, rituals belong to the most elusive phenomena of ancient social behaviour. As established stereotypical activities they are rarely described or explained by those who perform them; performative ritual texts—such as hymns and orations—do not survive in large numbers. And, if we can reconstruct some of the features of the rituals with the help of cult regulations or descriptions, we are rarely in a position to study their changes over longer periods of time (the 'dynamics of rituals')[9] and to understand their impact on performers and audiences.

Rituals are emotionally loaded activities; they generate and intensify emotions, sometimes as contradictory as the joy for a victory, the grief for the death of a beloved person, the pride for a heroic deed, and the fear of future dangers.[10] When a norm prescribes that only a boy whose parents are both still alive (*pais amphithalles*) shall have the honour to carry a sacred object and sing hymns during a festival,[11] every orphan in the city is bitterly reminded of his unfortunate situation; when a victorious athlete marches at the head of a festive procession, he is watched with envy by his defeated competitor, who attends the festival among the common citizens. This emotional dimension of war memorials, not as physical

---

[9] See the general remarks in Chaniotis 2005b.
[10] On rituals and emotions, see Kneppe and Metzler 2003; Chaniotis 2006 and 2010.
[11] See, for example, Sokolowski 1955, 88–92, no. 32, lines 19–21.

objects but as the stage for the ritualized commemoration of the salutary self-sacrifice of the war dead and the traumatic experience of war, presents a significant interpretative challenge.[12]

War memorials are also a complex historical phenomenon because they are connected with another elusive element of human behaviour: memory. When the six men and the four women of the grave peribolos were commemorated in the second century, no reference was needed either to their fathers' names or to the deeds that occasioned the construction of this unusual grave. All this was part of the collective memory of the Messenians, who had experienced this historical event together or had heard about it from eyewitnesses. Eventually every war memorial changes its character, at the latest sixty years after its inauguration, when it is no longer an object of memory—in the narrow sense of the word—but of tradition (or 'cultural memory').[13] The 'cultural memory' of a community is not the sum of the real memories of its members, but a limited set of selected events and persons of the past, about which the members of a community have the same elementary, and usually very abstract, knowledge (for example, 'the Persian Wars', 'the tyrannicides', 'the French Revolution', 'D-Day'). This elementary knowledge can be expressed through simple keywords, with which those who share it associate abstract ideas (freedom, victory, heroism, etc.) rather than specific historical facts. One of the main functions of the ritualized commemoration of war through commemorative anniversaries is to transmit this 'cultural memory' to future generations, thus forging civic identity.[14]

With a few exceptions—for instance, the battle of Kosovo of 1389 and Serbian identity—collective identities are constructed on the basis of the memory of victory, which of course does not exclude the traumatic memory of suffering, and not on the basis of failure and defeat. Around 220 BCE the Knossians attacked the city of Lyttos, which had been left defenceless since the armed men were participating in a campaign. As Polybius reports (4.54) the city was taken and destroyed completely, women and children were taken as captives; we do not hear another word about their fate. When the Lyttians came back to their city and saw what had happened, 'they were so much affected that none of them had the heart even to enter the native city, but after walking round it many times

---

[12] On rituals connected with burial within the city wall, see Schörner 2007, 114–42.

[13] On the distinction between 'collective memory' and 'cultural memory', see Chaniotis 2005a, 214–16 and 2009; see also Goebel, Chapter 7, this volume.

[14] On commemorative anniversaries and their function, see Chaniotis 1991. See also below, note 15.

bewailing and lamenting the fate of their country and themselves, turned their backs on it and retreated to Lappa'. From there, they continued the war and a few years later refounded their city and conquered all the small neighbouring cities, including their sworn enemy Dreros. One hundred years later (110 BCE), when the Lyttians concluded a treaty of alliance with Olous, one of the clauses stipulated that the new allies should be invited to the local festivals. Until a few years ago, the names of these festivals were not preserved on the fragments of this treaty. A new find reveals them:

> They shall come to the festivals, the Lyttians to Olous for the festival of Britomarpis and for the Theodaisia, and the Olountians to Lyttos both for the festival [*euameros*, 'the good day'] of the settlement of the city and for the 'good day' on which the Lyttians captured Dreros.[15]

The memory of destruction and loss was overlaid by the memory of survival, a new beginning, revenge, and victory.

These introductory remarks reveal the complexity of the study of the changing contexts of war memorials. A few selected examples will manifest the dynamic character of the ritualized commemoration of war.

Ritual and Civic Values

The 'good day' for the destruction of Dreros by Lyttos was one of the many festivals established in Hellenistic cities for the commemoration of war. Some of them were occasioned by victories of kings and were short-lived celebrations in the service of the good relations between a city and a king.[16] For instance, when the victory of Ptolemy IV at the great battle in Raphia was announced in Siphnos (217 BCE), the oboist Perigenes of Alexandria, who happened to be present,

---

[15] The old fragments of the treaty: Chaniotis 1996, 352–8, no. 60. The new fragment, the text of which was presented by Charalambos Kritzas, reads: [ἐ]ϱπόντων δὲ καὶ ἐς τὰς [ἑ]οϱτάς, οἱ μὲν Λύττιοι ἐς [Β]ολόεντα ἐς τὰ Βϱιτομάϱ[π]ια καὶ ἐς τὰ Θουδαίσια, ὡσαύτως δὲ καὶ οἱ Βολό[ν]τιοι Λυττόνδε ἔς τε τὰν [ε]ὐάμεϱον τᾶς καταβοικί[σι]ος τᾶς πόλιος κὴς τὰν εὐ[ά]μεϱον ἐν ᾆι οἱ Λύττιοι τὰν Δϱῆϱον ἧλαν.

[16] For example, the festival Antigoneia and Demetria was established in Samos upon the announcement of the victory of Demetrios at the sea-battle of Salamis in Cyprus in 306 BCE (*IG* XII.6 56; ἐπὶ τοῖς εὐαγγελίοις). The Athenians introduced in 304 BCE a sacrifice to Agathe Tyche and to Antigonos Monophthalmos and Demetrios Poliorketes after the latter's victory in the Peloponnese (*SEG* XXX 69).

rejoiced together with the others at the good news that had been announced and offered as a present to the city, to perform with his aulos alone for two whole days, wishing to demonstrate his good will towards the king and the queen as well as to our city.[17]

Similarly, celebrations for victories of the Romans, such as the competition in honour of the 'good tidings of the victory of the Romans' (εὐαγγέλια Ῥωμαίων νίκης), which was added to the Amphiaraia of Oropos after Sulla's victory over Mithridates VI (*c.*85 BCE),[18] served the same purpose of manifesting goodwill.

All Greek commemorative anniversaries have an aggressive character, and naturally this aggressive element is particularly clear in war anniversaries.[19] The citizens commemorated a victory over a foreign power, a barbarian, an internal or external enemy of freedom and constitutional order. The celebration of superiority and success, often with military overtones—which were expressed, for example, in contests—is intrinsically connected with the function of these celebrations as means by which identity is shaped, expressed, and transmitted. When the Athenians wanted to show Sulla who they were, they narrated the history of their great victories that rescued Greece and Greek culture;[20] when the Lyttians wished to strengthen their friendship with the Olountians, they invited them to the festivals that commemorated their success—the refoundation of their city and the sack of Dreros.[21] The events commemorated in most of these festivals could be understood as the beginning of a new era: the Persian Wars, the victories over the Gauls that established the rule of kings (Antigonos Gonatas, Attalos I), the refoundation of Lyttos, or the re-establishment of Thessalian autonomy (the *Eleutheria* of the Thessalian League). The commemorative anniversaries strengthened identities, and by doing so they also constructed otherness: they underlined the barriers that separated the Greeks from the barbarians (Amazons, Thracians, Persians, Gauls), and the free cities from the suppressive kings. Only commemorative anniversaries that were connected with the freedom or the rescue of a community (a *polis*, the community of the Greeks) were likely

---

[17] *IG* xii.5.481 + Suppl.; Stephanis 1988, 360, no. 2045. I give Stephanis' text, but I restore [μ]όνο[ς] instead of [μ]όνο[ν]: [συμπα]ρὼν δὲ καὶ Περιγένης Λεοντίσκου [Ἀλεξανδρεὺ]ς συνησθεὶ[ς] ἐπὶ τοῖς προσηγγελ[μ]ένοι[ς ἀγαθοῖ]ς ἐπιδίδωσιν τῆι πόλει, ὥστε αὐλῆσα[ι μ]όνο[ς ἐν] ἡμ<έ>ραις δυσίν, βουλόμενος ἀποδείκνυ[σ]θαι τὴ[ν] εὔνοιαν ἣν ἔχει εἴ[ς] τε τὸν βασιλέα καὶ τὴν [βασ]ιλι[σσαν κ]αὶ τὴν πόλιν τὴν ἡμετέραν.

[18] *I.Oropos* 521, 525, 529.

[19] Chaniotis 1991, 124–7, 140–1.

[20] Plutarch, *Sulla* 13.

[21] See above, note 15.

to be used by this community as part of its self-representation and identity, thus surviving for longer periods.

The Hellenistic Greeks inherited such festivals, which commemorated the battles of the Persian Wars (the anniversaries of the battles of Marathon and Salamis in Athens, the *Eleutheria* at Plataia), adding both an important festival with Panhellenic claims (the *Soteria* of Delphi, commemorating the defeat of the Gauls in 279 BCE) and numerous local festivals.[22] A contest in Larisa (ἀγὼν τοῖς προκινδυνεύσασιν ἐπὶ τῶν Στενῶν) honoured the cavalrymen who had risked (and lost?) their lives fighting at Stena, near Larisa, against King Perseus in 171 BCE. The programme of this contest was primarily military; the disciplines in which the Lariseans— and only the Lariseans—competed included races of men and children, horse races, a competition of trumpeters and heralds, bull-hunting, a torch race on horses, and contests in sudden attack of infantry and cavalry (προσδρομὴ πεζῶν, προσδρομὴ ἱππέων). A separate competition within this festival (προσδρομὴ Ἡγησαρέτῳ) honoured an individual, probably the commander, who lost his life in this battle.[23] The military overtones and the exclusive participation of citizens of Larisa suggest that this celebration was aimed at forging local identity and transmitting the values of the citizen-warrior to the young men. After an interruption (in the first century BCE), the Lariseans decided with a decree to re-establish the contest under Augustus,[24] but we know of only two celebrations before it disappeared again, this time forever, possibly because local military traditions had lost their significance as a factor of civic identity.

A commemorative festival for a victory was also celebrated in Kyzikos in the late first century.[25] The occasion was quite different; the festival did not commemorate a battle in or near Kyzikos, but Caesar's victory against Ptolemy XIII in Alexandria in 47/6 BCE. It was an 'annual thanksgiving contest in honour of the heroes, Asklepiades, the founder, and those who fought together with him in Alexandria in the war against Ptolemy'.[26]

---

[22] For the commemoration of the Persian Wars, Jung 2006; for the *Soteria*, Nachtergael 1977.

[23] *IG* ix.2.527, 531–3; *SEG* LIII 550; LIV 559 (there, erroneously attributed to the *Eleutheria*; the correct interpretation was suggested to me by Christian Habicht). For the history of this contest, see the remarks of J. Robert and L. Robert 1964, 176–82 no. 127; Helly 1983, 374–8.

[24] *IG* ix.2.531, lines 6–10. On the date cf. *SEG* LIII 550 (prosopographical remarks on Hegesaretos).

[25] *IGR* IV 159; J. Robert and L. Robert, *Bulletin épigraphique* 1964, 180.

[26] οἱ κατ᾿ ἐνιαυτὸν τιθέμενοι εὐχαριστήριοι ἀγῶνες Ἡρώοις, τῷ Ἀσκληπιάδῃ τῷ οἰκιστῇ καὶ τοῖς συναγωνισαμένοις αὐτῷ κατ᾿ Ἀλεξάνδρειαν ἐν τῷ κατὰ Πτολεμαῖον πολέμῳ.

Kyzikos owed these men its status as a free city, and this made a victory in
a distant war an important element of identity. The inscription attesting
this contest—an honorary decree for Asklepiades, grandson of Asklepiades
'the founder'—also mentions a competition (καταδρομή, 'incursion') in
honour of Oiniades, the 'founder's' son, probably again for a military
contribution, and a contest (probably a race), organized by the magistrates of the gymnasium. The starting point of this race was the *heroon*, a
grave monument near the gymnasium, probably the grave (or cenotaph)
of the Kyzikenes, who were killed in the *bellum Alexandrinum*.

War memorials (graves, trophies) are known to have served as the
starting point of races during rituals of military commemoration. An
honorary decree for the Athenian ephebes of 123/2 BCE mentions such a
race in the festival in honour of the war dead:

> On the *Epitaphia* they held a race in armour, both the race that starts at the
> *polyandreion* and the other obligatory races.[27]

This race seems to have been modelled after the famous race at the
Eleutheria of Plataia, another commemorative anniversary in honour of
war dead (cf. below). As early as the third century BCE (possibly earlier)
the pentaeteric *Eleutheria* included a race of men in full armour from the
trophy of the battle to the altar of Zeus Eleutherios (ὁπλίτης ἀπὸ τοῦ
τροπαίου or ὁ ἀπὸ τοῦ τροπαίου ἐνόπλιος δρόμος). The winner was
awarded the honorary title 'the best of the Greeks' (ἄριστος Ἑλλήνων).[28]
Of course, such races ultimately originate in contests in honour of the
dead, which reach back to Homeric times.

Such celebrations also included, of course, other rituals in addition to
the contests. The inscription from Kyzikos mentions a procession of the
boys and the young men who attended the gymnasium. The most detailed
description of the rituals of a commemorative anniversary of a battle is
given by Plutarch and concerns the battle at Plataia (479 BCE). Plutarch's
remark ('the Plataians observe these rites down to this very day') suggests
that the rituals, which he witnessed in the late first century CE, were of
older origin. The festival's name, *Eleutheria*, derives from Zeus Eleutherios,
the patron of freedom. But the focal point of attention in this festival was

---

[27] *IG* ii² 1006, line 22: ἐποιήσαντο δὲ καὶ τοῖς Ἐπιταφίοις δρό[μο]ν ἐν ὅπλοις, τόν τε ἀπὸ
τοῦ πολυανδρείου καὶ τ[οὺς ἄλλους] τοὺς καθή[κοντα]ς. This *polyandreion* was a cenotaph
in Athens commemorating the dead of Marathon: Parker 2005, 470.
[28] For Hellenistic evidence for this race, Moretti 1953, 117–121, no. 45 (early second century) and
151–6, no. 59 (*c.*20 BCE); *SEG* XI 338 (third century). Cf. Robert 1929.

not the god, but the war heroes and the idea of freedom, which explains why the service of slaves was not allowed on this occasion:[29]

> On the sixteenth of the month Maimakterion, which corresponds to the Boiotian month Alalkomenios, they held a procession, which is led forth, at break of day, by a trumpeter who sounds the signal for battle; wagons filled with myrtle and wreaths follow, then a black bull, then free-born youths who carry libations of wine and milk in jars and pitchers of oil and myrrh; for no slave is permitted to assist in this service, since the men had died for freedom; and at the end comes the chief magistrate of the Plataians, who may not at other times touch iron or dress himself with any other garment than white, but on this occasion wears a purple tunic, carries a water-jar from the seat of the city's magistrates, and marches, sword in hand, through the city to the graves. Then he takes water from the spring, washes with his own hands the stelae and anoints them with myrrh; then he slaughters the bull at the pyre and praying to Zeus and Hermes Chthonios he invites the brave men who died for Greece to come to the banquet and the offerings of blood. Then he mixes a mixer of wine and makes a libation saying: 'I drink to the men who died for the freedom of the Greeks.' The Plataians observe these rites down to this very day.

Races may express military values, and traditional rituals manifest the respect towards the war dead. To express civic values one needs, however, oral performances (hymns, acclamations, orations). The modern perception of rituals connected with the war dead has been shaped by Thucydides' description of the public burial of the warriors who fell in the first year of the Peloponnesian War.[30] The funeral oration, which he quotes (2.35–46) —regardless of the question of how closely it represents what Pericles said on that occasion—is the earliest surviving specimen of a particular group of performative ritual texts: the *epitaphioi logoi*. From the surviving funeral orations and the treatise of Menander Rhetor, it is easy to recognize some general features. The orators focused on aspects of civic identity; they associated the present deeds with past glories. Social roles were assigned: the youth should remember and emulate the deeds of the war dead; the men should fight; the women should mourn; the bereaved should be proud. Pericles' funeral oration prescribes emotions: pride, courage, moderate grief, and emulation.[31]

The importance of such oral elements during commemorations of war is quite clear. They represent a very dynamic element of celebrations,

---

[29] Plutarch, *Aristeides* 21.3; discussion in Chaniotis 1991, 131–3.
[30] Hornblower 1997, 294–316.
[31] Menander Rhetor 2.11 (418.5–422.4); Russell and Wilson 1981, 331–6. *Epitaphioi*, Loraux 1981; Ziolkowski 1981.

as their content can be continually adapted to changing contexts. The Larisean festival for the war dead at Stena included, at least in its latest phase, competitions in oratory and poetry (ἐγκώμιον λογικόν, ἐγκώμιον ἐπικόν, ἐπίγραμμα).[32] The texts probably referred both to the deeds of the warriors and to civic values. At the *Eleutheria* of Plataia, a rhetorical competition (*dialogos*, 'debate') took place between the representatives of Athens and Sparta, the two leading powers of the Greeks during the Persian Wars, who tried to prove in front of a Panhellenic jury that the contribution of their native city to the victory was more significant. It seems that this rhetorical contest was introduced in the second century, and continued to take place even in the Roman period.[33] An Athenian inscription preserves a fragment of a speech delivered on this occasion by an Athenian.[34] The personification of Athens is presented referring to the campaigns undertaken by the Athenians for the rescue of Greece and accusing Sparta of leaving the Hellenic alliance and not continuing the war against the Persians.[35]

We may assume that the visits of the Athenian ephebes to war memorials and their participation in commemorative anniversaries for wars and battles, described in late Hellenistic honorary decrees, were accompanied by oral performances (speeches, hymns, libations). These decrees praise those who had successfully finished ephebic training, demonstrating the virtues expected by the Athenians from their future citizens: diligence, endurance, obedience, discipline, piety, and respect towards ancestral traditions.[36] The festivals they attended included two commemorative celebrations for the two most important battles of Athenian history. The festival for Artemis Agrotera was the commemorative anniversary of the battle of Marathon; the sacrifice to Zeus Tropaios in Salamis commemorated the sea-battle of the Persian Wars. In addition to this, the ephebes also sacrificed to Athena Nike, the patron of military victory. On the *Epitaphia* they held races and performed exercises with weapons. They sailed to the trophy erected by the Athenians after the sea-battle at Salamis and sacrificed there to Zeus Tropaios. When they toured the frontier of

---

[32] *IG* ix.2.531, lines 43–8 (on this inscription see Petrovic 2009); *SEG* LIII 550, lines 14–15.

[33] On this *dialogos*, see Robertson 1986; Chaniotis 1988, 42–8.

[34] *IG* ii² 2788; Chaniotis 1988, 42–8, no. T10.

[35] For these accusations, see lines 18–19, μετὰ δὲ ταῦτα μόνης ἐμοῦ παρ[αμεινάσης ---] τετελειῶσθαι τὸν πρὸς τὸν Πέρσας [πόλεμον] ('after these events I remained alone — to complete the war against the Persians'); line 26, μὴ μετεσχηκέναι τῶν μετὰ ταῦτα κινδύνων ('they did not participate in the later dangers'). For the possible content of this fragmentary speech, see Chaniotis 1988, 45–8.

[36] For example, *IG* ii² 1006.

Attica, they visited the tomb of the war dead at Marathon; here, they crowned it and sacrificed 'to those who were killed in the war for the liberty of the Greeks'. Since prayers and hymns were part of the sacrifices, it is reasonable to assume that this tribute included some oral reference to the historical event, probably even an oration, as in their visit to the sanctuary of Amphiaraos, where they testified to (*historesan*) the ancestral claim of their city on this sanctuary:

> They made an excursion to the border of Attica carrying their weapons, acquiring knowledge of the territory and the roads [lacuna] and they visited the sanctuaries in the countryside, offering sacrifices on behalf of the people. When they arrived at the grave at Marathon, they offered a wreath and a sacrifice to those who died in war in defence of freedom; they also came to the sanctuary of Amphiaraos. And there they made clear our legitimate possession of the sanctuary, which had been occupied by the ancestors in old times. And after they had offered a sacrifice, they returned on the same day to our own territory. [37]

The sacrifices to the heroes and the war dead at Marathon and Salamis visualized the ideal of heroic death in combat; these memorials were an integral part of the rituals.

Commemorative anniversaries, which acquired and kept an important position in Hellenistic cities, share some common features. They always commemorated victories: the opponents were usually not ordinary enemies, but representatives of a different culture, that is, barbarians (the Persians, the Gauls) or enemies who threatened the freedom or the very existence of a community (the Antigonids); the war marked the rescue from a great danger and/or the beginning of a new era. The rituals performed on these occasions represented an element of continuity and stability, as more or less invariable, traditional actions. The celebrations also included, however, variable elements, such as the emotions of the participants, to which we now turn.

Emotional Contexts and Emotional Communities

Around 360 BCE (or perhaps somewhat earlier), during a period of continual war, the Thasians introduced a series of measures to honour those who fell for the fatherland.[38] Their names should be inscribed in a list of 'the Brave' (εἰς τοὺς Ἀγαθούς), to which the city regularly offered

---

[37] *IG* ii² 1006, lines 65–71; cf. Chaniotis 2008b, 143–4.
[38] Sokolowski 1962, 122–3, no. 64; new edition, including a new fragment by Fournier and Hamon 2007 (*SEG* LVII 820); cf. Parker 1983, 43; Ekroth 2000.

sacrifices. Their fathers and sons were invited to this sacrifice and were given a place of honour during the contests. The orphans received a full suit of armour from the city upon coming of age. The regulation contains an interesting detail:

> No one shall wear a sign of mourning for the brave men for more than five days. And it shall not be permitted to mourn them.[39]

A reason is not given, but taking into consideration other attempts of cult regulations to prescribe emotions,[40] the modification of norms was aimed at preventing displays of emotion that had been observed in the past. The magistrates, including the supervisors of the women (*gynaikonomoi*), were to exact fines from those who violated this law. A probable context is that of excessive mourning and the incongruity between the joyful celebrations for a victorious battle and the grief for those who were killed.[41] Proper honours should be paid to the war dead, but only for a limited period, so that the prevailing and sustainable emotion would be pride, not sorrow.

The ritualized commemoration of war is connected with emotional communities.[42] The smallest such community consists of the family and circle of friends of those who were killed in war—a community that needs to come to terms with the loss. This is the 'emotional community' envisaged by the Thasian law. However, the primary addressee of commemorations of war is the civic community of the living, which feels joy, pride, gratitude, and relief for the victory. A virtual addressee is the community of the dead, who need to be reassured that they did the right thing and that they will be remembered. The war dead often appear in their epitaphs proudly announcing that they have died for the fatherland or as brave warriors, without any feeling of pain or regret, but with a sense of honour and the knowledge that they have left behind undying glory:

> No enemy will claim to have seen me, in the battle of the spears, shamefully carrying the shield on my back. I have always faced the enemy and have erected two trophies. I died doing what is worthy of my ancestors. [43]

---

[39] Lines 3–4: πενθικὸν δὲ μηδὲν ποείτω μηδεὶς ἐπὶ τοῖς ἀγαθοῖς ἀνδράσιν πλέον ἢ ἐν πέντε ἡμέραις· κηδεύειν δὲ μὴ ἐξέστω.

[40] Chaniotis 2010.

[41] Cf. Sokolowski 1962, 123.

[42] On the concept of 'emotional community', see Rosenwein 2002. On the study of emotions in the Greek world, see most recently Cairns 2008.

[43] *I.Priene* 380; Merkelbach and Stauber 1998, 293, no. 03/01/05: [δυσμενέων δ' οὐδεὶς κ]αυχήσεται ἐν δορὸς αἰχμῆι | [ἐντροπαλιζομένο]ο ἰδεῖν σάκος ἀμφ' ὤμοισι· | [ἀλλὰ --- -]ρας ἐχθρῶν στὰς δισσὰ τρόπαια | [ἤγειρα· προγόνων δ' ἄ]ξια δρῶν ἔθανον.

Of course, these are not *their* words, but words written by the survivors. Exploiting the incapacity of the departed to express themselves, the authors of such epigrams manipulated the epitaphs in order to remove the anxiety caused by the fear of the unsatisfied dead.[44]

Finally, a quite different emotional community is the one that brings together the citizens and the foreign audience of the commemoration of war. The commemorative anniversaries of Lyttos have already been mentioned. When in the late second century BCE Lyttos concluded a treaty of alliance with Olous (110 BCE), it invited the Olountians to these two festivals that commemorated the refoundation of Lyttos and the capture of Dreros. It is usually impossible to study the emotional responses of different communities to the ritualized commemoration of war, because the sources are lacking. But to ignore this factor would create an erroneous impression of unchanging rituals.

An honorary epigram from Kyzikos (late second/early first century) presents a very instructive example of the interdependence of private emotions and public commemoration of the war dead. Metrodoros set up a bronze statue of his son Diopeithes, who was killed in a battle. The statue was dedicated to Sarapis and Isis, but probably not in a sanctuary of the Egyptian deities. Metrodoros underlines in the epigram the didactic nature of this statue: it should be an exemplum for the young men. From this I infer that Diopeithes' statue may have decorated a gymnasium:

> Lord of the universe and of the earth, Sarapis, seated on your high throne, and Isis, who wears on your head the crescent moon, to you Metrodoros has set up this superb work of the skill to cast bronze, an imprint of Diopeithes, represented in the armour of the god of war. Thus he demonstrates to the young men the manly spirit of his son, the spirit that he had when he marched against the killing phalanx of the enemies to defend the fatherland, having completed twice nine years.[45]

Metrodoros chose a public space for a private memorial, combining the private need to honour his own son with the public task of encouraging the young men to behave in a similar manner. By setting up his son's statue

---

[44] On the manipulation of the words of the dead in epitaphs, see the observations of Casey 2004.

[45] Merkelbach and Stauber 2001, 52, no. 08/01/40: [—] ὑψίθρονε κο[ίρ]ανε κό[σ]μου καὶ χθονὸ[ς Σάρα]πι, | ὄχουσά τε κρατὶ σελήνην ἀμφίκυρτον Ἶσι, | ὑμῖν τάδε καίρια τέχνης χαλκὸν εἰς καμούσης | ἱδρύσατο τῆς Θεοπείθους εἰκόνος τύπωμα } Ἐνυαλίου κατ᾽ ἔνοπλον σχῆμα Μητρόδωρος, | νέοισι τὸν ἄρσενα τέκνου θ[υμ]ὸν ἐκκαλύπτων, | ὃν ἔσχε δὶς ἐννέα πλήθων [τ]οὺς ἐτῶν ἀριθμοὺς | πάτρας ὑπὲρ εἰς φονόεσσαν δηΐων φάλαγγα.

in a public place, probably the gymnasium, Metrodoros not only displayed paternal pride, but also dissociated this monument from the narrow emotional community of the family and placed it into the circle of the emotional community of the young men who completed their military training and their civic education. It is quite possible that this statue was the focal point of rituals (for example, crowning) by the ephebes. The epigram's metre is very unusual. The poem consists of verses composed in the *paroemiacus* and the *ithyphallicus*, typical metres for processional songs and dances. Wilamowitz assumed that *paroemiacus* was the meter of martial dances.[46] The choice of the metre is related to the martial content of the poem, but it may also allude to the place where the statue was erected—a place of rhythmical movement, processions, and training of the young men in arms.

A similar interplay between public and private commemoration can be observed in a grave monument at Aphrodisias. An honorary decree for Kallikrates, son of Pythodoros, surviving in two copies, grants him the extraordinary honour of burial within the city wall (late first century BCE). A fragment of one of the two copies that can be partly reconstructed reveals that this honour is connected with the man's services during the wars of the late Republic:

> [since he] has preserved the public affairs in the most critical situations crises and [...] has served as stephanephoros and gymnasiarchos [... and] agoranomos in a most severe [famine ... and has held] offices not subject to account during the wars [... and has served] as envoy to the magistrates/generals in Rome [....] and in all kinds of dangers and affairs [... and] has fought against the enemy [killing?] sixty [of them] ... let it be allowed to him to be buried [in the gymnasium] ... .[47]

Kallikrates' grave may be the one that is still visible next to the bouleuterion of Aphrodisias.[48] There is no reason to assume that Kallikrates and his achievements were forgotten. In the first century BCE and in the early imperial period the military achievements of the Aphrodisians were the most prominent element of their self-representation, before the memory

---

[46] Wilamowitz-Moellendorf 1921, 381.
[47] Reynolds 1982, 150–1, no. 28: [... ἐν τοῖς] ἀνανκαιοτάτοις καιροῖς διατηρήσαντα [τὰ] κοινὰ καὶ [...] καὶ στεφανηφορήσαντα καὶ γυμνασιαρχή[σαντα ... καὶ] ἀγορανομήσαντα ἐν τῇ χαλεπωτάτῃ σε[ιτοδείᾳ ... καὶ τὰς] ἐν τοῖς πολέμοις ἀρχὰς ἀνυπευθύνους τε[λέσαντα ... καὶ πρεσ]βεύσαντα πρὸς τοὺς ἡγουμένους εἰς Ῥώμ[ην ...]λοις καὶ ἐν παντοδαποῖς κινδύνοις καὶ πρά[γμασιν ... καὶ καταγω]νισάμενον τοὺς ἐναντίους καὶ ἑξήκον[τα αὐτῶν ἀποκτείναντα? ...] ... συνκεχωρῆσθαι δὲ αὐτῷ καὶ ἐνταφ[ὴν ἐν τῷ γυμνασίῳ. Cf. ibid., 151–3, no. 29. Cf. Schörner 2007, 278–9.
[48] Chaniotis 2008a, 70–1. On this grave, see also Schörner 2007, 54–6 and 242–3 (no attribution).

of the wars of the late Republic faded away and the mythical past became the basis of Aphrodisian identity.[49] Kallikrates' military exploits, which were a cause of pride and gratitude for all the Aphrodisians and a role model for their youth until Augustus' time, had a different significance for his family: for his descendants, the memory of Kallikrates was connected with social prestige. This is why two generations later, when his honorary statue had collapsed or had been damaged, his homonymous grandson restored it.[50]

The responses of emotional communities to the commemoration of war are an elusive and very dynamic element. When Gerhard Schröder attended the sixtieth anniversary of D-Day (4 June 2004), joining the victors and lauding the 1944 Allied landings in Normandy as a symbol of the fight for freedom and democracy,[51] the presence of the first German leader to take part in D-Day festivities disturbed the 'emotional community' of the primary celebrants, the veterans. As is reported, Edwin Hannath, general secretary of the Normandy Veterans Association (NVA) in Britain, said he did not mind the presence of Mr Schröder as long as it was not intrusive, but his comments are revealing of mixed feelings.

> It was a French invitation —not British—and we can't do much about that. If he comes, he comes, as long as he doesn't bring his own contingent as well. We go there as a pilgrimage—we go to remember those that we left behind. As long as there is no encroachment, I don't suppose that anybody would mind. There won't be any aggro. As far as I was concerned, I was wounded in Normandy and I can still feel it now and it still hurts. I don't know how people feel when they haven't been in it. I lost two brothers and a brother-in-law in the war—one was only 15 and three-quarters. Do we just forget it? How do we feel? I don't know. I can always remember my mother's face, finding out about her two sons—I was nearly the third. I know the Germans were involved but, as far as we were concerned, they were the enemy. [52]

The German participation in this celebration ultimately changed its function. From the commemoration of a victory of specific countries against a specific enemy, it became a celebration of abstract ideals: freedom and democracy. Memory and meanings are as variable a factor in rituals as emotions.

---

[49] On this transformation of Aphrodisian identity, see Chaniotis 2003.

[50] Reynolds 1982, 151–3, no. 29: Καλλικράτης Μολοσσοῦ ἱερεὺς Μηνὸς Ἀσκαινοῦ καὶ Ἑρμοῦ Ἀγοραίου τὰς τῶν προπατόρων τιμὰς ἐπισκευάσας ἀποκαθέστησεν ('Kallikrates, son of Molossos, priest of Mes Askainos and Hermes Agoraios, has repaired and restored the honours, i.e. the honorary statues, of his forefathers').

[51] See, for example, www.goethe-bytes.de/dw/article/0,,1223570,00.html.

[52] See www.guardian.co.uk/world/2004/jan/02/france.germany.

Contested Memories, Changed Meanings

The Delphic festival of the *Soteria* ('the festival of the Salvation') com-memorated the defeat of the invading Gauls in 279 BCE. When the Delphic Amphictyony established the festival shortly after this event, Kos also established a thanksgiving sacrifice to Apollo, attributing the defeat of the Gauls to Apollo's miracle:[53]

> Whereas, the barbarians having made a campaign against the Greeks and against the sanctuary in Delphi, it is announced that those who came against the sanctuary have met with vengeance at the hands of the god and at the hands of the men who went to the aid of the sanctuary at the time of the barbarians' attack, and that the sanctuary has been preserved and, moreover, adorned with the arms of the attackers, and that most of the attackers perished in their battles with the Greeks [translated by Roger Bagnall and Peter Derow].

The festival's name (*Soteria*) derives from the epithet of Apollo Soterios, thus placing his salutary intervention in the foreground. In the mid-third century, the Aetolian League took over control of the Delphic sanctuary. The festival was reorganized under the auspices of the Aetolians, who shifted the focus from Apollo's miracle to their own contribution to the victory.[54] The epithet *Soter* ('the Rescuer') was no longer attributed to Apollo, but to Zeus. In 246/5 BCE the Aetolians sent envoys to Greek cities, in order to invite them to participate in the new festival.[55] We can gain an impression of their letter of invitation from the answers, which quote its formulations; for example the decree of Tenos:

> Whereas sacred envoys of the Aetolian Koinon and the general have arrived, bringing a decree, according to which they have decreed to establish the contest of the Soteria for Zeus Soter and Apollo Pythios, as a commemoration of the battle, which was fought against the barbarians who campaigned against the Greeks and the sanctuary of Apollo, a common sanctuary of the Greeks, and they invite the people of Teos to participate in the contest of the Soteria and in the sacrifice ... .[56]

---

[53] *Syll.*³ 398; Nachtergael 1977, 401–3, no. 1; Bagnall and Derow 2004, 34–5, no. 17. On the first phase of the *Soteria*, see Nachtergael 1977, 295–328.

[54] This has been rightly observed by Champion 1995.

[55] On the date and the context, see Nachtergael 1977, 223–41 and 328–38.

[56] *F.Delphes* III.1.482, lines 1–7 (Nachtergael 1977, 440–1, no. 23): [ἐπει]δὴ παραγεγόνασι θεωροὶ παρά τε του κ[οινοῦ τῶν Αἰτωλῶν καὶ τοῦ στρατηγοῦ κομί]ζοντες ψήφισμά τε καθ᾿ ὅ ἐψηφισμ[ένοι τιθέναι τὸν ἀγῶνα τῶν Σωτηρίων τ]ῶι τε Δὶ <τ>ῶι Σωτῆρι καὶ τῶι Ἀπόλλωνι τῶι Πυ[θίωι, ὑπόμνημα τῆς γενομ]ένης μάχης τῆς πρὸς τοὺς βαρβάρους τοὺς ἐπ[ιστρατεύσαντας ἐπί τε τοὺς Ἕλλην]ας καὶ τὸ ἱερὸν τοῦ Ἀπόλλωνος τὸ κοινὸν τῶ[ν Ἑλλήνων καὶ παρακαλοῦσι τὸν δῆμον τὸ]ν Τηνίων μετέχειν τοῦ ἀγῶνος τῶν Σ[ωτηρίων καὶ τῶν θυσιῶν ...]. Similar formulations are used in the decrees of a Cycladic polis (*F.Delphes* III.1.481, lines 3–10; Nachtergael 1977, 441–3, no. 24) and Chios (*F.Delphes* III.3.215, lines 4–10; Nachtergael 1977, 436–40, no. 22). On this phenomenon, i.e. answering a letter by adapting the formulations that were used in it (*Empfängerformular*), see Chaniotis 1999.

From the letter of Chios we may infer that the Aetolian envoys highlighted their own contribution to the victory:[57]

> we shall praise the Aetolian Koinon and crown it with a golden crown for its virtue, its piety towards the gods, and its bravery against the barbarians.

One of the communities that accepted the Aetolian invitation was Athens. The Athenian decree also adopted the formulations that we find in the other answers of Greek poleis, and which ultimately derive from the Aetolian letter, but with a significant difference: the Athenians praise the piety of the Aetolians, but it is only the Athenian military contribution that is explicitly mentioned in their decree:

> Whereas the Aetolian Koinon, demonstrating its piety towards the gods, has decreed to establish the contest of the Soteria for Zeus Soter and Apollo Pythios, as a commemoration of the battle, which was fought against the barbarians, who campaigned against the Greeks and the sanctuary of Apollo, a common sanctuary of the Greeks, and against whom the [Athenian] people sent the elite troops and the cavalry, in order to join the fight for the common rescue. [58]

For the Hellenistic Greeks, the victory over the Gauls had the same ideological significance as an element of self-representation and identity as the Persian Wars had for the classical Greeks.[59] In the competitive context of Hellenistic interstate relations the memory of this event was contested. During the time in which the Aetolians were reorganizing the *Soteria*, styling their federal state as the rescuer of Greece, and the Athenians were ensuring that *their* contribution was not forgotten, the Macedonian king Antigonos Gonatas also claimed his share of the glory in connection with the repelling of the barbarians.[60] Around 250 BCE, Herakleitos—an

---

[57] *F. Delphes* III.3.215, lines 18–20: ἐπαινέσαι δὲ καὶ τὸ κοινὸν τῶν Αἰτωλῶν καὶ στεφανῶσαι χρυσῶι στεφάνωι ἀρετῆς ἕνεκεγ καὶ εὐσεβε[ίας τῆς εἰς τοὺς θεοὺς] καὶ ἀνδραγαθίας τῆς εἰς τοὺς βαρβάρους. The expression 'they took over the war for the rescue of the sanctuary and of the Greeks' ([τὸν πόλεμον ἀνεδέ]ξαντο ὑπὲρ σωτηρ[ία]ς τοῦ τε ἱεροῦ καὶ τῶν Ἑλλ[ήνων]) in the decree of Smyrna (*F. Delphes* III.1.483; Nachtergael 1977, 443–5, no. 25) may refer to the Aetolians.
[58] *IG* ii² 680, lines 5–13 (Nachtergael 1977, 435–6, no. 21): ἐπειδὴ τὸ κοινὸν τὸ τῶ Αἰτ[ωλ]ῶν ἀποδεικνύμενον τὴν πρὸς τοὺς θεοὺς εὐσέβειαν [ἐψ]ήφισται τὸν ἀγῶνα τὸν τῶν Σωτηρίων τιθέναι τῶι Δι[ὶ τ]ῶι Σωτῆρι καὶ τῶι Ἀπόλλωνι τῶι Πυθίωι, ὑπόμνημα τῆ[ς μ]άχης τῆς γενομένης πρὸς τοὺς βαρβάρους τοὺς ἐπισ[τ]ρατεύσαντας ἐπί τε τοὺς Ἕλληνας καὶ τὸ τοῦ Ἀπόλλωνος ἱερὸν τὸ κοινὸν τῶν Ἑλλήνων, ἐφ᾽οῦς καὶ ὁ δῆμος ἐξέπεμπε[ν] τοὺς ἐπιλέκτους καὶ τοὺς ἱππεῖς συναγωνιουμέν[ους] ὑπὲρ τῆς κοινῆς σωτηρίας.
[59] For an analysis of the commemoration of the Galatian invasion, see Nachtergael 1977, 175–205. Cf. Chaniotis 2005a, 157–60, 220–1.
[60] On the ideological exploitation of Antigonos' victory at Lysimacheia, see Nachtergael 1977, 176–81.

Athenian citizen, agonothetes of the Panathenaia, and general of the
Macedonian garrison in Piraeus—dedicated to Athena Nike a monument
commemorating Antigonos' victory.[61] His initiative should be seen within
the context of the competition of kings, cities, and federal states for a
military glory that legitimized the claim on leadership. The setting of this
monument was carefully selected. Athena Nike, the patron of Athens and
of victory, was worshipped on the acropolis of Athens, where buildings
and sculptures commemorated the victories of Greeks and the Athenians
over the barbarians (the Amazons, the Trojans, the Persians). In this setting Herakleitos' monument subtly incorporated the victory of the
Macedonian king into the Greek traditions of military victories over the
barbarians and presented Antigonos not only as the saviour of the Greeks
from the barbarians but also as continuing Greek heroic traditions.

As we have already seen, the *Eleutheria* of Plataia presented another
stage for contested memories: Athenians and Spartans competed every
five years in a rhetorical contest over the privilege to lead the procession.
As we may infer from a surviving oration,[62] the subject of this competition was the appreciation of these cities' contribution to the victory and
to the freedom of the Greeks. The *Eleutheria* of Plataia are very instructive also as regards changes in the meaning of the commemoration of
war. For two centuries, this celebration reminded the Greeks of their common ideal of freedom. This message did not remain unchanged. During
the Chremonidean War (268–265 BCE) a new element was emphasized: the
concord of the Greeks. Chremonides, who proposed the decree concerning the alliance between Ptolemy II, Athens, Sparta, and other Greek
cities, reminded the Greeks that together 'they had fought many glorious
battles against those who wished to enslave the cities' (that is, against the
Persians), thus assuring freedom. Now that another enemy (Antigonos
Gonatas) threatened the freedom and the ancestral constitutions, the
Greeks should ally themselves with Ptolemy, the defender of 'the common freedom of the Greeks', to preserve concord (*homonoia*). A few years
later (*c*.261–246 BCE), during the celebration of the *Eleutheria*, the Greeks
who participated in this festival issued a decree in praise of Glaukon, an
Athenian in the service of Ptolemy II. He

---

[61] *IG* ii² 677, lines 3–6: ἀνατίθησι τῆι Ἀθηνᾶι τῆι [Νίκηι γραφ]ὰς (or [στήλ]ας) ἐχούσας
ὑπομνήματα τῶν [τῶι βασιλεῖ π]επραγμένων πρὸς τοὺς βαρβάρους ὑπὲρ τῆς τῶν
Ἑλλήνων σωτηρίας ('he dedicates to Athena Nike paintings/stelae containing memorials of the
king's deeds against the barbarians for the salvation of the Greeks'). See Nachtergael 1977,
180–1; Chaniotis 1988, 301 and 2005a, 220–1.

[62] See notes 33 and 34 above.

had contributed to making more lavish the sacrifice to Zeus Eleutherios and Concord and the contest which the Greeks celebrate on the tomb of the heroes who fought against the barbarians for the freedom of the Greeks.[63]

This is the earliest reference to an altar of Homonoia (*Concord*) standing next to that of Zeus Eleutherios[64] and serving as a reminder that freedom can best be defended through concord. We do not know if the cult of Homonoia was introduced in Plataia during the Chremonidean War or earlier, but we can be certain that during and after this war the emphasis of the *Eleutheria* was shifted from the idea of freedom to the combination of concord and freedom.

Commemorative anniversaries of wars and war memorials can be continually adapted to new circumstances. The memorial of the Holocaust in Washington is a good example of a memorial of Jewish suffering which in the cultural memory of the non-Jewish Americans has already been transformed into a monument of victory and an expression of their mission to save the rest of the world. Perhaps also the Vietnam memorial—a memorial of suffering connected with a military failure—will somehow be transformed into a memorial of bravery and missionary spirit.

The Persian Wars were still commemorated as late as the fifth century CE.[65] A pagan priest with the characteristic name of Helladios had an inscription written on the cenotaph of the dead of the Persian Wars in Megara. It records that his city still offered a sacrifice to these heroes. Rather than commemorating a victory of Greeks over Persians, or of freedom over slavery, Helladios' ultimate aim—I think—was to defy Christianity.

Bibliography

Austin, M. M. 2006. *The Hellenistic World from Alexander to the Roman Conquest: A Selection of Ancient Sources in Translation.* 2nd edn. Cambridge: Cambridge University Press.

Bagnall, R. S. and P. Derow. 2004. *Historical Sources in Translation: The Hellenistic Period.* 2nd edn. Oxford: Oxford University Press.

Cairns, D. 2008. 'Look Both Ways: Studying Emotion in Ancient Greek.' *Critical Quarterly* 50 (4), 43-62.

---

[63] Étienne and Piérart 1975; *SEG* XL 412 (Austin 2006, 135–6, no. 63).
[64] Thériault 1996, 102–22.
[65] *IG* vii 53. Cf. Schörner 2007, 261–2.

Casey, E. 2004. 'Binding Speeches: Giving Voice to Deadly Thoughts in Greek Epitaphs.' In *Free Speech in Classical Antiquity*, ed. I. Sluiter and R. M. Rosen. Leiden and Boston, MA: Brill, 63–90.

Champion, C. 1995. 'The Soteria at Delphi: Aetolian Propaganda in the Epigraphical Record.' *American Journal of Philology* 116, 213–20.

Chaniotis, A. 1988. *Historie und Historiker in den griechischen Inschriften: Epigraphische Beiträge zur griechischen Historiographie*. Stuttgart: Franz Steiner.

——1991. 'Gedenktage der Griechen: Ihre Bedeutung für das Geschichtsbewußtsein griechischer Poleis.' In *Das Fest und das Heilige: Religiöse Kontrapunkte zur Alltagswelt*, ed. J. Assmann. Gütersloh: Gütersloher Verlagshaus G. Mohn, 123–45.

——1996. *Die Verträge zwischen kretischen Städten in der hellenistischen Zeit*. Stuttgart: Franz Steiner.

——1999. 'Empfängerformular und Urkundenfälschung: Bemerkungen zum Inschriftendossier von Magnesia am Mäander.' In *Urkunden und Urkundenformulare im Klassischen Altertum und in den orientalischen Kulturen*, ed. R. G. Khoury. Heidelberg: C. Winter, 51–69.

——2003. 'Vom Erlebnis zum Mythos: Identitätskonstruktionen im kaiserzeitlichen Aphrodisias.' In *Stadt und Stadtentwicklung in Kleinasien*, ed. E. Schwertheim and E. Winter. Bonn: Habelt, 69–84.

——2005a. *War in the Hellenistic World: A Social and Cultural History*. Oxford: Blackwell.

——2005b. 'Ritual Dynamics in the Eastern Mediterranean: Case Studies in Ancient Greece and Asia Minor.' In *Rethinking the Mediterranean*, ed. W. V. Harris. Oxford: Oxford University Press, 141–66.

——2006. 'Rituals between Norms and Emotions: Rituals as Shared Experience and Memory.' In *Rituals and Communication in the Graeco-Roman World*, ed. E. Stavrianopoulou. Liège: Centre international d'étude de la religion grecque antique, 211–38.

——2008a. 'Twelve Buildings in Search of a Location: Known and Unknown Buildings in Inscriptions of Aphrodisias.' In *Aphrodisias Papers* 4: *New Research on the City and its Monuments*, ed. C. Ratté and R. R. R. Smith. JRA Supplement 70. Portsmouth, RI: Society for the Promotion of Roman Studies, 61–78.

——2008b. 'Policing the Hellenistic Countryside: Realities and Ideologies.' In *Sécurité collective et ordre public dans les sociétés anciennes*, ed. C. Brélaz and P. Ducrey. Entretiennes Hardt 54. Geneva: Fondation Hardt, 103–53.

——2009. 'Travelling Memories in the Hellenistic World.' In *Poeti Vaganti: Travel and Locality in Greek Poetic Culture*, ed. R. Hunter and I. Rutherford. Cambridge: Cambridge University Press, 249–69.

——2010. 'Dynamic of Emotions and Dynamic of Rituals: Do Emotions Change Ritual Norms?' In *Ritual Matters*, ed. C. Brosius and U. Hüsken. London: Routledge, 208–33.

Chiricat, E. 2005. 'Funérailles publiques et enterrement au gymnase à l'époque hellénistique.' In *Citoyenneté et participation à la basse époque hellénistique*, ed. P. Fröhlich and C. Müller. Paris: Droz, 9–37.

Ekroth, G. 2000. 'Offerings of Blood in Greek Hero-Cults.' In *Héros et héroïnes dans les mythes et les cultes grecs* (*Kernos Suppl.*, 10), ed. V. Pirenne-Delforge and

E. Suárez de la Torre. Liège: Centre international d'étude de la religion grecque antique, 263–80.

Étienne, R. and M. Piérart. 1975. 'Un décret du Koinon des Hellènes à Platées en l'honneur de Glaukon, fils d'Éteoclès, d'Athènes.' *Bulletin de Correspondence Hellénique* 99: 51–75.

Fröhlich, P. 2008. 'Les tombeaux de la ville de Messène et les grandes familles de la cité à l'époque hellénistique.' In *Le Péloponnèse d'Épaminondas à Hadrien*, ed. C. Grandjean. Bordeaux: Ausonius, 203–27.

Hamon, P. and J. Fournier. 2007. 'Les orphelins de guerre de Thasos: un nouveau fragment de la Stèle des Braves (*ca* 360–350 av. J.-C.).' *Bulletin de Correspondence Hellénique* 131, 309–81.

Helly, B. 1983. 'Les Italiens en Thessalie au IIe et Ier s. av. J.-C.' In *Les 'bourgeoisies' municipales italiennes aux IIe et au Ier siècles av. J.-C.*, ed. M. Cébeillac-Gervasoni. Paris and Naples: Editions du Centre national de la recherche scientifique, Centre Jean Bérard, 355–80.

Hornblower, S. 1997. *A Commentary on Thucydides*, vol. 1: *Books I–III*. Oxford: Oxford University Press.

Jung, M. 2006. *Marathon und Plataiai: Zwei Perserschlachten als 'Lieux de mémoire' im antiken Griechenland*, Göttingen: Vandenhoeck & Ruprecht.

Kneppe, A. and D. Metzler. eds. 2003. *Die emotionale Dimension antiker Religiosität*. Münster: Ugarit-Verlag.

Loman, P. 2004. 'No Woman, No War: Women's Participation in Ancient Greek Warfare.' *Greece and Rome* 51 (1), 34–54.

Loraux, N. 1981. *L'invention d'Athènes: histoire de l'oraison funèbre dans la 'cité classique'*. Paris: Mouton.

Ma, J. 2005. 'The Many Lives of Eugnotos of Akraiphia.' In *Studi ellenistici* 16, ed. B. Virgilio. Pisa: Giardini, 141–91.

Merkelbach, R. and J. Stauber. 1998. *Steinepigramme aus dem griechischen Osten*, vol. 1: *Die Westküste Kleinasiens von Knidos bis Ilion*. Stuttgart and Leipzig: K. G. Saur.

—— and —— 2001. *Steinepigramme aus dem griechischen Osten*, vol. 2: *Die Nordküste Kleinasiens (Marmarameer und Pontos)*. Leipzig: K. G. Saur.

Moretti, L. 1953. *Iscrizioni agonistiche greche*. Rome: Signorelli.

Nachtergael, G. 1977. *Les Galates en Grèce et les Sotéria de Delphes: recherches d'histoire et d'épigraphie hellénistique*. Brussels: Palais des académies.

Parker, R. 1983. *Miasma: Pollution and Purification in Early Greek Religion*. Oxford: Clarendon Press.

— 2005. *Polytheism and Society in Athens*. Oxford: Oxford University Press.

Petrovic, A. 2009. 'Epigrammatic Contests, *poeti vaganti*, and Local History.' In *Poeti vaganti: Travel and Locality in Greek Poetic Culture*, ed. R. Hunter and I. Rutherford. Cambridge: Cambridge University Press, 195–216.

Reynolds, J. 1982. *Aphrodisias and Rome*. London: Society for the Promotion of Roman Studies.

Robert, J. and L. Robert. 1964. 'Bulletin épigraphique.' *Revue des Études Grecques* 77, 128–259.

Robert, L. 1929. 'Recherches épigraphiques, I. Ἄριστος Ἑλλήνων.' *Revue des Études Anciennes* 31, 13–20 and 225–6.

Robertson, N. 1986. 'A Point of Precedence at Plataia: The Dispute between Athens and Sparta over Leading the Procession.' *Hesperia* 55: 88–102.

Rosenwein, B. H. 2002. 'Worrying about Emotions in History.' *American Historical Review* 107 (3), 821–45.

Russell, D. A. and N. G. Wilson. 1981. *Menander Rhetor: Edited with Translation and Commentary.* Oxford: Clarendon Press.

Schörner, H. 2007. *Sepulturae graecae intra urbem: Untersuchungen zum Phänomen der intraurbanen Bestattung bei den Griechen.* Möhnensee: Bibliopolis.

Sokolowski, F. 1955. *Lois sacrées de l'Asie Mineure.* Paris: de Boccard.

——1962. *Lois sacrées des cités grecques. Supplément.* Paris: de Boccard.

Stephanis, I. E. 1988. *Διονυσιακοὶ Τεχνῖται. Συμβολὲς στὴφ προσωπογραυία τοῦ θεάτρου καὶ τῆς μουσικῆς τῶν ἀρχαίων Ἑλλήνων.* Herakleion: Panepistemiakes Ekdoseis Kretes.

Themelis, P. 2000. *στὴυ προσοπογραφ ρωες καὶ ἥρῶα στὴ Μεσσήνη.* Athens: He en Athenais Archaiologike Hetaireia.

——2001. 'Monuments guerriers de Messène.' In *Recherches récentes sur le monde hellénistique: Actes du colloque international organisé à l'occasion du 60ᵉ anniversaire de Pierre Ducrey (Lausanne, 20–21 novembre 1998)*, ed. R. Frei-Stolba and K. Gex. Bern: Peter Lang, 199–215.

Thériault, G. 1996. *Le culte d'Homonoia dans les cités grecques.* Lyon and Québec: Maison de l'Orient méditerranéen, Editions du Sphinx.

Wilamowitz-Moellendorf, U. von. 1921. *Griechische Verskunst.* Berlin: Weidmann.

Ziolkowski, J. E. 1981. *Thucydides and the Tradition of Funeral Speeches at Athens.* New York: Arno Press.

4

Commemorating the War Dead of the Roman World

ALISON COOLEY

MONUMENTS COMMEMORATING WAR were a common sight in the Roman world, but war memorials as such—in other words, monuments drawing attention to the human cost of war, listing the names of individual casualties—are almost unknown.[1] The Romans did have access to the requisite information for creating war memorials: as we can see from papyri, military units kept official records listing the names of soldiers killed in action, and an inventory of each unit's personnel was drawn up every year, but they chose not to monumentalize this.[2] The Romans could have taken their cue from either classical Greece or the Hellenistic Greek East in choosing to set up monuments commemorating those who had been killed in war.[3] This would not have restricted them to evoking a single political or social system, since a whole variety of commemorative models was available, some focusing upon the citizen-body of the city-state, with others celebrating individual charismatic rulers.[4] As we shall see in this chapter, however, the Romans developed their own distinctive culture of commemoration, and this was one from which the idea of a monumental war memorial was virtually excluded.

Collective Commemoration: Two (Exceptional) Examples

In order to illustrate how alien war memorials were to the Roman way of thinking, let us begin by examining two exceptions to the rule of

---

[1] Hope 2003 and forthcoming.

[2] Fink 1971, no. 34: a casualty (?) list of legionaries, CE 115–17?; no. 63: a *pridianum* (?) of cohors I Hispanorum Veterana, *c.* CE 100.

[3] For classical Greece, Low 2003 and Chapter 2, this volume. For the Hellenistic world, Rice 1993; Chaniotis 2005, ch. 11 and Chapter 3, this volume.

[4] Low 2003, 99; Rice 1993, 254; Chaniotis 2005, 243.

Proceedings of the British Academy, **160**, 63–88. © The British Academy 2012.

non-commemoration of rank-and-file Romans fallen in battle. First of all, we turn to one of the most tumultuous moments in Roman internal politics at the end of the republic, and then to the period when Rome's empire reached its widest extent at the start of the second century CE under the emperor Trajan.

In the aftermath of the assassination of Julius Caesar in 44 BCE, Cicero delivered a series of speeches known as the *Philippics* in which he attacked Marcus Antonius, who, he feared, was trying to assume the dictator's mantle. His aim was to mobilize the Senate into outright opposition to Antonius by declaring him an outlaw. In the last of the speeches, *Philippic* XIV, Cicero addressed the Senate on 21 April 43 BCE, a significant date, still celebrated today as the birthday of Rome. This followed the battle of Forum Gallorum, in which it seemed at that time that Antonius had been substantially worsted. Cicero's speech responded to news of the victory over Antonius, but was delivered before the deaths of both consuls who had fought against Antonius were announced.

In his speech, Cicero proposed the construction of a public monument to honour the fallen and to provide a fitting place of burial for them.[5] It is quite possible that the Senate approved the proposal,[6] but the monument was never actually built, although the two consuls Hirtius and Pansa did receive public funerals, with public tombs on the Campus Martius, by order of the Senate.[7] In making this proposal, Cicero made a virtue of the fact that such treatment of wartime casualties would be an innovation. Towards the end of his speech, he apostrophized the dead with these words:

> And so, outstanding achievements have been performed by you, bravest of soldiers while you lived, and now truly also most blessed, because your courage will never be buried by the forgetfulness of those who are now alive, nor by the silence of posterity. For the Senate and People of Rome will have built almost with their own hands an everlasting memorial for you. Many armies on many occasions have been great and famous in the Punic, Gallic, and Italian wars, but to none of them has an honour of this kind been paid. [8]

It is important to appreciate, however, that Cicero's proposal to honour the fallen was not innocent of ulterior motives. Even though he claimed

---

[5] See Cicero *Philippic* IX.34 for the monument's function as a tomb.

[6] Dio Cassius 46.38.1: 'To those who had participated in the conflict and had died a public burial was voted, and also that all the rewards which they themselves would have received, had they lived, should be given to their sons and fathers.'

[7] Coarelli 1999; Macciocca 1999.

[8] Cicero *Philippic* XIV.33.

that he wanted to provide everlasting glory to the fallen soldiers and to alleviate the grief of bereaved families,[9] what he actually wanted was for the monument to serve as a visual condemnation of Antonius:

> Therefore it will be the relatives' greatest consolation that by this same memorial is proclaimed the courage of their kinsmen, the respect of the Roman people, the good faith of the Senate, and the memory of the cruellest war, in which had not the soldiers possessed such great courage, the name of the Roman people would have perished through the treachery of Marcus Antonius. [10]

Cicero's proposal for a war memorial was thus provoked by a particular set of circumstances, and illustrates clearly how the idea of such a memorial was alien to Roman culture, drawing instead upon classical Athenian precedents.[11] Indeed, Cicero's reply to a letter from Marcus Brutus implies that he realized that his proposal to honour the dead would seem excessive to some, but reveals that his real motivation was to condemn Antonius: 'I wanted there to be everlasting monuments of the public hatred towards the cruellest enemies'.[12]

Nor was this the only occasion on which Cicero tried to exploit the symbolic system of granting public honours for his own purposes of attacking Antonius. In *Philippic* IX, delivered in February 43 BCE, he sought to persuade the Senate to award Servius Sulpicius an honorific statue on the speakers' platform in the Forum as well as a public burial. Sulpicius had been sent on an embassy to Antonius during which he had died, and Cicero claimed that such honours were in accordance with Roman traditional practice whereby their ancestors 'wanted there to be a memorial for anyone whose actual embassy had caused his death, so that in dangerous wars men might undertake the duty of an embassy the more boldly'.[13] The big difference in the case of Sulpicius, though, was that Antonius had not killed him; he had simply succumbed to an ongoing illness whilst on his embassy. Undeterred, Cicero twisted the situation to such an extent that he claimed that Antonius had actually killed him, asserting that Antonius as good as killed Sulpicius by his own hands because Sulpicius died whilst on an embassy to him, and, of course, without Antonius there would have been no embassy. According to Cicero, 'without question he who was the cause of death has brought the death

---

[9] Cicero *Philippic* XIV.31 and 34.
[10] Cicero *Philippic* XIV.35.
[11] Sordi 1990, 174; Rüpke 1990, 249.
[12] Cicero *Letters to Brutus* I.15.9 = Shackleton Bailey (1980) no. 23; Sordi 1990, 172, 175.
[13] Cicero *Philippic* IX.3.

about'.[14] Consequently he tried to secure for Sulpicius honours usually awarded only to an ambassador killed by the enemy, arguing that 'I thus interpret our ancestors' intention to have been that they should assess the cause of death, and not investigate its character'.[15] The impression that Sulpicius had died in the course of duty was to be emphasized, according to Cicero's proposal, by an inscription on his statue base stating that he had died 'in the interests of the State'.[16] In this way, Cicero proposed such lavish honours primarily as a way of dishonouring Antonius: 'by presenting Sulpicius as heroically fallen in the service of the state, Cicero can slyly depict Antonius as a dangerous enemy of the republic'.[17] Indeed, Cicero intended that the statue should symbolize the Senate's condemnation of Antonius:

> Accordingly, I think it also relevant to the way in which posterity will remember these events that it is clear what the Senate's judgement was concerning this war; the statue itself will bear witness that the war was so serious that the death of an ambassador won an honourable memorial. [18]

In both cases—the honorific statue for Sulpicius and the war memorial— Cicero took advantage of the opportunity to propose unusual honours for those whom he represented as deceased heroes of the state as a way of stirring up hostility to Antonius. His eagerness to do this was the result of the ambiguous character of the fighting with Antonius: to be condemned if it was civil strife, but to be supported if it was war against a *hostis*, or public enemy.[19] As Cicero himself pointed out, 'if that blood was the blood of enemies, our soldiers showed the highest patriotism, but it was an appalling crime if it was the blood of fellow citizens'.[20] Such ambiguity may have made recruitment a particular problem, and Cicero was concerned not just with stirring up the Senate, but with enlisting the active fighting capacity of the common soldiers. This may explain his emphasis upon honouring the rank and file alongside their commanders.[21] Cicero's rhetorical strategy has been aptly termed the 'rhetoric of crisis'.[22] Throughout *Philippic* XIV, for example, Cicero refers to Antonius' men as

[14] Cicero *Philippic* IX.7.
[15] Cicero *Philippic* IX.3.
[16] Cicero *Philippic* IX.16.
[17] Hall 2002, 277.
[18] Cicero *Philippic* IX.7.
[19] Cicero *Philippic* XIV.21.
[20] Cicero *Philippic* XIV.6; cf. XIV.22.
[21] Cicero *Philippic* XIV.29.
[22] Hall 2002, 283–5.

'parricides', and Antonius himself as 'leader of brigands'.[23] Shamelessly he exaggerated the truth and by the extremes of his language goaded his audience into action to resist Antonius.

Whereas Cicero's proposal for a monument to commemorate the fallen in the civil war against Antonius was never actually executed, a unique example of a war memorial still stands at Adamclissi in modern Romania, in the Roman province of Moesia Inferior, about 50km from the coast of the Black Sea. The monument in question is a large altar—with sides about 12m long and 6m high—on whose external walls were inscribed the names of Romans killed in battle.[24] This altar is the only known example of a monument displaying a casualty list in memory of fallen Roman soldiers. The inscribed list is only partially preserved, but it began with a heading in larger letters, giving an emperor's name and titles,[25] followed by a declaration that the monument had been set up '[In …] memory of the most valiant [men who …] met their death in the service of the State'. [26] After this, the name of an officer was treated as a sub-heading, and then came columns listing the names of perhaps 3,800 casualties, including soldiers from Italy, Gallia Narbonensis, the Rhineland, and Noricum.[27] Roman military and social hierarchy was maintained in the location of the names, with the names of citizen legionary soldiers appearing on the front of the monument facing east, and peregrine auxiliaries being confined to the north side.

The most crucial part of the text is now missing, in this case the name of the emperor; consequently the altar's date and historical context have provoked much debate. The first possibility is that it commemorated soldiers killed fighting for the emperor Domitian towards the end of the first century CE. Literary sources record two military disasters somewhere in this region, when the provincial governor Oppius Sabinus was killed with his men in CE 85, and then the praetorian prefect Cornelius Fuscus in CE 86–87.[28] Alternatively, the casualties may have been incurred during

---

[23] Cicero *Philippic* XIV.27, 32.

[24] Gottlieb 1949, 8; Dorutiu 1961; Amiotti 1990; Hope 2003, 91–2; Stefan 2005, 442–4.

[25] Amiotti (following the editor of *CIL ad loc.*) assumes that the emperor concerned must have set up the monument himself: Amiotti 1990, 208.

[26] *CIL* III 14214; *ILS* 9107: *pro re p. morte occubu[erunt]*; with new fragments published by Dorutiu 1961.

[27] Dorutiu 1961, esp. 349–51; Poulter 1986, 524.

[28] For Oppius Sabinus, Suetonius *Domitian* 6.1. For Cornelius Fuscus' defeat, Dio Cassius 67.6.5, 68.9.3. Syme 1971, 73–83 argues that the prefect named upon the war memorial is not Cornelius Fuscus, but he does support a Domitianic date for the monument. For contemporary reactions to Fuscus' death, see Martial *Epigram* 6.76, Juvenal *Satire* 4.111–12.

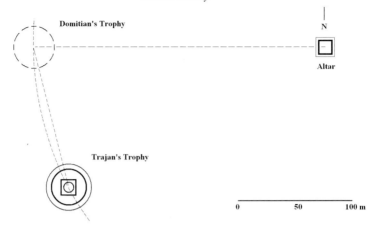

Figure 4.1 Map showing location of monuments at Adamclissi. (After A. S. Stefan *Les Guerres Daciques de Domitien et de Trajan* [Rome: Collection de l'École française de Rome, 2005], fig. 191)

Trajan's first Dacian campaign of CE 101/2.[29] Our problem is that we have no reliable accounts of either emperor's campaigns. Our historical sources for Domitian are distorted by the fact that after his assassination, writers were only too eager to trumpet his failures. For Trajan, we have only an epitome of Dio Cassius' history of this period, and although it is tempting to treat the spiral reliefs on Trajan's column as a historical narrative of his Dacian Wars, this is inappropriate given the generic character of many scenes, included for their ideological rather than documentary quality.[30] It is therefore possible to find arguments connecting the war memorial to both Domitian and Trajan.[31]

Above all, the altar needs to be interpreted in its topographical context. Figure 4.1 is a map showing the location of monuments at Adamclissi.[32] Close by the altar, about 250m to the west and sharing the

[29] Amiotti 1990, 212.
[30] Hannestad, 1988, 158.
[31] For a concise summary of the problem, Griffin 2000, 111. Poulter 1986 favours a Trajanic context for both monuments, and Picard 1957, 39 even offers a restoration of the altar's inscription so as to refer to Trajan's Dacian War. Dio Cassius Xiphilinus 68.8.2 states that, during the Dacian Wars, Trajan set up an altar to honour soldiers killed in action, and ordered annual ceremonies to be performed there. Although it is tempting to make a direct link between this and the altar at Adamclissi, the epitome is not detailed enough to allow for this; we do not know whether names were inscribed on this altar. On the other hand, the commanding officer, whose name is not preserved, is given two hometowns—Naples and Pompeii—which must reflect his relocation following Vesuvius' eruption in CE 79. This does not rule out a date of 101/2, but might favour 85–87. Syme 1971, 83 supports a Domitianic date.
[32] After Stefan 2005 fig. 191.

FIG. 2. RECONSTRUCTION DU TROPHÉE PAR M. FURTWÄNGLER.

Figure 4.2   Trajan's trophy at Adamclissi: reconstruction. (From T. Antonesco, *Le trophée d'Adamclissi* [Jassy: I.S. Ionesco, 1905], fig. 2)

same alignment, is a large circular structure; until recently, generally thought to be a mausoleum honouring the commander killed together with the men commemorated on the altar, it now seems more likely to be a victory trophy.[33] Too little of it remains to provide conclusive evidence for its function, but it appears to have been built at roughly the same time

---

[33] Poulter 1986, 525 argues that the circular structure is a victory monument, and that both this structure and the war memorial relate to the First Dacian War; on his interpretation, the later trophy then commemorates the final conquest of Dacia at the end of the Second Dacian War. The recent work of Stefan 2005, 442–4, argues convincingly that it fits the typology of a *tropaeum*, whereas no traces of human burials have been found.

as the altar, with which it shares a poor local limestone construction, as well as the same orientation. Only 200m from the altar is Trajan's massive victory trophy of CE 108/9, which gave its name to a nearby town and its inhabitants, who called themselves the *Traianenses Tropaeenses* (Fig. 4.2).[34] This huge circular monument—about 40m in diameter and 40m high—was once topped by a trophy, 4.75m high, at the base of which was the figure of a barbarian captive flanked by two mourning women. Around the top of the main cylinder were originally fifty-four metopes, with a crenellated parapet above, which was decorated with reliefs of bound captives and lions. The metopes portray the Romans' conflict with various barbarian opponents. Fragments of the monument's dedicatory inscription indicate that it was built under Trajan in CE 108/9.[35] It is much more conspicuous in the landscape than the war memorial, positioned as it is on a high plateau, so that it is visible from the Danube.

Whatever the exact dating of the three monuments, their juxtaposition makes a crucial point about the Roman culture of commemorating warfare. The location of the monuments is rather curious. The earlier war memorial may have been sited here not because of any direct link with a scene of fighting, but because this was a point where major roads met. In turn, Trajan's trophy was probably erected here not because this was where he himself had fought—it is in fact roughly 400km away from the focus of Trajan's Dacian Wars—but because it was intended to be a visual response to the earlier war memorial.[36] Indeed, the diversity of the barbarians depicted on the trophy's metopes argues against any close connection with the opponents encountered in Trajan's fighting further north. Careful differentiation in the clothing and hairstyle of the barbarians on the trophy identifies them as four different groups of inhabitants of the region around Adamclissi rather than of the area further north of the Danube, where Trajan's opponent, King Decebalus, was based.[37] Although Trajan's trophy must have drawn some of its significance from his success in the Second Dacian War against Decebalus, therefore, the metopes indicate that the monument also commemorates the defeat of barbarians around Adamclissi. Furthermore, Trajan's trophy was dedicated to Mars Ultor—

---

[34] On the *Tropaeum Traiani* and other monuments at Adamclissi, see Antonesco 1905; Barnea 1976; Bobu Florescu 1965; Borg 1991, 55–7; Gottlieb 1949; Hannestad 1988, 171–3; Poulter 1986, 524; Richmond 1967; Rossi 1972.

[35] *CIL* III 12467.

[36] Dorutiu 1961, 363.

[37] Syme 1971, 83; Coulston 2003, 413 traces non-Decebelan Dacians, Sarmatian Roxolani, Germanic Bastarnae, and Transdanubian migrants.

Mars the Avenger.[38] The choice of deity may well encapsulate the idea that this trophy commemorated victory for the Romans in a location where previously they had met with a serious defeat, and that Trajan had at last wreaked vengeance upon the barbarians who had earlier slaughtered Romans, whether in his own army or in Domitian's. Certainly, the later construction of Trajan's trophy indicates that the Romans were not content to leave a war memorial as the final word.

The most logical conclusion, however, is that both the earlier circular monument and the funerary altar were Domitian's.[39] If this is correct, Trajan's decision to demolish Domitian's victory monument, leaving only the altar commemorating his army's defeat, and to commission a victory monument in juxtaposition to it fits into the broader historical context of the relationship between these two emperors. One of the most striking features of Trajan's rule was the way in which he was presented as the 'best of emperors' in contrast to the tyrannical Domitian. Even though in many respects Trajan actually continued many of Domitian's projects, and although he had earlier supported Domitian during the revolt of Saturninus in CE 89, Trajan's public profile was built up, for example by Pliny the Younger, as being in sharp contrast to that of his predecessor.[40] An important part of the alleged differences between the two emperors was their military prowess. Pliny had developed this contrast as early as CE 100, before Trajan had even embarked upon his war in Dacia. In his speech to the Senate in praise of Trajan, Pliny confidently declared that 'at some time the Capitol will receive chariots that are not sham nor the images of a false victory, but a commander bringing home genuinely solid glory'.[41] Whereas Domitian was represented as having falsely celebrated triumphs at Rome for successes in Germany and Dacia,[42] Trajan was said to have put right Domitian's failures, for example by recovering the military standard lost by Cornelius Fuscus. If the memorial for the dead is Domitianic, therefore, we might hypothesize that Trajan was once again drawing attention to the way in which his troops had completed business left unfinished by Domitian by later building his huge trophy opposite it.

[38] *CIL* III 12467, with new fragment published by Gostar 1969.
[39] Stefan 2005, 443.
[40] Griffin 2000, 96, 97–8, 110.
[41] Pliny *Panegyricus* 16.3.
[42] Dio Cassius Xiphilinus 67.9.6: Domitian's triumph popularly criticized as really being a funeral of those who had died in Dacia and in Rome.

The Shameful Dead? Battlefield Burial and Commemoration

These two exceptions, then, only emphasize that the monumental war
memorial was not part of the repertoire of Roman commemorative culture. It has been suggested that in modern times it was the sheer scale of
casualties in the First World War that inspired the ubiquitous setting up
of war memorials during the 1920s in Britain, after hundreds of thousands had perished, representing about 2 per cent of the male population.[43] In France, too, the scale of involvement among the country's
population, with about a fifth of the population being mobilized, of
whom 1,450,000 died, resulted in virtually every family in every village
feeling the impact of the war. Consequently 38,000 monuments were set
up throughout the country on the initiative of the local communities
themselves, albeit with official encouragement.[44] The Romans, however,
also suffered comparatively high losses during the Second Punic War
(218–201 BCE), when as many as 16 per cent of all adult males in Italy may
have been killed, but we find no official commemoration of the war dead,
despite the fact that they had perished in resisting the Carthaginian invasion of Italy.[45] The lack of monumental commemoration of Rome's war
dead might therefore seem to tally well with the recent conclusions of
Tonio Hölscher's examination of the artistic representation of warfare in
Greece and Rome. He concludes: 'Romans do not much care for their
fallen dead, because death in war—except for some great heroes of the
past—was not glorious but shameful.'[46] In part, he suggests, this attitude
was a response to the professionalization of the Roman army during the
imperial period. There are several reasons, however, why this explanation
does not adequately reflect Roman attitudes to those killed in battle.[47]

At times of utter disaster Roman soldiers were left unburied, but this
did not reflect a sentiment that their deaths were in any way shameful. On
the contrary, in Virgil's depiction of the Underworld, those who had died
fighting for their country were granted a peaceful afterlife in the Elysian
Fields.[48] During the Second Punic War, the Carthaginian general Hannibal
inflicted a number of grave defeats upon the Romans in Italy, most notably

---

[43] Borg 1991, ix; Rich 1993, 45, n.1.
[44] Prost 1997, 308–9.
[45] Santosuosso 1997, 183; Rich 1993, 45.
[46] Hölscher 2003, 14.
[47] Hope forthcoming deals in detail with this issue, so here I simply add a few additional
observations.
[48] Virgil *Aeneid* 6.660.

at Lake Trasimene and at Cannae. In both cases, practically the whole army was wiped out, rank and file and generals alike. The few survivors were in no condition to think of anything more than their own personal survival. At Cannae, for example, Polybius claims that about 73,000 Roman infantry and cavalry died, with only about 3,470 escaping. In that case, we must picture Roman casualties falling during that one August afternoon at a rate of over 100 per minute.[49] The one surviving consul fled from the scene as quickly as he could with just seventy cavalrymen.[50] Some two centuries later, in CE 9, the German leader Arminius and his men annihilated three legions and their commander, P. Quinctilius Varus, together with three cavalry squadrons and six auxiliary cohorts, in the Teutoburg Forest, and their bones lay unburied until another Roman army led by Germanicus came onto the scene a few years later, and buried them.[51] Archaeological work on the Kalkrieser–Niewedder depression in north-western Germany, where Varus and his men were wiped out, has brought to light not just military weapons, but also everyday items, such as gaming counters, scissors and razors, tools for working wood and leather, as well as medical instruments and writing implements.[52] This is indicative of the thoroughness with which the Roman troops were destroyed.

In general, Roman literary sources rarely mention the burying of the dead after a battle, even whilst recording casualty figures. We even find only a handful of private tombstones for soldiers killed in action, set up usually by family members, but sometimes by comrades.[53] Some such monuments remained cenotaphs—as in the case of M. Caelius killed in the Varus disaster—whilst others included the name of the fallen soldier in a family funerary monument.[54] Repatriation of remains for burial was not the norm, nor was the state usually involved in setting up tombs.

---

[49] Hanson 1995, 49.

[50] Polybius 3.116–17. Livy 22.49.14–15 records 47,700 casualties, and 50 cavalry escaping with Terentius.

[51] Tacitus *Annals* 1.60–2; Suetonius *Gaius* 3.1–3; Clementoni 1990.

[52] Schlüter 1999.

[53] For example, *CIL* X 3886 = *ILS* 2225, a father commemorating his two sons who had served with Julius Caesar, one of whom was killed in action; *CIL* V 4371 = *ILS* 2065, Iulius Festus, killed in a barbarian war, commemorated by his brother; *CIL* XI 1196 = *ILS* 2284, casualty of the CE 69 civil war buried by his comrades; *CIL* III 6418 = *ILS* 2259, set up by an heir. Hope 2003, 85–9; Keppie 2003. Compare Haynes 1999, who discusses the ways in which auxiliary soldiers developed stronger ties to their families, friends, and colleagues than to the state.

[54] For M. Caelius, *ILS* 2244; for L. Silicius Saturninus, killed in Numidia, commemorated along with his mother by his brother at Lepti Minus, *CIL* VIII 22899 = *ILS* 9088; for Tadius Exuperatus, killed in Germany, commemorated along with his mother by his sister, *RIB* I 369.

Exceptions to this rule include the high-profile burials of members of the imperial family who died whilst serving abroad. The ashes of both Germanicus and Trajan were escorted back to Rome and buried with great pomp. An arch erected in Germanicus' honour at Rome in the Circus Flaminius bore an inscription that described his death as incurred in the service of the state.[55] Trajan's ashes were interred at the base of his column, an exceptional burial within the city's sacred boundary. In both cases, Rome devised new ways of honouring imperial princes who were represented as having died in service, even though their deaths were not actually the direct result of enemy attack.[56]

When burial of the dead is mentioned in literary sources, they do not record the norm. Historians like Livy do not narrate the burial of the rank and file, since they were primarily interested in the deeds of great men, and even the burial of generals killed in action is recorded only in exceptional circumstances. For example, Livy mentions burial of commanders killed following the act of self-sacrifice known as *devotio*, by which a Roman commander ceremonially 'devoted' himself to death as a way of bringing destruction upon the enemy. By charging into the midst of the foe when the Romans seemed to be about to lose a battle, a commander might give up his life to save his men. Livy gives a dramatic account of the *devotio* of Publius Decius in 340 BCE during a battle against the Latins. After uttering a formal prayer, declaring 'I devote the legions and auxiliaries of our enemies together with myself to the gods of the Underworld and to Earth', Decius rode into the midst of the Latins, spreading confusion far and wide, eventually to fall beneath a shower of missiles.[57] This episode is later mirrored by his son in 295 BCE during a battle against Samnites and Gauls. Following his father's example, Decius once again devoted himself. His body could not be found the next day, and was retrieved only on the day following that, under heaps of dead Gauls; he was given an honorific funeral and eulogy by his colleague.[58] For Livy, then, reporting the honorific burial of these two commanders suited his dramatic purposes, but he does not as a general rule mention the Romans' burial of casualties of any rank.

By contrast, Livy does mention several times Hannibal's burial of his own dead. For example, he states that the Carthaginian general buried

[55] Tabula Siarensis fragment 1, line 18: *ob rem p[ublicam] mortem obisset.*
[56] Compare, too, the burial of the Elder Drusus at Rome in 9 BCE and the honours accorded him: Tacitus *Annals* 2.7.2; Dio Cassius 55.1–2.
[57] Livy 8.9–10.
[58] See Livy 10.28.15 for the act of *devotio*, 10.29 for his burial.

about 8,000 of his dead after Cannae, whilst Polybius records that after the battle of Trasimene, Hannibal allowed his troops to rest and paid last honours to those of the highest rank among his dead.[59] Even more surprisingly, a recurring theme is Hannibal's burial of Roman generals after having cut their forces to pieces. At Trasimene, Hannibal is said to have tried to bury the Roman commander Flaminius, but failed to find his body. Later on, after the battle of Cannae, Livy is more hesitant, stating only that some sources say that Hannibal recovered and buried the dead Roman consul Lucius Aemilius, but he is more definite that Hannibal did later actually bury the consul Marcellus in 208 BCE.[60] Whereas the Roman historian could take for granted how the Romans would treat their own dead, Hannibal's treatment of the dead was of more interest to his Roman audience. The later epic poet Silius Italicus, too, contrasts Hannibal's humane treatment of both Carthaginian and Roman dead with the brutality of a Roman general who displays to him upon a pike the head of his brother Hasdrubal.[61]

The burial of the dead, or lack of it, during civil war also attracts comment from literary historians, as a means of heightening the sense of pathos as Romans slaughter Romans. Tacitus draws a vivid picture of the aftermath of the battle of Bedriacum in northern Italy of CE 69, when Vitellius' men defeated Otho's. The victors nursed the wounds of relatives from the opposite side, and sought out for burial the bodies of kinsmen who had fought for the enemy. He describes how 'vanquished and victors burst into tears, cursing with unhappy pleasure the lottery of civil war; in the same tents they nursed wounds, some of their brothers, others of their kinsmen … Nor was there anyone so immune from the tragedy that he did not mourn some death'.[62] Even so, Tacitus comments, most of the fallen lay unburied. He thus sets up for himself an opportunity for characterizing the ruthless Vitellius, who himself had not been a combatant in the battle. On visiting the scene of battle some forty days later, Vitellius viewed the mutilated corpses, severed limbs, and rotting bodies of both men and horses; but, Tacitus reveals, 'Vitellius did not avert his gaze nor did he shudder at so many thousands of unburied citizens'.[63] Tacitus, then, chose

---

[59] Livy 22.49; Polybius 3.85.5—compare Livy 22.7.5 for Trasimene.
[60] Livy 22.7.5 for Flaminius; 22.52.6 for L. Aemilius; 27.28.1 for Marcellus.
[61] See Silius Italicus *Punica* 10.504–78 for Hannibal's burial of a Roman general and of his own dead after Cannae; 15.387–96 for Hannibal's burial of the fallen consul Marcellus; 15.813–14 for Hasdrubal's head.
[62] Tacitus *Histories* 2.45.
[63] Tacitus *Histories* 2.70.

to describe what had happened to the Roman fallen in this particular battle since it allowed him to evoke feelings of horror in his audience at the outcome of the battle itself, as well as at the character of Vitellius.

Given, therefore, that literary sources tended to focus only upon exceptional circumstances, it was certainly not the norm for Roman soldiers to lie unburied on the battlefield, despite the fact that we might gain this impression by looking purely at the comments made by Roman historians.[64] On the contrary, it is clear that the Romans did regard it as of the utmost importance that their fallen should receive a decent burial. A mid-first-century CE handbook on generalship—the *Strategikos* of Onasander—dedicated to a prominent Roman, Q. Veranius, makes it quite clear that it was a prime duty of a general to gather up and bury his dead. Onasander states that whether victorious or defeated, the general should see to burying his dead immediately. He describes it as a 'holy act of reverence for the dead and a necessary example for the living', concluding that if the dead are not buried, soldiers may believe that their own bodies will be neglected in the event of death. Failure to bury the fallen could seriously affect the army's morale.[65] Significantly, it is Julius Caesar, ever conscious of his image as ideal general, who relates how he spent three days tending to the wounded and burying the dead after the battle at Bibracte against the Helvetii.[66] The norm for Roman casualties was for them to be gathered up and cremated all together on the battlefield.[67] Exceptionally, the people of Nursia added an inscription upon the tumulus set up for casualties in the civil war stating that they had 'fallen in defence of liberty', and thereby incurred the wrath of the young Octavian.[68] Even so, there was no expectation that the fallen would receive monumental commemoration either on the battlefield or at Rome.

The lack of Roman war memorials does not, however, reflect any sense of undervaluing men who had lost their lives in battle. Instead, the lack of war memorials may reflect a distinctive attitude to public duty and service on the part of the Romans.[69] In his account of the death and public funeral of the tyrannicide Brutus, Dionysius of Halicarnassus indulges in a brief excursus upon the tradition of delivering eulogies at funerals. His aim is

---

[64] Compare also Tacitus *Annals* 4.73 for comment on a Roman general leaving his dead unburied.

[65] Onasander *Strategikos* 36.

[66] Caesar *Gallic War* 1.26.

[67] Rüpke 1990, 203; Giorcelli 1995, 238–40; Hope 2003, 87–8. For cremation, Pliny the Elder *Natural History* 7.54.187; for battlefield burial, Appian *Civil War* 1.43, 2.82.

[68] Suetonius *Augustus* 12.1

[69] Dionysius of Halicarnassus *Roman Antiquities* 5.17.4–6.

to prove that the Romans, not the Greeks, were the first to institute the custom of delivering a eulogy at a public funeral. Whether or not Dionysius is strictly correct does not matter. What matters is his insight into the fundamental difference in attitude between Rome and Athens in particular. He comments that the Romans delivered a funeral oration for any public benefactor, whereas the Greeks—notably the Athenians—reserved such praise for those killed in war. Whereas the Athenians valued most of all the way in which a man met his death, for the Romans, a man's contribution to the state did not have to be judged purely on his death in battle:

> For, whereas the Athenians seem to have ordained that these orations should be pronounced at the funerals of those only who had died in war, believing that one should determine who are good men solely on the basis of the valour they show at their death, even though in other respects they are without merit, the Romans, on the other hand appointed this honour to be paid to all their illustrious men, whether as commanders in war or as leaders in the civil administration they have given wise counsels and performed noble deeds, and this not alone to those who have died in war, but also to those who have met their end in any manner whatsoever, believing that good men deserve praise for every virtue they have shown during their lives and not solely for the single glory of their death.[70]

Commemorating Victory and Defeat

If we were to focus exclusively upon the monumental commemoration of warfare, we might suspect the Romans of only ever commemorating their successes. Traditionally, the aftermath of a victorious battle saw the Romans gather up the weapons of their defeated foe and dedicate them in the form of a trophy on the battlefield. This relatively simple form of commemoration gradually took on grander dimensions, culminating in huge monumental trophies sculpted in stone, such as at La Turbie, near modern Monaco, celebrating Augustus' subjugation of the Alpine tribes. At Rome, it was common practice for the victorious general to pay for a monument commemorating his victory by selling off the spoils of war; this was known as dedicating *ex manubiis*.[71] During the Republic, members of Rome's elite competed for prestige by dedicating temples alongside the triumphal route. Once Augustus had set the pattern for one-man rule, however, the pattern of competition among the elite was altered, so that

[70] Dionysius of Halicarnassus *Roman Antiquities* 5.17.5 (Loeb translation); Briquel 1990, esp. 142–3.
[71] Aulus Gellius *Attic Nights* 13.25.26.

instead of competing with fellow senators, emperors tried to rival their
predecessors by constructing increasingly lavish buildings paid for *ex
manubiis*, culm inating with the Flavian Amphitheatre (or Colosseum)
and Trajan's Forum, the grandest forum ever built in the capital.[72]
Furthermore, triumphal arches decorated with images of barbarian defeat
can still be seen, not only in Rome but in many different provinces too.

The public commemorative art displayed on such monuments sometimes depicts scenes of Roman vulnerability, and even admission of short-
term defeat. Victory monuments celebrating Trajan's Dacian Wars, for
example, acknowledge that the Romans met with fierce opposition. On
Trajan's column at Rome, we see Roman prisoners being tortured by
Dacian women (scene 45; fig. 4.3) and the battlements of a Dacian fortress decorated with severed heads on stakes—presumably trophies of
unfortunate Roman soldiers (scene 25; fig. 4.4).[73] On Trajan's trophy at
Adamclissi too, several metopes depict Dacians on the attack. Although
there is no doubt that the Roman troops will be victorious in the end, the
survival of individual Roman soldiers is sometimes in question. One
Roman soldier is shown facing an opponent armed with his lethal curved
sword, which he is raising not in defeat, since it is the inner part of the
blade that bears its cutting edge, but with which he is trying to attack the
Roman (metope 21; fig. 4.5). In another scene (metope 37; fig. 4.6), we see
a Roman soldier taking up a defensive position, as another Dacian adopts
a different manoeuvre in attacking his Roman foe, even though one of his
comrades lies dead on the ground and another simply looks back on the
scene.[74] Nevertheless, the only dead bodies depicted are those of Rome's
opponents. We might conclude, then, that the Roman culture of commemoration involved ignoring Roman casualties, and emphasizing only
Roman victory.

Such a conclusion, however, is over-reliant on one type of commemoration, as expressed via 'material' objects. The extensive project directed
by Pierre Nora on French *lieux de mémoire* reminds us that monuments
are only one facet of any culture of commemoration, and that 'immate-
rial' constructions of memory are equally important.[75] In Nora's defini-
tion, a *lieu de mémoire* is 'any significant entity, whether material or

---

[72] Alföldy 1995; Packer 2001.
[73] Rossi 1972, 63 suggests that these may be the decaying heads of Domitian's men; see too a
commentary on this scene by Lepper and Frere 1988, 72.
[74] Bobu Florescu 1965, 497.
[75] Nora 1996, xvi.

Figure 4.3   Trajan's column, scene 45: torture of Roman prisoners. (From C. Cichorius, *Die Reliefs der Traiansäule* [Berlin: De Gruyter, 1896–1927], plate 117)

Figure 4.4   Trajan's column, 25: battlements of Dacian fortress displaying severed heads. (From C. Cichorius, *Die Reliefs der Traiansäule* [Berlin: De Gruyler, 1896-1927], plate 64)

non-material in nature, which by dint of human will or the work of time has become a symbolic element of the memorial heritage'.[76] Included among his case studies are geographical places, historical figures, monuments and buildings, literary and artistic objects, emblems, commemorations, and symbols.[77] The lack of war memorials in Roman culture does not mean that the Romans refused to acknowledge military defeats, but that they developed a different culture of commemoration, whereby Roman military disasters were incorporated into the state's religious calendar.

Rome's response to heavy casualties in warfare was not to remember the individuals who had lost their lives, but to lament a serious reversal in Rome's fortunes and to seek to win back the gods' support. Military disasters caused the Romans to turn to the gods with special sacrifices and prayers in order to try to avert divine displeasure. In times of protracted crisis the Romans summoned new deities from abroad in order to boost their divine protectors: their response to Hannibal's continued success in ravaging Italy was to escort from Phrygia the aniconic black stone thought

[76] Nora 1996, xvii.
[77] Kritzman, 1996, x.

Figure 4.5   Trajan's trophy at Adamclissi: metope 21 (inv. 17). (Photograph by J. J. Coulston)

Figure 4.6 Trajan's trophy at Adamclissi: metope 37 (inv. 34). (Photograph © Christian Chirita)

to represent the Great Mother of the Gods and to establish her cult on the Palatine.[78] After Cannae, the Romans even offered human sacrifices, contrary to their usual custom.[79]

The nadir in the whole of Rome's history was considered to be the city's sack by the Gauls in 390 BCE. The military defeat at the River Allia which allowed the Gauls to sack Rome was designated in the state calendar as a day of ill omen. Livy explains how the Senate

> then began to deliberate about days of ill omen. The 18th July, which was notorious for a double disaster, since on this day the Fabii had been slaughtered at the Cremera and then the atrocious battle was fought at the Allia which led to the destruction of the City, they named the Day of the Allia after the latter disaster, and distinguished it by the fact that no business should be carried out whether public or private.[80]

The disaster at the Allia was synchronized with another at the Cremera, when 300 Fabii had been killed by the Etruscans.[81] Consequently, 18 July was commemorated each year, and no business of any kind was transacted.[82] The anniversary was long-lived: it was observed by Romans well into the imperial period, being included in inscribed calendars dating from the first centuries BCE and CE.[83] In the Augustan period it was far from an obscure anniversary: in Ovid's irreverent didactic poem *The Art of Love*, the poet wittily suggests that the day of the Allia is actually a good day for lovers, since a man cannot be expected to buy presents for his mistress on a day when all the shops are shut.[84] In CE 69, criticisms were made of the doomed emperor Vitellius for taking up his position as *pontifex maximus* on this day, and Plutarch attests to contemporary Roman observance of this anniversary in the early second century CE: 'But this day of the Allia is regarded by the Romans as one of the unluckiest' (*Camillus* 19.8).[85] Even writers of late antiquity remained conscious of the day's significance.[86] Nor was the day observed only in Rome itself: in Pisa, the town council decreed that the death-day of Augustus' heir and

---

[76] Nora 1996, xvii.

[77] Kritzman, 1996, x.

[78] Livy 29.10.4–8; 29.14.5–14.

[79] Livy 22.57.6; Plutarch *Roman Questions* 83 = *Moralia* 283F–284C.

[80] Livy 6.1.11.

[81] Plutarch *Camillus* 19.1; for *Fasti Antiates Ministrorum*, Degrassi 1963, 208.

[82] Cicero *Letter to Atticus* 9.5.2; Festus s.v. 'religiosus' p. 348L.

[83] For *Fasti Antiates Maiores* 84–55 BCE, Degrassi 1963, 15; for *Fasti Amiterni* post-CE 20, Degrassi 1963, 189; for *Fasti Antiates Ministrorum* CE 23, Degrassi 1963, 208.

[84] Ovid *Art of Love* 1.413.

[85] Compare Tacitus *Histories* 2.91; Suetonius *Vitellius* 11; Plutarch *Roman Questions* 25 =

the town's patron Gaius Caesar should be treated on a par with the *dies Alliensis*.[87] In this way, his death was represented as a crisis of the utmost order for the Roman state. In dealing with this one disaster, then, the Romans did not seek to hide their defeat, but developed a distinctive way of commemorating it.

Admittedly, the Day of the Allia was of unique significance since it marked the only occasion when the city of Rome itself was attacked and sacked, and when the Romans even contemplated moving their capital to Veii. Nevertheless, other disasters were also commemorated in the calendar, as can be seen in the inscribed calendars surviving from the late republic and early imperial periods. Anniversaries of both military success and failure were marked in the calendar. Some festivals commemorated the foundation of temples at Rome, which had been dedicated as the result of vows made to the gods by generals hard-pressed in the heat of battle. The dedicatory days of the temples of Castor and Pollux, of Concord, and of Jupiter Victor—temples all founded after a battlefield vow—were still recalled many generations later.[88] Games too might be celebrated to recall past victories, such as the Games for Sulla's Victory at the Colline Gate. These began on 26 October and culminated on 1 November, the actual date of the battle.[89] Other festivals, however, commemorated failure. Most notably, 8 June was the dedicatory day of the temple of *Mens* ('Good Sense') on the Capitol. This temple had been established in the aftermath of the catastrophe at Trasimene to remind the Romans of the lack of *mens* demonstrated by the Roman general Gaius Flaminius, which had resulted in his defeat by Hannibal in that battle.[90] Finally, we can see that such anniversaries continued to weigh upon Roman sensibilities in an example of the ill fortune associated with a day being reversed by later success: 6 October marked the date of a defeat at Arausio (modern Orange) in 105 BCE, but in 69 BCE the general Lucullus vowed to change the luck of the day, and did so, winning a battle against Tigranes in Armenia.[91]

During the imperial period, however, we do not find fresh military disasters being added to the calendar, despite the notoriety of some disasters, notably the slaughter of Varus' legions. The only hint of some sort of

Moralia 269E–270D.

[86] Minucius Felix 7.4; Sidonius Apollinaris 9.244.

[87] *CIL* XI 1421 = *ILS* 140.

[88] For Castor and Pollux, 27 January, see Degrassi 1963, 403; Concord, 5 February, Degrassi 1963, 406; Jupiter Victor, 13 April, Degrassi 1963, 440.

[89] For *Ludi victoriae Sullanae*, see Degrassi 1963, 526; Scullard 1981, 196.

commemoration of that disaster comes in Florus, who alleges that it occurred on the anniversary of the battle of Cannae.[92] Instead, new entries commemorate only success, such as Trajan's Dacian and Parthian victories, which appear in Ostia's calendar.[93] This is perhaps because the emperor's personal prestige was now at stake, as the leader under whose auspices all battles were fought.

Conclusion

Roman public monuments commemorating warfare might depict temporary reversals in Roman fortunes, but ultimately their message was of Roman victory. It was not usual to commemorate the human cost of war through memorials. Cicero's proposal for just such a memorial was never accomplished, and was made as a self-consciously novel measure, intended to draw attention to the crisis faced by the Roman state under attack from Marcus Antonius. Practical considerations perhaps discouraged such a practice and certainly made repatriation of remains too difficult logistically. Instead, the war dead could expect a decent burial en masse with their comrades on the battlefield. Nevertheless, the funerary altar inscribed with the names of the fallen at Adamclissi does indicate that the Romans could have pursued this sort of commemoration of their dead, had they wished to do so. The juxtaposition of the funerary altar at Adamclissi with what appear to be two victory trophies shows, however, that even in this exceptional case, the Romans chose to end on a triumphal note.

The Romans' choice not to commemorate their war dead with memorials was not because it was too difficult, nor because of a sense of shame or lack of concern for the dead. Even though they did not monumentalize individual losses, the Romans did not ignore defeat. Festivals incorporated into the state calendar recalled notorious defeats, and the Day of the Allia in particular was commemorated for many generations. The Roman response to military disaster, then, was to look forwards, and to attempt to win back the gods' support in order to prevent future disasters. It is worth noting, however, that there was a shift from Republic to Principate. Once emperors ruled at Rome, their military disasters did not enter the calendar, only their victories. Furthermore, Augustus set the precedent for emperors to monopolize the image as war heroes, reserving

---

[90] *Fasti Maffeiani*, post-8 BCE, Degrassi 1963, 77; Degrassi 1963, 467; Scullard 1981, 148.
[91] Plutarch *Lucullus* 27.7.
[92] Florus 2.30.35.

for themselves the supreme celebration of the triumph. Only emperors like Domitian who were officially condemned after falling from power were depicted as failing in war. The tendency during the imperial period for the Romans to play down military disasters, therefore, was not the result of the professionalization of the army and the sentiment that those killed were simply doing their job. Rather it reflected the higher stakes at risk for an emperor, in contrast to generals during the Republic, since his whole authority could have been undermined if he was seen to have suffered great military losses: this in turn might have implied that he had lost the support of the gods.

Note. I would like to thank Polly Low and Graham Oliver for inviting me to participate in this colloquium, and the British Academy and its staff for their hospitality. Members of the audience raised several interesting issues in response to my paper, to which I have endeavoured to respond in this revised version. I am also grateful to Val Hope for sharing her unpublished work on the topic of Roman war dead with me and to Jon Coulston for providing a photograph of the Adamclissi metope.

Bibliography

Alföldy, G. 1995. 'Eine Bauinschrift aus dem Colosseum.' *Zeitschrift für Papyrologie und Epigraphik* 109, 195–226.

Amiotti, G. 1990. 'Il "monumento ai caduti" di Adamklissi.' In *'Dulce et decorum est pro patria mori': la morte in combattimento nell'antichità*, ed. M. Sordi. Milan: Università Cattolica del Sacro Cuore, 207–13.

Antonesco, T. 1905. *Le trophée d'Adamclissi*. Jassy: I. S. Ionesco.

Bargagli, B. and C. Grosso. 1997. *I Fasti Ostienses: documento della storia di Ostia*. Itinerari Ostiensi 8. Rome: Soprintendenza Archeologica di Ostia.

Barnea, I. 1976. 'Tropaeum Traiani.' In *Princeton Encyclopaedia of Classical Sites*, ed. R. Stillwell. Princeton, NJ: Princeton University Press, 937.

Bobu Florescu, F. 1965. *Das Siegesdenkmal von Adamklissi Tropaeum Traiani*. Bucharest: Akademie der Rumänischen Volksrepublik.

Borg, A. 1991. *War Memorials from Antiquity to the Present*. London: Leo Cooper.

Briquel, D. 1990 'La morte di Lucio Giunio Bruto: sull'origine e lo sviluppo della leggenda di Bruto.' In *'Dulce et decorum est pro patria mori': la morte in combattimento nell'antichità*, ed. M. Sordi. Milan: Università Cattolica del Sacro Cuore, 127–43.

Chaniotis, A. 2005. *War in the Hellenistic World*. Oxford: Blackwell.

Clementoni, G. 1990. 'Germanico e i caduti di Teutoburgo.' In *'Dulce et decorum est pro patria mori': la morte in combattimento nell'antichità*, ed. M. Sordi. Milan: Università Cattolica del Sacro Cuore, 197–206.

Coarelli, F. 1999. 'Sepulcrum: A. Hirtius.' In *Lexicon Topographicum Urbis Romae*, Vol. 4: *P–S*, ed. E. M. Steinby. Rome: Quasar, 290.

Coulston, J. C. N. 2003. 'Overcoming the Barbarian: Depictions of Rome's Enemies in Trajanic Monumental Art.' In *The Representation and Perception of Roman Imperial Power*, ed. L. De Blois et al. Amsterdam: J. C. Gieben, 389–424.

Degrassi, A. 1963. *Inscriptiones Italiae XIII.ii—Fasti et Elogia: Fasti Anni Numani et Iuliani.* Rome: Istituto Poligrafico dello Stato.

Dorutiu, E. 1961. 'Some Observations on the Military Funeral Altar of Adamclissi.' *Dacia* n.s. 5, 345–63.

Fink, R. O. 1971. *Roman Military Records on Papyrus.* Cleveland, OH: Cape Western Reserve University Press, for the American Philological Association.

Giorcelli, S. 1995. 'Il funus militare.' In *La mort au quotidien dans le monde romain*, ed. F. Hinard. Paris: de Boccard, 235–42.

Gostar, N. 1969. 'Les inscriptions votives du monument triomphal d'Adamclissi.' *Latomus* 28, 119–25.

Gottlieb, C. 1949. 'The Monument of Adamklissi.' MA dissertation, University of London.

Griffin, M. 2000. 'Nerva to Hadrian.' In *Cambridge Ancient History*, Vol. 11, ed. A. K. Bowman et al. 2nd edn. Cambridge: Cambridge University Press, 84–131.

Hall, J. 2002, 'The *Philippics.*' In *Brill's Companion to Cicero: Oratory and Rhetoric*, ed. J. M. May. Leiden: Brill, 273–304.

Hannestad, N. 1988. *Roman Art and Imperial Policy.* Aarhus: Aarhus University Press.

Hanson, V. D. 1995. 'From Phalanx to Legion 350–250 BC.' In *The Cambridge Illustrated History of Warfare*, ed. G. Parker. Cambridge: Cambridge University Press, 32–49.

Haynes, I. 1999. 'Military Service and Cultural Identity in the *auxilia.*' In *The Roman Army as a Community*, ed. A. Goldsworthy and I. Haynes. *JRA* Supplement 34. Portsmouth, RI: Society for the Promotion of Roman Studies, 165–74.

Hölscher, T. 2003. 'Images of War in Greece and Rome: Between Military Practice, Public Memory, and Cultural Symbolism.' *Journal of Roman Studies* 93, 1–17.

Hope, V. M. 2003. 'Trophies and Tombstones: Commemorating the Roman Soldier.' In *The Social Commemoration of Warfare*, ed. R. Gilchrist. *World Archaeology* 35 (1), 79–97.

—— forthcoming. 'Soldiers of Death: The Practical and Symbolic Treatment of the Roman War Dead.' In *Good Deaths, Bad Deaths*, ed. D. Burton. London: Institute of Classical Studies.

Keppie, L. 2003. '"Having Been a Soldier": The Commemoration of Military Service on Funerary Monuments of the Early Roman Empire.' In *Documenting the Roman Army*, ed. J. J. Wilkes. *BICS* Supplement 81. London: Institute of Classical Studies, 31–53.

Kritzman, L. D. 1996. 'Foreword: In Remembrance of Things French.' In *Realms of Memory: Rethinking the French Past*, Vol. 1: *Conflicts and Divisions,* directed by P. Nora, ed. L. D. Kritzman. Translated by A. Goldhammer. New York: Columbia University Press, ix–xiv.

Lepper, F. and S. Frere. 1988. *Trajan's Column: A New Edition of the Cichorius Plates.* Gloucester: Alan Sutton.

Low, P. 2003. 'Remembering War in Fifth-century Greece: Ideologies, Societies, and Commemoration beyond Democratic Athens.' In *The Social Commemoration of Warfare*, ed. R. Gilchrist. *World Archaeology* 35 (1), 98–111.

Macciocca, M. 1999. 'Sepulcrum: C. Vibius Pansa.' In *Lexicon Topographicum Urbis Romae*, Vol. 4: *P–S*, ed. E. M. Steinby. Rome: Quasar, 30.

Nora, P. 1996. 'From Lieux de mémoire to Realms of Memory.' In *Realms of Memory: Rethinking the French Past,* Vol. 1: *Conflicts and Divisions*, directed by P. Nora, ed. L. D. Kritzman. Translated by A. Goldhammer. New York: Columbia University Press, xv–xxiv.

Packer, J. E. 2001. *The Forum of Trajan in Rome: A Study of the Monuments in Brief.* Berkeley: University of California Press.

Picard, G. C. 1957. *Les trophées romains.* Paris: de Boccard.

Poulter, A. G. 1986. 'The Lower Moesian Limes and the Dacian Wars of Trajan.' In *Studien zu den Militärgrenzen.* Roms 3. 13 Internationaler Limeskongreß. Stuttgart: Konrad Theiss Verlag, 519–28.

Prost, A. 1997. 'Monuments to the Dead.' In *Realms of Memory: Rethinking the French Past,* Vol. 2: *Traditions*, directed by P. Nora, ed. L. D. Kritzman. Translated by A. Goldhammer. New York: Columbia University Press, 306–30.

Rice, E. 1993. 'The Glorious Dead: Commemoration of the Fallen and Portrayal of Victory in the Late Classical and Hellenistic World.' In *War and Society in the Greek World*, ed. J. Rich and G. Shipley. London and New York: Routledge, 224–57.

Rich, J. 1993. 'Fear, Greed and Glory: The Causes of Roman War-making in the Middle Republic.' In *War and Society in the Roman World*, ed. J. Rich and G. Shipley. London and New York: Routledge, 36–68.

Richmond, I. A. 1967. 'Adamclissi.' *Papers of the British School at Rome* 35, 29–39.

Rossi, L. 1972. 'A Historiographic Reassessment of the Metopes of the Tropaeum Traiani at Adamklissi.' *Archaeological Journal* 129, 56–68.

Rüpke, J. 1990. *Domi Militiae: Die religiöse Konstruktion des Krieges in Rom.* Stuttgart: Franz Steiner Verlag.

Santosuosso, A. 1997. *Soldiers, Citizens and the Symbols of War from Classical Greece to Republican Rome, 500–167* BC. Oxford: Westview Press.

Schlüter, W. 1999. 'The Battle of the Teutoburg Forest: Archaeological Research at Kalkreise near Osnabrück.' In *Roman Germany: Studies in Cultural Interaction*, ed. J. D. Creighton and R. J. A. Wilson. *JRA* Supplement 32. Portsmouth, RI: Society for the Promotion of Roman Studies, 125–59.

Scullard, H. H. 1981. *Festivals and Ceremonies of the Roman Republic.* London: Thames & Hudson.

Shackleton Bailey, D. R. 1980. *Cicero Epistulae ad Quintum fratrem et M. Brutum.* Cambridge: Cambridge University Press.

Sordi, M. 1990. 'Cicerone e il primo epitafio romano.' In *'Dulce et decorum est pro patria mori': la morte in combattimento nell'antichità*, ed. M. Sordi. Milan: Università Cattolica del Sacro Cuore, 171–9.

Stefan, A. S. 2005. *Les guerres daciques de Domitien et de Trajan: architecture militaire, topographie, images et histoire.* Rome: Collection de l'École française de Rome.

Syme, R. 1971. *Danubian Papers.* Bucharest: Association internationale d'études du sud-est Européen.

5

Two Neoclassical Monuments
in Modern France:
The Panthéon and Arc de Triomphe

AVNER BEN-AMOS

Introduction: Monuments and Meaning

THE PANTHÉON AND THE ARC DE TRIOMPHE: two neoclassical, national monuments that were created, respectively, during the reigns of Louis XV and Napoléon Bonaparte. During most of the nineteenth and twentieth centuries, they were considered France's two most important national monuments, representing the different facets of French national identity. Their meanings were never stable: at times they were seen as representing opposite values; at other times they were seen to complement each other. However, they were always at the centre of the national imagination.

This chapter traces the 'parallel lives' of these two monuments, as they evolved after the French Revolution, and attempts to explain their relationship in terms of the changing and conflictual nature of French national identity. However, before expounding the main facets of that identity, let us consider the question of the meaning of a monument. The first place historians usually look for this meaning is in the monument's form—the material it is made of, its location, shape, and style. This is what Antoine Prost did in the first part of his article on the French monuments commemorating the Great War, in which he distinguished between patriotic, funerary, pacifist, and conservative memorials according to their locations, the figures that appeared on them and their gestures, and the inscriptions that were displayed on the socle.[1] In the second part of the article, Prost analysed the Armistice Day ceremonies that took place at war memorials, and concluded that, together, the ceremonies and the

---

[1] Prost 2002.

Proceedings of the British Academy, **160**, 89–112. © The British Academy 2012.

monuments constituted a republican cult of the fallen soldiers, a kind of civil religion that celebrated the ideals of the republic.

However, because Prost was interested in a typological analysis of the monuments and the ceremonies, he looked neither into the interaction of a specific monument with a specific ceremony, nor at the impact that the performance of a ceremony could have had on the meaning of a monument. As I intend to demonstrate in this chapter, in certain cases it is impossible to determine this meaning without taking into account the symbolic usage of the monument during a ceremony.

The ceremony has its own meaning, conveyed through speech, music, movement, decoration, and the manipulation of objects, which can be distinct from that of the monument. Moreover, ceremony constitutes a special, high-intensity time, different from the regular existence of the monument in everyday life.[2] At least while it lasts, therefore, the ceremony has the power to charge the monument with a special meaning. Certainly, this power is not unlimited, and the shape of the monument determines the range of possible meanings of the ceremony. Nevertheless, within these limits, the monument can acquire many different connotations, some of which were never imagined by its designer. The overall meaning that emerges during the ceremony is, then, the result of an interaction between the time (of the ceremony) and the space (of the monument) in which the former usually carries more weight because of the intensity of the performance.

This is why I trace the evolving meaning of the Panthéon and the Arc de Triomphe through studying their ceremonial history. I also pay attention to the formal modifications the monuments underwent, usually after a change of political regime, but the main emphasis is on the events in which the monuments played a major symbolic role. This chapter is limited to the study of the official usage of the monuments from the time of their creation, between the mid-eighteenth and early nineteenth centuries, to the end of the Third Republic (1940). The picture that eventually emerges is, of course, one-sided, since the ceremonies are seen through the lenses of the intentions of the authorities that organized them. However, when possible I also make references to the attitude of the forces of the political opposition, who, at times, had a totally different view of the events.

---

[2] For the transformative power of a ceremony, see Moore and Myerhoff, 1977, 3–24; Handelman 1990.

That the Panthéon and the Arc de Triomphe could represent the national identity for such a long period needs to be explicated. An obvious explanation would be that they were the only monuments that continually served as settings for major national ceremonies—that is, they remained 'active' throughout the period under study. But this still begs the question since what has to be explained is the reason for their use by successive regimes. Part of the answer seems to lie in their complex architectural form, which rendered them open to different interpretations and made them adaptable to various usages. However, other complex monuments, such as the Invalides, never achieved the same prominent status. An additional factor, then, is the fit, at a certain historical moment, between a monument and the political and cultural viewpoint of a regime, which makes the former a preferable vehicle for expressing the ideology of the latter. In the case of modern France, it was mainly the various republican regimes that made use of these two monuments, since they stood for the republican version of national identity.

Yet the relationship between these monuments and French identity should be regarded as exceeding mere reflection. As Colette Beaune observed in her book about the birth of the French nation '[the] representations of power are themselves powerful'.[3] Since the 'nation' is a political and cultural construct, its symbolic representation in monuments, ceremonies, and images makes it a palpable object, comprehensible to a population that wishes to imagine itself as a unified community.[4] Symbolic representations of the nation, such as monuments, therefore have a creative power as well: they give substance to abstract concepts and enable the spectators to identify themselves with this large and remote entity. Moreover, each particular representation is also a statement about the nature of the nation. Hence quarrels about symbolic representations are actually quarrels about the 'correct' identity of the nation, and the winner of such a quarrel is in a position to impose his or her views concerning this identity.

The different facets of the French national identity may be characterized by using two concepts developed by the anthropologist Mary Douglas, who observed that the life of a community is organized along two different dimensions: grid and group.[5] The grid defines the inner hierarchy within the community and the rules governing the allocation of roles; it is

[3] Beaune 1985, 344. For the relationship between symbols and political power, see also Geertz 1983, 121–46.
[4] See Anderson 1991, 1–36.
[5] Douglas 1982, ch. 4.

expressed mainly in political terms. The group, on the other hand, defines the community as a self-contained unit, with a common identity, and is usually manifested culturally. At times the energy of the members of the community is directed inwardly, to transform the grid, that is, to operate in the political arena, while at other times it is directed outwardly, to confront an external enemy. These two variables relate to each other, and together they may explain the behaviour of the members of the community in a given situation. For example, facing an external threat that affects the entire community, the grid will tend to be egalitarian, with the emphasis placed on the common traits of all the members.

The words used to portray national identity in the French case do not correspond exactly to the terms used by Douglas. The two most common words, *nation* and *patrie*, that became popular in the eighteenth century, stood for the people and the territory. As David Bell explained, 'both referred to the entity known as France, but the first signified above all a group of people sharing certain important, binding qualities, while the second was used in the sense of a territory commanding a person's emotional attachment and ultimate political loyalty'.[6] At times, the nation was clearly a grid concept, as in Abbé Sieyès' celebrated pamphlet *What Is the Third Estate?*, published on the eve of the French Revolution. Sieyès maintained that the nation was the origin of all laws, adding that 'what is not part of the Third Estate is not part of the nation',[7] thus excluding from sovereignty the king, the higher clergy, and the aristocracy.[8] The political and legal nation came into being when the Estates General was replaced by the National Assembly on 17 June 1789, and reasserted itself three days later through the Tennis Court Oath. Likewise, the fatherland was clearly a group concept, as was manifested in the words of the 'Marseillaise', originally named 'The War Hymn of the Army of the Rhine', which stated that *la Patrie* was in a position to demand the lives of its children when it was fighting the enemy.

However, the two concepts each had more than one meaning. At the battle of Valmy, in September 1792, the French soldiers cried 'Vive la Nation!', and when they went on to the conquest of Europe they did it in the name of 'La Grande Nation'. On the other hand, the fatherland was the term for the (grid) entity that was supposed to take care of the education of the children through close surveillance, according to Lepelletier's

[6] Bell 2001.
[7] Sieyès [1789] 1988, 41.
[8] For the concept of the nation before and during the French Revolution, see also Nora 1989.

educational plan.[9] This is why, in order to translate Douglas's abstract concepts into the concrete language of late modern France, I use the term 'republican' to denote the (grid) struggle for popular sovereignty, whereas the (group) urge to confront—usually by military force—other countries is referred to as 'patriotic'. Regarding the two neoclassical monuments that are the subject of this chapter, I argue that, although each of them had a complex meaning, on the whole the Panthéon represented the republican dimension of French national identity, while the Arc de Triomphe stood for the patriotic dimension. Throughout the nineteenth and twentieth centuries these two dimensions were, in turn, emphasized by French governments, which also used the two monuments to express their republican or patriotic preferences. In fact, the relationship between republicanism and patriotism, as well as that between the two monuments, can be described as a see-saw movement: when one was ascendant, the other was on the wane, and vice versa.

The Births of the Monuments

The Panthéon began its life in a patriotic context in 1744, during the War of the Austrian Succession, in the course of which Louis XV became seriously ill. The king prayed to Sainte Geneviève for recovery, and after regaining his health promised the canons of the abbey of Sainte-Geneviève to rebuild their old and ruined church that stood on a dominant hill on the left bank of Paris. Sainte Geneviève was an apt patron for the king's prayers as she was an early version of Jeanne d'Arc: a simple shepherdess who lived in the mid-fifth century and averted by her prayers the imminent attack of Attila the Hun on Paris. She became the patron saint of Paris, representing the devotion of the common people to fatherland and Church.

   The grandiose ceremony of laying the cornerstone of the new church, in which the king played a dominant role, took place in 1764. The choice of the date was not accidental: a year after the French defeat in the Seven Years' War, the king attempted to ameliorate his image, which was tarnished by military failure and constant criticism of his reign. He had already embarked on an ambitious building programme in Paris and the provinces, and the new and imposing edifice was to be its summit. It was designed by Jacques-Germain Soufflot, one of the advanced architects of

---

[9] See Baczko 1982, 352.

the period, who planned a gigantic basilica in the shape of a Greek cross, an immense dome in the manner of Saint Peter's Cathedral in Rome, and a vast crypt for the burial of the canons. However, faithful to the neo-classical style of the eighteenth century, it would also have Corinthian columns supporting a large portico with a triangular fronton—to make it resemble a Greek temple. It was to become a monument proclaiming the perpetuity of the Christian religion while simultaneously celebrating the French monarchy, the protector of the fatherland. Because of its impressive size, shape, and location, it was referred to as a Temple of the Nation even before its completion.[10]

When the French Revolution began in 1789, the Christian and patriotic edifice had not yet been consecrated, and soon the revolutionaries turned it into a republican monument by associating it with the cult of great men. The emblematic figure of the great man was promoted by the eighteenth-century *philosophes* as a counter-model to the king and the nobility. Unlike the pillars of the Old Regime, great men did not inherit their titles, nor were their titles given to them by God; they merited them on the basis of their talents, which were employed in the service of humanity. Great men were, usually, 'intellectuals'—scientists, philosophers, and writers—although legislators or orators could also join their ranks, providing that their acts contributed to the progress of humankind.[11] And last but not least: great men, overwhelmingly, were not women. Upon his death, the great man crossed the threshold to immortality—not that of a Christian afterlife, but the memory of future generations. This notion of non-transcendental eternity was developed by Diderot, who postulated a sacred posterity that would replace 'the other world of religious men' and whose task would be to judge the merit of the citizen and to decide whether—and how—to commemorate him.[12] As we shall see, the exact nature of this posterity was hotly debated in the nineteenth and twentieth centuries, but more often than not it was represented by the republican side of the French identity.

Like a ceremony, the body itself of a great man was capable of transforming the meaning of a monument. The relationship between these two factors—ceremony and the actual body—should be considered as complementary: as noted above, a ceremony was a unique, intense event, limited in time but capable, through the participation of a large crowd and

---

[10] This expression is mentioned in a work on Soufflot published in 1785; quoted in Rabreau 1989, 48.

[11] For the figure of the great man in eighteenth-century France, see Ozouf 1984; Bonnet 1998.

[12] Quoted in Bonnet 1986, 220.

the accounts by various media, of making a forceful impact upon the popular imagination; the presence of a hero's body on the premises of a monument created, on the other hand, a more subdued yet continuous, long-term effect. At times, a grave became a place of pilgrimage, like that of the Unknown Soldier under the Arc de Triomphe, but even if it did not attract many visitors, its powerful presence put its stamp on the public image of the monument. For example, the presence of Émile Zola's body in the Panthéon marked it as a 'Leftist' monument, belonging to the winning side in the Dreyfus affair. In addition, the transfer of his body to the monument in 1908 had its own significance, for it was done through an impressive state ceremony that served as a victory celebration for the Dreyfusards.

How do we explain the importance of the presence of the remains of a hero within a monument? Whether republican or patriotic, the hero was, first, a pedagogical figure by means of which the values he had incarnated could be inculcated to the population. His heroic acts and way of life became exempla which everyone was supposed to follow. However, the emphasis on the physical presence of the dead body and on the monument that 'wrapped' it indicated that the function of the hero's corpse was more than pedagogical. The dead turned the monument into a kind of sacred gate to the other world—that of the ancestors—from which the community could draw its strength.[13] This is why at special collective moments, either of crisis or of celebration, the values of the community would be reaffirmed through a ceremonial visit to the monument.

The first person to be buried in the Panthéon was the revolutionary leader Comte de Mirabeau, who died prematurely on 2 April 1791. For his sake the Constituent Assembly decided to turn the church of Sainte-Geneviève into the Temple of the Great Men two days after his death, specifying the rules governing the selection of the persons who would be buried there.[14] The rapidity of the decision was a sign that the idea of a collective place of burial for the great men of the French nation was ripe, and that the revolutionaries had waited only for the right opportunity to change the status of the monument. Indeed, in 1734, Voltaire had put forward Westminster Abbey, where the great men of the British nation were buried, as an exemplary educational edifice. In 1756, a year after the

---

[13] See Bloch and Parry 1982.

[14] *Archives parlementaire*, 4 April 1791, 543–4. The main rule was that only the legislative body had the right to decide who had merited the honour, but in any case it could not award it to one of its members; this could be done only by the next legislature. Mirabeau was an exception because of the grief over his premature death.

laying of the cornerstone, the journal *Le Mercure* suggested the creation
of a national pantheon, where the mortal remains of the nation's great
men would be consecrated, in the future church of Sainte-Geneviève; it
was even envisaged that the bodies of Descartes and his disciple Rohault,
who were buried in the old church of Sainte-Geneviève, would be
transferred to the new edifice after its completion.[15]

Although Mirabeau's funeral inaugurated the Panthéon and opened a
new tradition, it was not an innovative event. The popular orator died a
Catholic, and his impressive funeral, which took place two days after his
death, was religious. It included the clergy, the government of Louis XIV,
the National Assembly, the constituent bodies, the royal army, the national
guard, representatives of the Paris Commune, various republican and
patriotic clubs, and an enormous crowd of all classes who gathered to
watch the procession.[16] Since the Panthéon still kept its religious emblems,
the funeral should be seen as a moment of transition between the old and
the new identities of the monument—a traditional event that signalled its
transformation into a republican temple.

Mirabeau was a revolutionary, yet the title of great man hardly fitted
this manipulative politician, and his death, more than anything, seemed
to have served like a pretext for creating the new temple. Better suited to
the title of 'great men' were the two men of letters who, for the revolutionaries, incarnated the spirit of the new 'era of liberty', and were natural
candidates for pantheonization: Voltaire and Rousseau. They were mentioned in the 1791 Panthéon bill, and the final decree specified that
although the monument was destined for the great men of the new, post-
1789 era, an exception could be made for certain figures who had died
before it.[17] There was no doubt about the identity of these 'exceptions',
and these two 'fathers' of the revolution were indeed transferred to the
Panthéon in due course. But whereas Voltaire's pantheonization was quick
to come (11 July 1791), that of Rousseau had to wait until the end of the
period of the Terror (11 October 1794). The ceremonies, however, had
much in common. Both men of letters died in 1778, and their pantheonizations were less events of mourning than civic apotheoses that celebrated
the egalitarian ideals of the revolution. They were secular ceremonies,
and the main emphasis in both processions was on the great men and their

[15] MacManners 1985; Etlin 1984, 49; Deming 1989, 108.
[16] *Le Moniteur universel*, 6 April 1791, 42.
[17] *Archives parlementaire*, 4 April 1791, 536, 543–4.

work: their statues, with laurel crowns, and signs with the titles of their major books were carried amidst large crowds.[18]

Two other revolutionary heroes of a very different sort were buried in the Panthéon in the period between the burials of the two *philosophes*. They were the two 'Martyrs of Liberty', the deputy of the National Convention Michel Lepelletier and the radical journalist Jean-Paul Marat, who were assassinated by counter-revolutionaries. Although their funerary ceremonies, on 24 January 1793 and 21 September 1794 respectively, were more emotionally charged than those of the *philosophes*, all these events contributed to the identification of the Panthéon with the republican nation of Abbé Sieyès. Nevertheless, the political instability of the revolutionary period caused these transfers to be effective in a rather limited way. The decision to immortalize contemporary revolutionary leaders in addition to the pre-revolutionary great men backfired: the bodies of Mirabeau and Marat were removed from the Panthéon after the period of the Terror, due to changes in the government.

Another sign of the new identity of the Panthéon was the changes in the façade and the exterior of the monument, introduced by the architect Quatremère de Quincy. The fronton was covered with an allegorical relief, sculpted by Jean-Guillaume Moitte, depicting the Fatherland surrounded by Virtue, Liberty, and Genius, above an inscription 'To the Great Men— The Grateful Fatherland'. All Christian imagery was removed from the interior, which became more sombre and serene after the abolition of the large lower windows with their colourful stained glass. De Quincy planned to introduce an army of allegorical statues to inhabit the void that he had created. The citizen entering the edifice would follow an itinerary of initiation to republican values, culminating with a statue of the fatherland.[19] However, this ambitious plan was never carried out, and while the bodies of great men were deposited in the crypt, the main space of the monument remained empty.

The Arc de Triomphe, like the Panthéon, was born in a context of war, but in contrast to the Temple of the Great Men it continued to bear the patriotic mark of hard-won battles and heroic soldiers. After Napoléon Bonaparte's stunning victory in the battle of Austerlitz (2 December 1805), in which he succeeded in dissolving the armies of the Third Coalition (Britain, Austria, and Russia), he decided to build an Arc de Triomphe to the glory of his Grand Armée. He had been crowned exactly

[18] *Le Moniteur universel*, 13 July 1791; Guénot 1989.
[19] Naginski 1992.

a year earlier as Emperor Napoléon I in a magnificent ceremony at Notre Dame cathedral, and it was not surprising that he wanted to celebrate his victory in the style of the Roman emperors. His first choice for the location of the monument was Place de la Bastille, an empty space and a sacred revolutionary site, which was also on the route traditionally taken by the armies returning from the east. However, his minister of the interior, Nompére de Champagny, convinced him that the top of Chaillot hill, known also as Place de l'Étoile, was a better choice since it was vaster and higher—from there the large monument would be seen from afar. Another advantage was that it was situated at the end of the axis along the central alley of the Tuileries gardens, visible from the central pavilion of Tuileries palace, thus glorifying the Parisian residence of the emperor. [20]

This unique location had already attracted several architects, who had earmarked it for extravagant monuments, such as a gigantic elephant that would contain dance and concert halls (Jean-Etienne Ribaut, in 1758); a large, white marble obelisk (Ange-Jacques Gabriel and Jean-Rodolphe Perronet, in 1762); and a huge arch, dedicated to 'General Peace, Year X' (Balzac, 1802). Building a grand Arc de Triomphe in Place de l'Étoile seemed, therefore, to fulfil an architectural dream of the eighteenth century. The task of planning the monument was entrusted to two eminent architects, Jean-François-Thérèse Chalgrin and Jean-Arnaud Raymond, and the first stone was laid on 15 August 1806, the birthday of Napoléon. The arch was modelled after the Arch of Titus, built in Rome by Emperor Domitian after the death of his brother, Emperor Titus Vespasianus (BE 81), to celebrate the latter's success in crushing the Jewish rebellion of CE 67–70. The reference to the Roman Empire accorded with the imperial image that Napoléon wished to project, and the colossal arch, with its two massive piers, immense entablature, and reliefs that would show battle scenes was clearly the right vehicle for the glorification of the emperor and his army. However, Napoléon did not live to see the finished monument. He died in exile in 1821, while the Arc de Triomphe was inaugurated in 1836, after two regime changes and several modifications to the initial project.

The first ceremonial usage of the arch took place in rather non-military circumstances—the solemn entrance into Paris of the new empress, Marie-Louise de Habsbourg (1 April 1810). Chalgrin, who had in the meantime become the sole master of the project, had a temporary wooden

---

[20] Gaillard 1998, 26.

structure built upon the foundations of the arch, covered with painted cloth, which created a *trompe l'oeil* effect of the completed arch. After the fall of the empire in 1814 and the advent of the Bourbon Restoration, the building of the arch was halted since it was identified with Napoléon. However, the construction was resumed by Louis XVIII in 1823 in order to commemorate the first military victory of the regime—that of the king's nephew, Louis-Antoine de Bourbon, Duc d'Angoulême, in the Spanish campaign. Afterwards, the design of the arch was altered several times, by each new architect who was put in charge of the project, until it acquired its final form under the July Monarchy.

When the Arc de Triomphe was finally inaugurated, on 29 July 1836, its grandiose form corresponded to the initial plan of Chalgrin, but the reliefs and inscriptions were produced under the guidance of Adolphe Thiers, the minister of the interior, and an art critic who had a predilection for the periods of the Revolution and the empire.[21] Since the new king, Louis-Philippe of Orléans, presented himself as the inheritor of the ideals of the Revolution and the empire, the arch became a monument that paid homage to the victorious armies of these regimes, and the reliefs presented either allegorical or historical scenes that glorified them. The most important among them were the lower reliefs representing 'The Departure of the Volunteers', known also as 'La Marseillaise', by François Rude, and 'Napoléon's Triumph', by Jean-Pierre Cortot. In addition, names of major victories and important army officers from the periods of the Revolution and the empire were engraved on the piers of the monument, thus turning it into a commemorative site as well.

The inauguration of the monument took place on the sixth anniversary of the July Revolution (29 July 1836), but the ceremony was modest. After the failed assassination attempt by Fieschi during the previous anniversary celebration (28 July 1835), Louis-Philippe feared another attempt on his life, and did not take part in the celebration. Moreover, he wished to avoid offending the foreign powers that might have resented seeing their past humiliations inscribed on the walls of the arch. As a result, only Thiers, who had become the president of the council, and the Comte d'Argout, the minister of finance, participated in the ceremony. Nevertheless, a large crowd of Parisians came, attracted by the orchestra that played revolutionary and imperial military airs during the day and by the magnificent gaslight illumination of the arch during the night.[22] In

---

[21] Thiers had already published a monumental history of the French Revolution, and would later publish a history of the Consulate of Napoléon and the First Empire.
[22] Fernandes et al. 2000, 16.

spite of the king's reticence, the arch soon became an important element in the growing cult of Napoléon, and the 'return of the ashes' of 1840 only augmented the popularity of the late emperor.[23]

The Monuments until the Third Republic

The coming to power of Napoléon in 1799 changed the status of the Panthéon, and opened a period that lasted until the early years of the Third Republic (1885), during which the monument played only a marginal role in France's official symbolic system. The various regimes that succeeded the First Republic—the First Empire, the Bourbon Restoration, the July Monarchy, and the Second Empire—were hostile, in varying degrees, to the egalitarian ideals of the Revolution and, consequently, either refrained from using the monument that represented those ideals, or changed its nature. Yet the fact that each regime busied itself anew with determining the characteristics of the Panthéon was testimony to the importance of the edifice.

Under Napoléon, the function of the Panthéon—burial place of the most important figures of the nation—was fulfilled by the Invalides, the army hospital whose church received the body of Turenne, Louis XIV's renowned general (22 September 1800), as well as the bodies of several generals of the empire. It was also the symbolic home of the newly created Legion of Honour, thus becoming a prominent patriotic monument. However, the monument on Sainte-Geneviève hill was far from neglected, and its fate reflected Napoléon's ambiguous attitude towards the legacy of the Revolution. Having signed the Concordat in 1801, he could not ignore the wish of the Catholics to regain their deconsecrated church, but he also wanted to recompense his loyal civil servants. The solution was to create a hybrid institution that would serve both sides, the Church and the emperor, but would ultimately be under the control of the latter. A decree published on 20 February 1806 stipulated that the Panthéon would become a church, renamed, according to the original vow of Louis XV, after Sainte Geneviève. But the next article stated that the church would 'preserve the destination that was given to it by the Constituent Assembly, and [would] be dedicated to the burial of great dignitaries'.[24] Although

---

[23] For the cult of Napoleon, see Ménager 1988; Hazareesingh 2004a.
[24] Quoted in *Journal officiel de la République française—Chambre des députés*, 6 March 1881, 419.

the Panthéon was restored to the Church, its main function remained civic, with a certain militarist dimension.[25]

But the civic notions of Napoléon were not those of the Revolution. The term 'great man' that appeared in the inscription on the fronton was absent from the Napoleonic decree, and in its place the term 'dignitary' was used. Napoléon preferred the loyal functionary, whose basis for immortality was the title conferred upon him by the emperor, to the independent spirit, the benefactor of humanity whose figure contrasted with that of the monarch. Becoming a dignitary no longer depended on belonging to the nobility, as it had in the Old Regime, and under Napoléon the way to high office was open to people of merit, but the main criterion of selection was still arbitrary: the goodwill of the emperor. Whereas during the Revolution burial in the Panthéon was an exceptional honour, under Napoléon it became almost automatic for those who died while occupying high positions of power. The list of the dignitaries whose bodies were deposited there during the First Empire—all in the period that followed the decree—is indicative of Napoléon's intentions. Of forty-two burials, nineteen were of senators who also occupied other positions in the imperial administration, fifteen were generals and other high-ranking army officers, four were ministers, three were cardinals, and one was a duke. Besides Marshal Lannes, who died in 1809 in the battle of Essling, the other dignitaries were obscure figures who did not fit contemporary notions of the great man. For himself and his family, Napoléon reserved the privilege of a burial at the Basilica of Saint-Denis, where a special vault was prepared for them, thus placing the Bonapartes in the ancient tradition of French monarchy.

The Bourbon Restoration, the most reactionary regime of the post-revolutionary period, adopted a policy towards the Panthéon that countered those of the Revolution and the First Empire. Louis XVIII had already ordered all revolutionary and Napoleonic signs to be removed from it on the morrow of his royal entry to Paris (3 May 1814), but the episode of the Hundred Days delayed the execution of the order. After the king's return to power in 1815 the Panthéon finally closed its gates to both great men and dignitaries, and the revolutionary inscription as well as the sculptured fronton by Moitte were taken down. The edifice was officially reconsecrated on 3 January 1822, Sainte Geneviève's day, and subsequently it was handed over to the order of the Missionaires de

---

[25] For the Panthéon in the nineteenth century, see Bergdoll 1989; Exposition: Paris, Panthéon 2002.

France. With its republican connotations totally effaced, it could serve the legitimist vision of the Bourbons.

The July Revolution of 1830, which put a citizen-king, Louis-Philippe of Orléans, on the throne, changed the status of the Panthéon yet again, this time in accord with the revolutionary image of the new regime. On 26 August 1830 the previous laws of the First Empire and of the Restoration were abrogated, and the original inscription was restored on the fronton. The king also appointed a committee that was to determine the criteria for the transfer of great men to the Panthéon, and to decide on the minimal delay between death and transfer, in order to avoid the embarrassing de-pantheonizations of the French Revolution. In addition, a new sculptured fronton was commissioned from David d'Angers, to replace that of Moitte. The young, liberal sculptor planned a 'progressive' relief, which described the allegorical figures of *la patrie*, liberty, and history distributing laurel wreaths to great men of the eighteenth and nineteenth centuries, among whom were Voltaire, Rousseau, Mirabeau, Manuel, and Lafayette.

The Panthéon was also at the centre of the first anniversary of the Revolution (28 July 1831): a commemorative ceremony was celebrated there for the victims of the fighting, and a bronze plate with their names was affixed on an inside wall. Yet soon afterwards the regime's enthusiasm for the renewed egalitarian monument waned. The republican opposition began to gather strength, and on the occasion of General Lamarque's funeral (5 June 1832) an attempt was made to bring the body of the popular leader to the Panthéon. The police blocked its way, and the ensuing insurrection, which lasted for two days and spread over a large part of Paris, was suppressed by force. The Panthéon never received the body of a great man during the reign of Louis-Philippe, and when David d'Angers' fronton was finally unveiled in 1837 it was done in a discreet manner, and after several modifications that attenuated its republican message.

While the Panthéon returned to the shadows, the Arc de Triomphe remained a favourite Orleanist monument, playing a major role in the 'return of the ashes' of Napoléon (15 December 1840). The initiative to bring the body of the emperor to Paris from St Helena was taken by Thiers, who became the president of the council again in March 1840, and attempted to boost the popularity of the regime by associating it with the cult of Napoléon. The long maritime voyage of the coffin gave the government and the Parisian population ample time to prepare for the ceremony, which was, indeed, unprecedented in its size and splendour.[26] The

---

[26] For the 'return of the ashes', see Tulard 1986; Humbert 1990.

sumptuous procession, with the magnificent hearse at its centre, passed through the Arc de Triomphe on its way to final burial in the Invalides in the presence of an enormous crowd, estimated at about three-quarters of a million. Although the event did not increase public support for the regime, which fell as a result of the February 1848 Revolution, it certainly contributed to the consolidation of the cult of Napoléon, and helped to launch the political career of his nephew, Louis-Napoléon Bonaparte.

The Second Republic, born after the 1848 Revolution, prefigured the Third Republic in its attempt to use both the Arc de Triomphe and the Panthéon to represent the patriotic and republican dimensions of its identity, respectively. On the one hand, the decorated arch played a role in the Festival of Brotherhood (20 April 1848), in which the provisional government distributed flags to units of the national guard and the army who were positioned along the Champs Élysées. On the other hand, the regime planned to reopen the gates of the Panthéon, while accentuating its universal dimension. It renamed the edifice the Temple of Humanity, and the painter Paul Chenavard was commissioned to prepare a series of murals that would depict the history of the human race from biblical times to Napoléon, including episodes from the development of the major religions.[27] However, the regime was short-lived, and the *coup d'état* of the elected president, Prince Louis-Napoléon, on 2 December 1851 (the anniversary of the crowning of Napoléon and the battle of Austerlitz) put an end not only to the republic but also to the efforts of Chenavard.

Louis-Napoléon's model was clearly the First Empire of his uncle, but during the Second Empire the alliance between State and Church was even stronger. Hence the radical change in the status of the Panthéon. Four days after the *coup d'état*—a rapidity that indicated the importance of the matter for him—Louis-Napoléon published a decree stipulating that the church of Sainte-Geneviève would be given back to the Catholics, as in the period of the Restoration. The inscription mentioning great men was removed again, and the remains of Sainte Geneviève were transferred from Notre Dame on the saint's day in an impressive religious procession that was part of the inaugural ceremony (3 January 1853). The Panthéon ceased to be the state necropolis, and was replaced by the Invalides, which the 'return of the ashes' had turned into a Napoleonic monument, and where Napoléon's body received a permanent, majestic tomb in 1861. At the same time, the arch became one of the main attractions of the official national festival of 15 August – the birthday of Napoléon, which happened

[27] See Grunewald 1977.

to coincide with the Catholic festival of the Assumption. This was the main annual celebration of the Second Empire, and in accord with the militarist image that Louis-Napoléon projected, wishing to be associated with his famous uncle, the army played a major role in the festivities. Hence also the importance of the arch which was especially illuminated and decorated for the event, with a giant eagle—the symbol of Napoléon— placed on its top.[28]

The Monuments during the Third Republic

The Third Republic, which replaced the Second Empire after the defeat in the battle against Germany at Sedan on 2 September 1870, was more heterogeneous in its world view. It was the only regime since the French Revolution that succeeded in combining the republican and patriotic aspects of French identity, a success that partially explains its longevity (1870–1940). Consequently, it used both the Panthéon and the Arc de Triomphe in its official, state rituals, but did not give them equal weight. In the first period, up to the First World War, the main efforts of the regime were dedicated to the consolidation of its republican basis, against the forces of the conservative opposition that wished to turn back the clock and re-establish some form of monarchist rule. In the second period, after the war, the emphasis was placed on conflicts with external enemies and on grappling with the painful memories of fallen soldiers, while giving their death a meaning. Thus, in the first period, the Panthéon was usually at the centre of attention, while in the second period it was the arch.

Unlike the other regimes of the nineteenth century, the Third Republic did not precipitate change in the status of the Panthéon. Although the regime officially turned republican in 1870, it was actually governed by non-republican forces, and the republicans attained control only in 1879. The republican group that controlled the regime at first, the 'Opportunists', claimed to carry on the ideals of the French Revolution, but did not advocate social revolution and was apprehensive of any rapid change. Thus, despite its anti-clericalism, it was at times ready to accommodate the Church and did not wish to upset Catholic public opinion by provocative symbolic action. In addition, although the regime was driven by the patriotic desire to recover Alsace and Lorraine, the territories that had been lost to Germany in the 1870–71 war, it refrained from any steps that could

---

[28] For the celebration of 15 August, see Truesdell 1997; Hazareesingh 2004b.

have been interpreted as bellicose, knowing the weakness of the French army. Lastly, since the regime tried to identify the republic with the nation in order to enhance its legitimacy, it appropriated different segments of the national past and underlined their common denominators.

This is why the regime waited until 1885, when the death of Victor Hugo, the epitome of a republican 'great man', gave it the opportunity to change the status of the Panthéon yet again, and also transform the identity of the Arc de Triomphe.[29] Hugo, the venerated writer and republican militant, was a 'natural' candidate for pantheonization. However, he died without the last sacrament of the Church, and had demanded a secular funeral in his will. In order that the edifice on Sainte-Geneviève hill could receive his body, the building had to be taken out of the hands of the Church, desacralized, and rededicated to the republican cult of great men. Consequently, after deciding that Hugo would be given a national funeral, the government decreed on 27 May 1885 that the Panthéon would be restored to its original function. But Hugo was also associated with the cult of Napoléon, whom he admired, and with the arch, about which he had written in his early poetry. His body lay, therefore, in state under the magnificently decorated arch, from where the impressive funeral procession departed to the Panthéon, whose Christian emblems had been hastily removed. French public opinion was divided about the ceremony. The Church and the Catholic press protested against the 'godless' funeral and the desacralization of Sainte-Geneviève church, while the extreme Left denounced the ceremony as a bourgeois manipulation. However, the huge crowd, estimated at more than a million people, remained calm and respectful, and the event surpassed in its magnitude the Napoleonic 'return of the ashes' in 1840. The funeral also had long-term consequences for the two monuments that it symbolically connected. After being associated mainly with Bonapartism, the Arc de Triomphe was 'rehabilitated' as a patriotic monument with which the republicans could identify, while the Panthéon became definitely a secular monument, where great men of successive republican regimes would be buried.

Despite the abrupt change in the status of the Panthéon in May 1885, the process of its interior redecoration, begun after the establishment of the Third Republic, continued with some modifications. The project initiated by the monarchist Philippe de Chennevières, who became the general director of the arts at the ministry of public instruction in 1873, included mural paintings that would depict the 'religious-national history of

---

[29] For Hugo's funeral, see Ben-Amos 1984.

France'. It was a return to the original intention of Louis XV, who envisaged the church as a religious monument that would also emphasize the role of the French monarchy as the protector of the nation.[30] In the late 1870s and early 1880s the republicans gradually modified the project so that it became less religious and more civic; this was done through the introduction of allegorical subjects such as Family, Work, and Fatherland. But on the whole the main themes remained Christian. The various religious murals, which were under construction until the first decade of the twentieth century, thus coexisted with the secular pantheonizations as a testimony to the ability of the Third Republic to represent the entire gamut of French history.

After Hugo's funeral, the Panthéon continued to play a major role in the civic rituals of the regime. The centenaries of the First Republic (1892) and of Hugo's birth (1902) were celebrated there in a majestic way, and several bodies of 'great men' were buried in the crypt. The first burial took place on the occasion of the centenary of the French Revolution, which coincided with the tense period of the ascension of the popular General Boulanger, who posed a threat to the republican regime. In order to accentuate the patriotic and military image of the republic, the bodies of three revolutionary army officers were ceremoniously transferred to the Panthéon (4 August 1889). Together with them was transferred the body of deputy Jean Baudin, who died in 1851 on a Parisian barricade opposing the *coup d'état* of Louis-Napoléon, thus becoming a republican martyr.[31] The next pantheonizations were those of Sadi Carnot, the president of the republic who was assassinated by an anarchist (1894), and Marcelin Berthelot, the renowned chemist who served as minister in several republican governments (1907). The last person to be buried in the Panthéon before the First World War was Émile Zola, who died and was buried in 1902, but whose body was transferred to the monument in 1908 in order to celebrate the final acquittal of Captain Dreyfus. The transfer ceremony took place in spite of the vociferous protests of the anti-Dreyfusards on the extreme Right, but it marked the Panthéon as a 'Leftist' and anti-militarist edifice.

The First World War unified the country behind the 'Sacred Union' government, at least for a while, and thus shifted the emphasis from the grid to the group. The war also brought changes in the respective places of the Panthéon and the Arc de Triomphe in the symbolic system of the Third Republic. The first sign was the reburial of Rouget de Lisle, the

---

[30] See Vaisse 1989.
[31] For the centenary celebration, see Ory 1984.

celebrated revolutionary author of the 'Marseillaise', which took place during the war, on Bastille Day (14 July 1915), as part of the government effort to boost public morale.[32] At first, it was decided to transfer the body to the Panthéon, but due to legal complications the Invalides was chosen instead. On the day of the ceremony, de Lisle's coffin, which was exhumed at the cemetery of Choisy-le-Roi, was brought to the Arc de Triomphe, where it was placed on a gun carriage from the time of the French Revolution that stood beneath Rude's relief. From there it was taken to the Invalides in an imposing civic and military procession, accompanied, in the air, by a formation of war aeroplanes. The two Napoleonic monuments were thus symbolically connected, but this time in the service of the patriotic republic which, as in the time of the French Revolution, fought the German enemy.

After the war, the arch clearly eclipsed the Panthéon, although the latter did not completely disappear from the rituals of the republic. On the first Bastille Day after the war (14 July 1919) the Allies' victory was celebrated by a French and international military parade that began at the arch and went down the Champs Elysées to Place de la Concorde. To mark the occasion, the government erected a temporary cenotaph near the arch which commemorated the fallen soldiers. However, the bereaved families and the war veterans insisted on a permanent, symbolic grave for those soldiers who had died in battle and had not received a decent burial, and the Chamber of Deputies voted to transfer the body of an unknown soldier to the Panthéon.[33] Since the fiftieth anniversary of the Third Republic was to be celebrated in the same year, the government decided to combine the two commemorations, hoping thereby to enhance the popularity of the regime: the heart of Leon Gambetta, one of the founding fathers of the republic, would be transferred to the Panthéon, together with the body of the Unknown Soldier, in a single solemn procession that would depart from the Arc de Triomphe.[34]

Again, the war veterans constituted a pressure group that rejected the burial of the Unknown Soldier in the crypt of the Panthéon—a close, sombre, and rarely frequented place, where he would be one among many, some of whom were second-rate figures. Their unique brother in arms deserved to rest alone under the Arc de Triomphe, an open and elevated structure that dominated Paris, situated in the heart of a busy and modern

[32] See Ben-Amos 2000.

[33] *Journal officiel de la République française—Chambre des députés, Documents*, 17 October 1919, 3169.

[34] For the figure of Gambetta and the transfer of his heart, see Ben-Amos 2002.

part of the city, where his memory would be kept alive.[35] They were joined
by the Right, which considered the Panthéon as 'polluted' by the body of
Zola, and finally the government gave in and decided that the Unknown
Soldier would indeed be buried under the arch. The ceremony, which took
place on Armistice Day (11 November 1920), was therefore modified. The
body of an Unknown Soldier—ceremoniously chosen from among several
unidentified bodies—together with the heart of Gambetta, departed in a
procession from Place Denfert-Rochereau to the Panthéon, and then to
the arch. While the body of the Unknown Soldier remained at the arch,
Gambetta's heart returned 'clandestinely' to the Panthéon, under the
cover of darkness, where, after several years, it was taken out of its simple
wooden box and placed in an ornamental marble urn at the entrance to
the crypt.

As in the case of Hugo's funeral, the arch and the Panthéon were associated through this ceremony, but in the ensuing period the former got
most of the limelight. First, the body of the Unknown Soldier received
better treatment than Gambetta's heart. The grave, in the open, under the
flagstone of the arch, where it was accessible to the public, was officially
inaugurated on 28 January 1921, and the inscriptions on the ground
beside it underlined the connection between the heroic sacrifice of the
soldiers, the republican regime, and the French victory in the war.[36] In
addition, from Armistice Day 1923 until the Second World War the daily
ceremony of the lighting of the flame at the grave, in memory of the fallen
soldiers, attracted large crowds. The official annual ceremony of Armistice
Day also took place at the arch, and important foreign visitors were often
taken to place a wreath on the grave. Another occasion on which the arch
drew an enormous crowd, of several hundred thousand people, was the
funeral of Marshal Foch, one of the heroes of the First World War, when
his body lay there in state (27 March 1929).[37] In consequence, between the
two world wars, the Arc de Triomphe became the focal point of the group
dimension of the national identity, as a monument that expressed the
country's pride over its patriotic victory and its mourning.

In the same period, the Panthéon accentuated its 'Leftist' image after
the transfer of the body of the socialist leader, Jean Jaurès, on 23 November

---

[35] For the war veterans' organizations and the cult of the Unknown Soldier between the world
wars, see Prost 1977.

[36] The text of the inscriptions reads: 'Here lies a French soldier who died for the Fatherland', '4
September 1870, the proclamation of the Republic', '11 November 1918, Return of Alsace and
Lorraine to France'.

[37] For the funeral of Marshal Foch, see Ben-Amos 1999.

1924. This transfer was decided by the new coalition of the Cartel of the Left, constituted by the radicals and socialists who won the elections of May 1924. The transfer marked the tenth anniversary of the assassination of Jaurès on the eve of the First World War by an extreme-Right fanatic, who opposed his anti-war campaign, but it was also meant to cement the forces of the coalition. The procession, which departed from the Chamber of Deputies (Palais Bourbon) to the Panthéon, included, beside the official part, numerous workers' delegations, and was followed by a communist counter-demonstration that was perceived by the Right as a revolutionary menace. Thus the anti-militarist image of the Panthéon was fixed for the period between the two world wars, and even the transfer of the body of Paul Painlevé (October 1933), who had served twice as war minister, did not change this.

The longevity of the Third Republic enabled the meaning of the two monuments to settle, though certain nuances, too, were introduced. Thus, the transfer of the bodies of the three revolutionary officers to the Panthéon in 1889 added a military–patriotic dimension, while the tomb of the Unknown Soldier added a mournful, inward-looking dimension to the victorious–patriotic Arc de Triomphe. But, on the whole, the monuments continued to represent, respectively, the grid and group dimensions of the national identity. The regime of Vichy, which replaced the Third Republic after the defeat by the Germans in 1940, constitutes a sort of test case. On the one hand, it rejected the ideals of the French Revolution, and regarded this event as the beginning of the nation's decline and the source of all its troubles. On the other hand, being dependent upon the German occupier, it could not celebrate the French military victories of the previous century and a half. Hence the absence of both the Panthéon and the Arc de Triomphe from the state rituals of Vichy, and their replacement by religious edifices such as Notre Dame cathedral.[38] After the Second World War, the two monuments returned to the public sphere and were used by the Fourth and the Fifth Republics in their official ceremonies. However, these events drew much less attention than before. In contrast to earlier periods, there was a near consensus around the republican nature of the regime, and no serious threat from external enemies. France seemed secure, both in terms of its (republican) grid and its (patriotic) group. The need to reaffirm its identity through the recurrent usage of the monuments was less urgent than before and as a result the enthusiasm of the public— for or against the state ceremonies—was on the wane. The

---

[38] For the commemorative state rituals of the regime of Vichy, see Ben-Amos 1998.

Panthéon and the Arc de Triomphe are still at the centre of state ceremonies, but these ceremonies are no longer at the centre of French public life.

Bibliography

Anderson, B. 1991. *Imagined Communities: Reflections on the Origin and Spread of Nationalism*. London: Verso.

Baczko, B. ed. 1982. *Une education pour la démocratie: textes et projets de l'époque révolutionnaire*. Paris: Garnier.

Beaune, C. 1985. *Naissance de la Nation France*. Paris: Gallimard.

Bell, D. 2001. *The Cult of the Nation in France: Inventing Nationalism, 1680–1800*. Cambridge, MA: Harvard University Press.

Ben-Amos, A. 1984. 'Les funérailles de Victor Hugo: apothéose de l'événement spectacle.' In *Les lieux de mémoire*, vol. 1: *La République*, ed. P. Nora. Paris: Gallimard, 473–522.

——1998. 'La Commémoration sous le regime de Vichy: les limites de la maîtrise du passé.' In *La France démocratique: combats, mentalités, symbols*, ed. C. Charle et al. Paris: Publications de la Sorbonne, 397–408.

——1999. 'Les funérailles du maréchal Foch: le retour de la Grande Guerre.' In *La mort du roi: essai d'ethnographie politique comparée*, ed. J. Julliard. Paris: Gallimard, 231–58.

——2000. 'The *Marseillaise* as Myth and Metaphor: The Transfer of Rouget de Lisle to the Invalides during the Great War.' In *France at War in the Twentieth Century: Propaganda, Myth and Metaphor*, ed. V. Holman and D. Kelly. New York: Berghahn, 22–48.

——2002. 'A French Great Man's Last Rites: The National Funeral of Leon Gambetta and the Transfer of His Heart to the Panthéon.' In *Language and Revolution: Making Modern Political Identities*, ed. I. Halfin. London: Frank Cass, 341–63.

Bergdoll, B. 1989. 'Le Pantheón/Sainte-Geneviève au XIXe siècle: la monumentalité à l'épreuve des revolutions idéologiques.' In *Le Panthéon, Symbole des revolutions*. Paris: Picard, 175–233.

Bloch, M. and J. Parry. 1982. 'Introduction: Death and the Regeneration of Life.' In *Death and the Regeneration of Life*, ed. M. Bloch and J. Berry. Cambridge: Cambridge University Press, 1–44.

Bonnet, J.-C. 1986. 'Les morts illustres, oraison funèbre, éloge académique, nécrologie.' In *Les lieux de mémoire*, vols 2–3: *La Nation*, ed. P. Nora. Paris: Gallimard, 217–41.

——1998. *Naissance du Panthéon: essai sur le culte des grandes hommes*. Paris: Éditions Fayard.

Deming, M. 'Le Panthéon révolutionnaire.' In *Le Panthéon, symbole des revolutions*. Paris: Picard, 97–150.

Douglas, M. 1982. *Natural Symbols: Explorations in Cosmology*. New York: Pantheon.

Etlin, R. 1984. *The Architecture of Death: The Transformation of the Cemetery in Eighteenth-Century Paris*. Cambridge, MA: MIT Press.

Exposition: Paris, Panthéon. 2002. *Le Panthéon de Napoléon*. Paris: Éditions du patrimoine.

Fernandes D., G. Plum, and I. Rouge. 2000. *Arc de Triomphe de l'Étoile*. Paris: Éditions du patrimoine.

Gaillard, M. 1998. *L'Arc de Triomphe*. Amiens: Martelle.

Geertz, C. 1983. 'Centers, Kings and Charisma: Reflections on the Symbolics of Power.' In *Local Knowledge: Further Essays in Interpretive Anthropology*. New York: Basic Books, 121–46.

Grunewald, M.-A. 1977. *Paul Chenavard et la decoration du Panthéon de Paris en 1848*. Lyon: Musée des Beaux-Arts.

Guénot, H. 1989. 'De L'Île des Peupliers au Panthéon: la translation des Cendres de Rousseau (11 Octobre 1794).' *Études Jean-Jacque Rousseau* 3, 101–25.

Handelman, D. 1990. *Models and Mirrors: Towards an Anthropology of Public Events*. New York: Cambridge University Press.

Hazareesingh, S. 2004a. *The Legend of Napoléon*. Cambridge: Cambridge University Press.

——2004b. *The Saint-Napoléon: Celebrations of Sovereignty in Nineteeth-Century France*. Cambridge, MA: Harvard University Press.

Humbert, J.-M. ed. 1990. *Napoléon aux Invalides: 1840, le retour des cendres*. Paris: Musée de l'armée.

MacManners, J. 1985. *Death and the Enlightenment: Changing Attitudes to Death in Eighteenth-Century France*. Oxford: Clarendon Press.

Ménager, B. 1988. *Les Napoléon du peuple*. Paris: Aubier.

Moore, S. and B. Myerhoff. 1977. 'Secular Ritual: Forms and Meanings'. In *Secular Ritual*, ed. S. Moore and B. Myerhoff. Assen: Van Gorcum, 3–24.

Naginski, E. 1992. 'Un parcours initiatique pour le citoyen: le "Chemin de Croix" de Quatremère de Quincy au Panthéon.' In *Le progrès des arts réunis 1763–1815*, ed. D. Rabreau and B. Tollon. Bordeaux: CERCAM, Universite Michel de Montaigne, 329–36.

Nora, P. 1989. 'Nation.' In *Critical Dictionary of the French Revolution*, ed. F. Furet and M. Ozouf. Translated by A. Goldhammer. Cambridge, MA: Harvard University Press, 742–52.

Ory, P. 1984. 'Le centenaire de la Révolution française.' In *Les lieux de mémoire*, vol. 1: *La République*, ed. P. Nora. Paris: Gallimard, 523–60.

Ozouf, M. 1984. 'Le Panthéon.' In *Les lieux de mémoire*, vol. 1: *La République*, ed. P. Nora. Paris: Gallimard, 139–66.

Prost, A. 1977. *Les anciens combattants et la société française 1914–1939*, vol. 3. Paris: Presses de la Fondation nationale des sciences politiques.

——2002. 'War Memorials of the Great War: Monuments to the Fallen'. In *Republican Identities in War and Peace: Representations of France in the 19th and 20th Centuries*. Translated by J. Winter with H. McPhail. Oxford: Berg, 11–43.

Rabreau, D. 1989. 'La Basilique Sainte-Geneviève de Soufflot.' In *Le Panthéon, symbole des revolutions*. Paris: Picard, 37–96.

Sieyès, E. J. [1789] 1988. *Qu'est-ce que le tiers-état?* Paris: Flammarion.

Truesdell, M. 1997. *Spectacular Politics: Louis-Napoléon Bonaparte and the Fête Impériale, 1849–1870*. Oxford: Oxford University Press.

Tulard, J. 1986. 'Le retour des cendres.' In *Les lieux de mémoire*, vols 2–3: *La Nation*, ed. P. Nora. Paris: Gallimard, 81–110.

Vaisse, P. 1989. 'La peinture monumentale au Panthéon sous la IIIe République.' In *Le Panthéon, symbole des revolutions.* Paris: Picard, 252–8.

6

Naming the Dead,
Writing the Individual:
Classical Traditions and
Commemorative Practices in the
Nineteenth and Twentieth Centuries

GRAHAM OLIVER

OVERFAMILIARITY WITH CONTEMPORARY COMMEMORATIVE CULTURE can give
the wrong impression of the unusual state of remembrance that has pre-
vailed in the last century and a half: the listing of the war dead and the
commemoration of the dead combatants of modern society is not typical
of the treatment that most societies have offered to their war dead.[1]
Historians can trace, often in some detail, the origin and development in
the nineteenth and twentieth centuries of the ideas and development of
mass commemoration of the war dead of the American Civil War and the
First World War.[2] One of the best documented births is that of the
Imperial War Graves Commission, now the Commonwealth War Graves
Commission. The story of this organization has been told in several
places.[3] The Commission (CWGC) is responsible for maintaining the
cemeteries and monuments of the Commonwealth's war dead from the
major conflicts of the twentieth century. The ranked slabs of (usually)
Portland stone set in well-tended cemeteries have been seen on television
broadcasts and visited by thousands. The information on which the
CWGC's activity depends can be examined via an online database: the
name of any of the war dead can be searched for and the location of the

---

[1] Faust 2006, 996 makes the point well for the USA since the American Civil War.
[2] For the American Civil War, Blight 2004 (on Memorial Day); Faust 2006 and 2008. On the
commemoration of the war dead in the First World War, numerous books exist but Winter 1985;
Becker 1988; Prost and Winter 2004, 235–62; and Winter 2006 are noteworthy. On the association
of war memory and popular culture, see now Keren and Herwig 2009.
[3] Longworth 1985; Ward 1989; Ware 1937.

Proceedings of the British Academy, **160**, 113–134. © The British Academy 2012.

tomb or record of the name, and often other associated information, can be found.[4]

For some individual war dead, the commemoration overseen by the War Graves Commission may have been the only form of remembrance. But many families will have performed their own rituals. Indeed, because the War Graves Commission came into being officially only in May 1917, families and communities undertook their own commemorative ceremonies. Consider, for example, one of the victims of the battle of Coronel, Britain's major naval catastrophe of the First World War.[5] Among the many who died when HMS *Good Hope* was sunk by the German ships led by von Spee on 1 November 1914 was Lt-Commander Godfrey John Benyon. A photograph of the ship's officers, taken two weeks before their death, arrived in England a month after the ship was lost and was published on the front page of the *Daily Graphic* to celebrate the sinking of two of the German ships responsible for the loss of the *Good Hope*.[6] It was several months before Benyon's widow, his son, newborn daughter, mother-in-law, and sister-in-law returned in May 1915 to Britain from Bermuda on RMS *Transylvania*, dodging German submarines. At the time they had left New York newspaper boys were calling out the news of the sinking of the *Lusitania*. Once the family had settled back in England, it was a few months before Benyon's death was commemorated with the dedication of a small stained-glass window in the local church in Windsor a year after his death, appropriately on All Saints' Day 1915. Whether the commemoration of Benyon on the Portsmouth naval memorial performed any further role in the mourning of his loss is difficult to assess.[7] As a story of remembrance, however, this example is one of many that illustrate how little the mourning of the war dead may have related to the later official memorials erected. Benyon's family no doubt had access to means that others were unlikely to have enjoyed. But for the ratings, the hundreds of other dead sailors commemorated on the Portsmouth memorial, the listing of their names certainly secured some lasting form of recognition.[8]

---

[4] Searches are possible at www.cwgc.org. For records of those who died for France, see also www.memoiredeshommes.sga.defense.gouv.fr.

[5] Bennett 2001.

[6] *Daily Graphic*, Saturday 12 December 1914.

[7] On the Portsmouth memorial, see, for example, Boorman 2005, 38–41. The Benyon story is based on documents that have been passed down from my father's family. It is as good an example as any of the function of commemoration and the role that individuals can play in contributing to collective memory.

[8] Winter 1995, 78–116.

The story told here of Benyon illustrates well one aspect that lay at the heart of the War Graves Commission: the desire for individualization and family commemoration set against, or alongside, the state's formal monumentalization and commemoration of the large number of individuals on a collective list and memorial for the dead. This tension was expressed particularly by the surviving families of the war dead in the First World War. They came up against the Commission's wish that the state should retain control over some forms of commemoration. The Commission prevented the burial of remains of the war dead by the surviving family and wanted to discourage family members searching for and returning remains of the war dead from (invariably) northern France and Belgium to England. Among the principal problems that the War Graves Commission addressed was the tension between individual (and family) and state; this caused considerable friction in the early years of the Commission.

The idea of commemorating all one's war dead first developed in the modern era after the American Civil War and was pioneered in a more comprehensive way during the First World War by the War Graves Commission. The development is an important one and led during the latter half of the nineteenth and twentieth centuries to a 'memory boom'.[9] It is worth pausing to think about the stress laid by the nation state on the commemoration of the individual war dead in the last 150 years, for this is a phenomenon that is peculiar to the relatively recent past. Typically, the war dead before the twentieth century would have received little form of post-mortem attention after the disposal of the bodies. But attention paid to the performance of rituals and the commemoration of the individual war dead that eventually became a feature of the American Civil War, and later the Imperial War Graves Commission, was not without parallel. If we look back through history, before the rise of the Roman Empire, to classical Athens, we find a society that paid similar attention to the commemoration of the individual war dead. As it happens, our understanding of the commemoration of the war dead in the classical (see Chapter 2) and Hellenistic periods (see Chapter 3) has moved on considerably as the respective contributions to this volume will have demonstrated. But if we look back to the time when debate raged about the disposal of the war dead in the First World War, for instance, the most familiar models on which society could draw for such large-scale commemorative cultures were neither contemporary, nor recent, but ancient.

---

[9] See Winter 2006 for the use of this term.

In what follows I review the presence of classical Athenian commemorative culture in the *mentalités* of those who were closely associated with the establishment of the Imperial War Graves Commission in the early twentieth century. I then review briefly the general absence of similar cultures of commemoration of the individual war dead in the period before the nineteenth century. Finally I suggest that since the early twentieth century, the ideas that drove the commemorative practices that developed after the American Civil War, and the principles on which the commemorative culture of the Imperial War Graves Commission was established, have had an indirect influence on subsequent forms of remembrance. In short, this chapter argues that the widespread remembrance of the individual war dead within the framework of the community—or the state here—owes a great deal to the legacy of ancient Greek culture.[10]

Kenyon and Commemoration: *Mentalités* and Perceptions of Antiquity

It is appropriate to focus on the role that Sir Frederic Kenyon played in the establishment of the War Graves Commission, particularly in a volume that is published by the institution to which he himself gave so much. Within the overall history of the War Graves Commission, emphasis has been placed rightly on individuals such as Fabian Ware, Reginald Blomfield, or Lutyens. The influence of the classical world on the forms of commemorative cultures that the War Graves Commission established has accounted largely for the architectural forms.[11] Little has been done to review the role of Kenyon, and, as far as I am aware, his interaction with the evidence for the commemoration of the war dead in antiquity has not been explored.[12]

Kenyon offers a route into exploring how the commemoration of the war dead during the classical era might have influenced the formation of

---

[10] Rood 2007 explores the ancient Greek models that were echoed by the celebration of victory and commemoration after the battle of Waterloo. The contrast between the treatment of the mass of individual war dead in the early nineteenth century and the commemorative practices that were introduced a century later illustrates the change that took place.

[11] See Stamp 2006, 56–71 on Lutyens' classical borrowings and pp. 194–5 for a bibliography. Blomfield 1932, 179 avoided 'any association with any particular style ... above all ... the sentimentalism of the gothic' but wrote about Greek architecture. On the Graeco-Roman influences, see also Borg 1991 and, in more general terms, Curl 1980.

[12] See Longworth 1985.

attitudes to commemorative practices in British society at the end of the nineteenth and in the early twentieth centuries. Let us consider whether Kenyon's perception of commemorative culture could have been affected by his own intimate involvement in antiquity. It is argued here that Kenyon's *mentalités* were imbued with the commemorative culture of classical Athens, and that this knowledge and understanding would have had a major impact on shaping Kenyon's attitudes that proved to coincide so closely with those of Fabian Ware, making the Academician Kenyon well suited to his future role in the War Graves Commission.

Kenyon is well known within the British Academy as one of its most successful presidents (1917–21): an award (the Kenyon Medal) bears his name. But to historians and experts of twentieth-century commemoration in Britain and its Empire, Kenyon is best known as the author of *War Graves: How the Cemeteries Abroad Will Be Designed, Report to the War Graves Commission*, which became known as *The Kenyon Report*.[13] To others, Kenyon is known as the director of the British Museum and, in particular, as former keeper of manuscripts, and author of many important papyrological publications.

It is to this last role that I turn first. Arguably the most important of those papyri that Kenyon published at the end of the nineteenth century was the so-called *Constitution of the Athenians* attributed to Aristotle.[14] Kenyon wrote the first major commentary on the Aristotelian *Constitution of the Athenians* and, among his many publications, he was also translator of that work. The *Constitution of the Athenians* gives a brief history of archaic and classical Athens and an overview of the institutions of the Athenian city at the time of the work's composition, which was sometime around 330–320 BCE.[15] In its description of Athenian politics in the middle of the fifth century, at the very time when the democracy was becoming stronger and more deeply rooted in a broader section of society, we hear about the large numbers of war dead that the Athenians were suffering. At this time the Athenians played a major role in leading the Greeks' defence against the Persians and had established themselves as an imperial power in the process. The text describes, in probably *c.*460 BCE, the losses suffered by the Athenians. Kenyon's translation reads: 'the mass of the people suffered great losses by war'.[16] It is worth noting that the modern authority on this text, P. J. Rhodes, offers a slightly less colourful

---

[13] *The Kenyon Report*, Kenyon 1918.
[14] Kenyon 1891.
[15] See Rhodes 1993 for a full, modern commentary; Rhodes 1984 for a modern translation.
[16] Kenyon 1907, 48, translating Aristotle *Constitution of the Athenians* 26.1.

translation, which adheres more closely to the original Greek: 'In addition, many had been killed in war.'[17] The difference is interesting not least because Kenyon's translation 'mass of the people' anticipates his translation a few lines later that refers to the impact of the losses on the lower and upper classes. For the purposes of our interest in Kenyon's own perceptions of the commemoration of the war dead in classical Athens it is worth reproducing the complete translation he offered for the relevant passage:

> The soldiers for active service were selected at that time from the roll of citizens, and as the generals were men of no military experience, who owed their position solely to their family standing, it continually happened that some two or three thousand of the troops perished on an expedition; and in this way the best men alike of the lower and the upper classes were exhausted.[18]

This passage is clearly attractive to us in terms of the common issues it raises for examining the commemoration of war dead in societies past and present. How were soldiers recruited? How representative was military service among the citizen population? How did casualties affect social groups? Of course all these issues were important in the First World War and of considerable relevance to the War Graves Commission, as we shall see shortly.

When Kenyon published the new Aristotelian *Constitution of the Athenians*, it was already possible to understand a great deal about the Athenian commemoration of war dead. A good classical education would have ensured that the nineteenth-century gentleman was familiar with Thucydides' *Histories*, an account of the Peloponnesian War and the build-up of Athenian imperial strength in the fifty years (*c*.478–431 BCE) that led up to the war's outbreak. At the end of the opening year of the war, in the winter of 431/0, the Athenians honoured their war dead with a public burial at which the leading politician offered a speech.[19] Thucydides introduces the occasion and offers a version of the speech made by Pericles, the 'Funeral oration' (Thucydides, *Histories* 2.35–46).[20] The

---

[17] Rhodes 1984, 69.
[18] Kenyon 1907, 48, translating Aristotle *Constitution of the Athenians* 26.1. Rhodes 1984, 69 reads: 'At that time military service was based on selective conscription, and the generals who commanded were men lacking in experience of war but honoured because of their forebears' reputations, thus it regularly happened that two or three thousand of the men sent out were killed, and the casualties fell on the better sorts of both the ordinary people and the wealthy.'
[19] Hornblower 1991, 292 follows Jacoby 1944 in stressing that the occasion was very much a religious one in which the dead were honoured with a heroic cult.
[20] I use the Crawley translation in Strassler 1996.

funeral oration of Pericles formed an essential part of classical education: Lincoln's Gettysburg address (19 November 1863) made several allusions to some of the sentiments expressed by Pericles.[21] There is a strong argument that Pericles' fifth-century speech influenced Lincoln's in the nineteenth century.[22]

But, in addition to that literary evidence, we know a great deal about the monumental commemoration of the war dead—the archaeology of commemoration. The Athenian war dead were commemorated by civic memorials—stone monuments carrying lists of the Athenian dead, their names arranged on stone tablets (stelae) according to the tribe to which each individual belonged. In such lists the Athenian war dead are never given one part of the name that was widely used to identify an individual: the patronymic. Nor were citizens on the lists distinguished by the demotic, the third element in Athenian nomenclature more familiar in the later classical period.[23] One form of this kind of monument might be a single stone slab (stele) on which the Athenian war dead are listed by tribe—the headings in larger letters here – and below each heading the individual's name; no patronymic or demotic is given. In one particular inscription (*IG* i³ 1162) we have two separate campaigns commemorated in the 440s BCE in the two columns that dominate the stone: one campaign fought in the Chersonese (the left-hand column) and the other at Byzantium (the right-hand column); at some later point, presumably in the same year, the dead from other campaigns were added (see Figure 2.2 in Chapter 2 of this volume; the end of the left-hand column shows the dead in the Chersonese and the later addition of the dead in other wars).

These monuments list the names of the dead, individually. The names are arranged by one of the most important subgroups of the city, a sub-group that served also as the military unit of organization in which citizens fought and ultimately died: the tribe. The monuments of the Athenians are therefore civic but essentially military. For the tribe served as the critical reference point for participation in Athens on the level of the state, or *polis*. In the Agora at the heart of the city of classical Athens, the so-called Monument of the Eponymous Heroes was used to post notices

---

[21] On classical education in the nineteenth century, see, for example, Stray 1998.

[22] See Wills 1992. For the indirect influence of Pericles on more recent oratory via Lincoln, see e.g. Stow 2007. For Lincoln's contact with Pericles' funeral oration, see Stow 2007, 195, n. 1.

[23] The demotic refers to the third element of an Athenian name (name, patronymic, demotic). A deme (a village) was where an Athenian citizen's male ancestor had originally been registered, a necessary condition to qualify for citizenship.

for the tribes of the Athenians, including calls to arms of age groups of Athenians within each tribe.[24]

Unfortunately we have no way of calculating the numbers of war dead that the Athenians suffered on an annual basis. The evidence of the *Constitution of the Athenians* suggests that in the mid-fifth century annual losses were particularly high. The remains of the inscribed monuments bearing the lists of the war dead are rarely preserved completely and only a small fraction of the monuments that must have once been set up for the war dead at Athens have survived.[25] It is clear that many of these monuments stood for long periods in antiquity—the writer Pausanias in the second century CE saw monuments of Athenian war dead that had been set up three or four hundred years earlier and describes them.[26]

A fortunate survival among the epigraphical record is a single stele, which records the names of 177 Athenians who had died fighting as part of the tribe Erechtheis.[27] The number of war dead—and let us remember that there were ten tribes—ties in with the evidence of the *Constitution of the Athenians* that indicates that two or three thousand Athenians were dying on campaign at the time of Kimon, in the mid-fifth century.[28] The monument for the Erechtheis, if typical of casualties in that year, would suggest losses of between 1,500 and 2,000 men.

We cannot be certain that the monuments listed all the dead but the Athenians paid particular importance to collecting all the bodies of their dead and this suggests the commemoration sought to be exhaustive in listing all the dead, even adding those whose deaths followed the earlier setting up of the monument. In 425, during the Peloponnesian War, the Athenians fought their neighbouring Corinthians in a battle on Corinthian territory. They inflicted heavy casualties on the enemy and killed a Corinthian general (Lykophron). The Athenians collected their dead and withdrew by boat from the territory in which they had fought. However, Nicias the general learned that two of the dead were missing, and so halted the fleet and sent a herald to the enemy to ask for the return of the two bodies (Plutarch, *Life of Nicias* 6.4–5).

When Kenyon published *The Constitution of the Athenians*, the funeral oration of Pericles, the Athenian treatment of the war dead, and the evidence of the stone monuments listing the war dead were already familiar

---

[24] Aristotle *Constitution of the Athenians* 53.7, 61.3.
[25] Clairmont 1983 gathers the material together.
[26] On the reliability of Pausanias, see Habicht 1998.
[27] Meiggs and Lewis 1988, 33 (IG i³ 1147; Figure 2.6).
[28] Aristotle *Constitution of the Athenians* 26.1.

to those studying ancient history. In Paris, nice examples of the inscribed lists of the war dead were well known from the collection in the Louvre (IG i³ 1147 and 1190), and in London some fragmentary lists were included among the collection of Greek inscriptions housed in the British Museum.[29] Although it is not certain, it is more than likely that these monuments would have been known to Kenyon in the 1890s. In 1909 Kenyon became the director and principal librarian of the British Museum, holding the post until 1931. It is hard to imagine that he was unaware of the monumental background to the Athenian commemoration of the war dead when he worked on the *Constitution of the Athenians*.

I have tried to establish strong grounds for believing that Kenyon was aware of the commemorative practices of classical Athens. Let us now consider his role in helping to shape the commemorative culture that was pioneered by Fabian Ware during the First World War. During the war years, Kenyon's career reached new heights: he served as president of the British Academy from 1917. In this capacity his presidential address of 4 July 1918 sets out clearly his expressed wish that the Academy, a relatively new institution, should serve to represent and reflect the ideas of the intellectual community alongside the Royal Society:

> The Academy must be ready to undertake any service required of it by the State, and to justify its claim to represent the best scholarship of the nation ... The State should regard the Academy as its natural resort when advice is needed on matters which come within its scope.[30]

Kenyon envisaged several scenarios that defined how he saw 'The position of an Academy in a civilised state'—the title of his presidential address.

The address revealed his ambitions for the Academy but also reflected the services that he was performing for the state. For in the previous year, at a meeting of the Imperial War Graves Commission on 20 November 1917, Kenyon was appointed adviser to the Commission. The Commission had been in existence for only six months, having received a royal charter on 21 May 1917 following the Imperial War Conference. Kenyon was given the responsibility of writing a report for the government, *War Graves: How the Cemeteries Abroad Will Be Designed*.[31] Needless to say, government-sponsored reports are not always unbiased, and the institutional background to Kenyon's Commission, the youth of the Academy,

---

[29] Text and photographs of the monuments for the Athenian war dead in the British Museum collection had been published in the first of a series of volumes by Revd E. L. Hicks in 1874.

[30] Kenyon 1917–18, 47.

[31] Kenyon 1918.

and his own desire to enhance the Academy's status are relevant factors in assessing his own role.

Although this is well-trodden ground, some background to the report and the Imperial War Graves Commission is necessary. The Commission was built largely on foundations laid by Fabian Ware. His role in its history can be found in a report he submitted twenty years after the Commission was created, in 1937.[32] The Commission's origins are also explained in Longworth's history of it: Fabian Ware is the protagonist of the story and rightfully holds centre stage[33]. Kenyon's contribution is seen to be rather marginal. For it was Ware's Graves Registration Unit that in 1916 had become the Directorate of Graves Registration and Enquiries before finally being transformed into an imperial institution in 1917, with responsibilities for all parts of the British Empire. The Prince of Wales presided over the Imperial War Graves Commission; its first chairman was Lord Derby, with Fabian Ware, the vice-chairman.

Kenyon had not been the first choice as adviser to the Commission. Ware had initially approached Sir Charles Holmes, director of the National Gallery. Holmes had at first accepted Ware's invitation to serve on the Commission but then declined on the grounds that his duties prevented him spending enough time on the Commission and he recommended Kenyon.[34] In Holmes's view, Kenyon's position as director of the British Museum was one which could more easily sustain the distractions of service on the Commission. At a meeting in London on 25 August, Ware asked Kenyon to consider the position of chairman to the Advisory Committee for the War Graves Commission. Two days later Kenyon accepted, identifying his own military experience throughout the war as an appropriate qualification.[35] In the preface to Kenyon's report, Fabian Ware explained that Kenyon's appointment 'was made with a view to focusing, and, if possible, reconciling the various opinions on this subject [designs of monuments and cemeteries] that had found expression among the armies at the front and the general public at home, and particularly in artistic circles'.[36]

---

[32] Ware 1937.

[33] Longworth 1985.

[34] For Holmes's initial acceptance, see CWGC WQ8 Pt 2 Box 1001, letter from Holmes to Ware, 21 April 1917; for his later refusal, CWGC WQ8 Pt 2 Box 1001, letter from Holmes to Ware, 10 May 1917.

[35] For Ware's invitation to meet Kenyon, see CWGC WG1 Box 2017, letter 22 August 1917; for Kenyon's acceptance of the offer, CWGC WG1 Box 2017, letter 27 August 1917.

[36] Kenyon 1918.

One of the central controversies was the commemoration of the individual, and Kenyon's role was to some extent that of fixer, a respected academic who would be able to communicate the central principles of the Commission and settle the differences between the artists and architects involved in the Commission.[37] Notwithstanding the several artistic differences, one of the causes of discontent was addressed by one of the central principles of the Commission, 'that no distinction should be made between officers and the men lying in the same cemetery in the form or nature of the memorials'. What Kenyon called the 'equality of treatment', some might regard as the denial of individuality.[38]

It is well known that during the First World War relatives wished to set up their own memorials to the war dead. Some wished to return the remains of the dead to England for burial. The British Army had no clear policy concerning the treatment of the dead in the war and the large number of casualties exacerbated this situation. Fabian Ware had, on his own initiative, taken steps first in tandem with the Red Cross but later within the structures of the army to record where the dead had been buried. The absence of any clear policy and the overwhelming needs of the war campaign itself meant that there was no real framework or organization and so the burial and commemoration of the dead developed rather haphazardly. The number of requests for information about the dead, and the desire to mourn and visit the grave of lost ones, lies behind the creation of the War Graves Commission and the institutionalization of Ware's project.

The Commission, reinforced by Kenyon's report, insisted on one principle—equal treatment of the war dead. It is well worth reviewing how Kenyon justifies and supports the principle of equality. He was influenced not only by the principles of the Commission but also, like others involved in the Commission, by his visit to northern France.[39] Kenyon recognized clearly that money and good taste would foster good individual monuments. However, he also understood that such a scenario did not reflect the likely reality of commemoration that would result if private money were allowed to effect the construction of monuments in cemeteries of the war dead. For if that were to happen, 'In the large majority of cases, either no monument would be erected, or it would be poor in quality; and

---

[37] Ware describes the role as 'arbiter in matters of artistic taste' in a memo to the chairman of the Imperial War Graves Commission: CWGC WG1 Box 2017, memo, 22 October 1917.
[38] Kenyon 1918, 8.
[39] Compare Lutyens, see Stamp 2006, 67–70.

the total result would be one of inequality, haphazard and disorder.'[40] In other words, one argument for equality of treatment was to avoid the over-importance that the wealthy would assume in military cemeteries if they were allowed to erect monuments and commemorate their relatives in such locations.

The fear was, Kenyon explained, that if such individually selected and constructed monuments were allowed to multiply, the war cemeteries would become 'a collection of individual memorials'.[41] By the early nineteenth century, the image of public cemeteries had become fairly well established. Public cemeteries in England had been established from the 1820s and typically were full of individualized monuments presenting a varied landscape of different shapes, sizes, and forms of monument. However, both the Commission and Kenyon recognized—or argued—that to allow such individual monuments to be set up would repress the representation of the poorer elements of society: 'The monuments of the more well-to-do would overshadow those of their poorer comrades.'[42] Such individualization was felt inappropriate in the space that the War Graves Commission sought to control, the military cemetery: the Commission did not wish to see the spectre of the now familiar late Georgian and Victorian cemeteries that had developed since the 1820s with their varied monuments, some of which were neglected.[43]

Nevertheless, and this is a crucial condition, it was felt appropriate that 'private' memorials should be set up, but in a different space—not on the battlefield sites nor in the cemeteries but *at home*. This was an important concession to individualization in the commemoration of the war dead. However, no corpses were to be repatriated. Kenyon wrote in his report: 'The place for the individual memorial is at home, where it will be constantly before the eyes of relatives and descendants, and will serve as an example and encouragement for generations to come.'[44] That statement merely echoed the already-voiced opinion of Ware.[45] Kenyon therefore reinforced the guiding principles that Ware had devised for the War Graves Commission.

The War Graves Commission was not set up to repress the commemoration of the individual, but it sought a way to accommodate the individual

---

[40] Kenyon 1918, 6.
[41] Kenyon 1918, 6.
[42] Kenyon 1918.
[43] Curl 1980, ch. 7.
[44] Kenyon 1918.
[45] Scott 2010, 28.

within the framework of the community of the dead under the direction of the state. The standard commemoration was always to be individual burial and individual headstone. That choice was intended to allow the relatives to express their emotions for the dead: 'the individual headstone, marking the individual grave, will serve as centre and focus of the emotions of the relatives who visit it' runs Kenyon's report.[46] Ultimately, such efforts to recognize individuals in death required individuals to be identifiable. The commemoration of the individual required that the death and the identity of the dead individual be known and communicated. In modern warfare such information and transfer of knowledge could be problematic. Identification tags were introduced in the American Civil War. In European armies they were introduced towards the end of the nineteenth century: most armies used identity tags in the First World War which reduced enormously the number of individual dead that could not be identified.[47]

Despite the efforts taken to acknowledge individuals and allow for some individuality in military cemeteries, these commemorative contexts belonged essentially to the group. Figure 6.1 shows a detail from the Thiepval memorial on which individuals are listed not by rank but by military unit:

> The sacrifice of the individual is a great idea and worthy of commemoration, but the community of sacrifice, the service of a common cause, the comradeship in arms which have brought together men of all ranks and grades—these are greater ideas that should be commemorated in those cemeteries where they lie together.[48]

Of course, the War Graves Commission could have repressed the individual even further. The headstones marking individual graves allowed the individual to be commemorated—they were better adapted for decoration with flowers (as well as easier to maintain and satisfactory in effect). And despite the lack of individuation in terms of the form and inscription of the memorial, such as at Thiepval, *the commemoration of, and concern for the recording of, every individual* displays a real concern to include every individual in the commemorative process. There is of course a tension between this concern for the individual and the desire to set the individual within the framework of a wider community.

[46] Kenyon 1918.
[47] For the USA, Sledge 2005, 97–9; for Britain, Longworth 1985, 19.
[48] Kenyon 1918, 6217.

Figure 6.1   Detail from the Thiepval Monument. (Photograph by G. Oliver)

If we return to ancient Greece, individual tombstones for the Greek
war dead honoured by the city are the exception: military honours existed
but individual funerary monuments were not the norm.[49] The group dom-
inates—the *polis* or city-state and also the military group (the tribe) to
which the individual belongs determine the order of commemoration in
Athens in the fifth century. Certainly this is the understanding that would
have circulated among those who were aware of the fifth-century BCE evidence looking back from the early twentieth century.[50] However, in Athens,
for example, it was indeed possible for individuals to be commemorated
as individuals or as part of a family in a space away from the special areas
reserved for monuments to the war dead. The monument for the young
Athenian cavalryman Dexileos occupies such a space in the Kerameikos
in a prominent plot that was surrounded by other private monuments.[51] In
theory, the public honour or heroization of the war dead at least ensured
that the burial and the monumentalization of the individual's death were
not forgotten. Indeed, it cannot be certain that in normal circumstances
all Athenian individuals would have had their own death commemorated
on an inscribed monument because of the prohibitive cost for the poorer
members of society. The provision of a permanent grave marker for the

---

[49] *IG* ii² 5226a seems to be an example of an individualized monument in honouring an Athenian
who lost his life in a conflict on behalf of the city.

[50] Low 2003 and Chapter 2, this volume, demonstrate how a much more varied view of practices
must be adopted.

[51] *IG* ii² 6217. This monument, however, had been found in the late 1800s.

war dead was guaranteed by the public funeral rites.[52] The culture of commemoration in classical Athens did not prevent the individual war dead from being commemorated monumentally, separately from, and in addition to, the public honour conferred on him by the state at the civic burial in the *demosion sema*.

The similarities between remembrance in classical Athens and the guiding principles of the War Graves Commission allow us therefore to review the commemoration of the individual war dead. The 'total commemoration' of the war dead that has become familiar to us now because of the work of the CWGC—rows of headstones of the identified and unidentified bodies of the war dead and lists of names of the unrecovered bodies of the fallen—is virtually without precedent in post-antique culture. Such practices can be glimpsed only from the mid-nineteenth century onwards (in the American Civil War) before it flourishes (and then not everywhere) from the First World War onwards. In the absence of earlier models of such practice, we have seen how the ancient world may have offered a useful reference point for the educated minds of the time, particularly given that so many had a classical education in the late nineteenth and early twentieth century.

The Absence of the Commemoration of the Individual War Dead in Past Societies

It is a challenge to argue, however, that no historical cultures from the Roman Empire through to the mid-nineteenth century witnessed the centralized mass commemoration of their war dead in the monumental form that can be found in classical Athens, late nineteenth-century USA, and early twentieth-century Britain (and its empire). But when one turns to, for example, medieval England it is difficult to see such signs of ritual. Certainly individuals might have been recorded in chantries or by anniversaries, but there seems little to suggest something similar to the Athenian practice developed by the CWGC.[53] Borg's study of war memorials suggests that the institutions that had developed such commemorative processes might have included hospitals established as charities.[54]

---

[52] On the cost of commemoration in Athens, see Oliver 2000.
[53] Daniell 1998, 177.
[54] Borg 1991, 66. The notable feature of Borg's survey is the paucity of parallel evidence from the medieval and early modern periods.

It has become a common motif to contrast the later nineteenth-century practice with that which marked the early nineteenth-century disposal of the dead following the battle of Waterloo.[55] Edmund Blunden's opening remarks to Fabian Ware's *Immortal Heritage* not only contrast the commemorative practices of Wellington's time with those of the First World War but also lay emphasis on the role of the individual: 'it has been the faith of the Commission that those who fought and died in 1914–18 were ... several and separate personalities ... each claiming individual comprehension'.[56]

France in the early nineteenth century displayed little interest in listing the names of ordinary citizens who had died for the state.[57] The Arc de Triomphe carried the names of high-ranking officers and battles, but for the lowly citizen where does one turn? *La colonne de juillet* in the Place de la Bastille, for example, has a list of those who fell, but then the names of the victims of that particular event in 1830 carried particular significance.[58] Certainly there is a real case for reviewing the evidence for the centralized commemoration of the war dead. The evidence is elusive and even as far back as the Roman imperial period the evidence for lengthy lists of the war dead such as those found at Adamclissi are the exception that proves the rule.[59]

Developing the Commemoration of the Individual War Dead

This chapter has so far attempted to draw a close association between the commemorative culture of the Greek *polis* or city-state of the classical period and the self-conscious development of a centrally organized commemoration machinery that became the Commonwealth War Graves Commission. The association can be identified in the conscience of the agents, or at least one prominent agent, who had participated in the development of the Commission. Although we have not explored the *mentalités* of other agents such as Ware, the chapter has attempted to move Kenyon back to a more prominent role. There seems to be a strong case then for thinking further about the common features shared by those societies that developed centralized commemoration of the civic war

---

[55] Stamp 2006, 74–5; Borg 1991, 55.
[56] Blunden, Preface to Ware 1937.
[57] See Ben-Amos, Chapter 5, this volume.
[58] Ben-Amos 2000, 101–6.
[59] See Cooley, Chapter 4, this volume; Bobu Florescu 1965.

dead. The attention paid to the listing of the war dead, or the determination to ensure proper rituals that lay great emphasis on the shared and non-discriminatory treatment of the dead, is striking.

Following on from the nineteenth-century American policy of burying the dead soldiers after the 1865–71 Civil War, and the creation of the Imperial (now Commonwealth) War Graves Commission, there has been a real growth in commemorative cultures of the named war dead. But not everywhere in the recent past has behaved in the same way: twentieth-century Russia is an interesting case study. The treatment of the war dead and the experience of combatants has been the subject of important academic studies.[59] Greater access to information following the collapse of the Soviet system has provided new evidence as details about casualties and operations during the Great Patriotic War became known.[61] In theory Soviet soldiers were to have worn identity tags, but the decree passed in 1941 requiring this was cancelled the following year. Sources reveal that casualty figures and details were rarely complete. The often very heavy casualties in a highly mobile war combined with the inconsistent use of tags will have made recovery operations very difficult. The work of the Imperial War Graves Commission demonstrates the enormous effort and will that commemoration on such a scale requires.[62]

Soviet Russia created few monuments that *list* the war dead but it was rich in memorials.[63] Dedicated cemeteries with ranks of headstones are not a feature of this landscape. However, an organized heroic cult surrounding combatants was actively developed. And this is one of the features of Merridale's research that has described the impact of the hero culture on young Soviets.[64] Change did occur and as a result of casualties in the Afghan War a significant reaction to the losses and a need to commemorate the dead spread in the last decades of the twentieth century.[65] However, the proportion of Soviet citizens affected by loss in the Afghan War was relatively small compared with those Americans affected by the death of soldiers in Vietnam.[66]

Of course the changing context of the fragmenting power of the Soviet state also played an enormous role. The change in commemorative practice

[60] Merridale 1999, 2000, and 2005.

[61] Sella 1992, esp. 64–6.

[62] Sella 1992, 65.

[63] Merridale 2005, 324.

[64] Merridale 2000, 363–6. For the impact of the glorification of war in Britain in the later nineteenth and twentieth centuries, see Paris 2000.

[65] Alexievitch 1992; Galeotti 1995.

[66] Galeotti 1995, 30.

is marked in the aftermath of the Afghan War when, several years later, memorials listing the dead appeared in several Russian cities. Vologda is said to have provided 2,149 soldiers of whom 81 are listed on the panels of a monument erected to commemorate the dead. Another memorial at Yekaterinberg has organized the list of names in accordance with the year in which they died (see Figure 6.2). At Petrozavodsk in Karelia a monument listing fifty-five dead continues to serve as an active focus of remembrance for those who have dedicated flowers and cigarettes to the dead (see Figure 6.3). These memorials can clearly perform a role within the community and serve as a medium for mourning and remembrance. This contrasts starkly with the treatment of the bodies of the dead who arrived back from Afghanistan in zinc coffins (thus the name 'Zinky Boys'): the bodies were often not allowed to be buried in war cemeteries and the 'graves were scattered around in the hope that their numbers would have less impact, and the headstones seldom specified where or why death had occurred'.[67]

Figure 6.2   Monument for the Afghan War, Yekaterinberg. (Photograph courtesy of Christel Müller)

[67] Alexievich 1992; quotation, Merridale 2000, 366.

Figure 6.3   Monument for the Afghan war dead, Petrozavodsk. (Photograph by G. Oliver)

Conscription and high numbers of casualties link many of the conflicts in which the widespread and organized commemoration of the individual war dead developed. But these two factors alone are not sufficient: common to the American Civil War, First World War, and perhaps too the wars of the first half of the fifth century BCE in Athens was a shared need for mourning by those who suffered loss and for the dead to be acknowledged.[68] If these needs combine with an acceptance by a central authority (such as a state) to recognize its collective responsibility for a commemorative culture for the dead, then we may find it more likely that the remembrance of the individual will be given more importance.

When Blunden compared the work of the War Graves Commission with the past he looked back to a time when such concerns did not exist: 'the ancients regarded the soldier in the mass, and felt no difficulty in consigning him accordingly without name or detail into some common sepulchre'. But Blunden's ancients cannot be the Greeks or the Athenians of the classical era. It is much more likely that he was thinking of the Napoleonic era. For when we compare ancient and modern commemorative cultures we find a much greater affinity in their treatment of the individual war dead.

---

[68] See Ricoeur 2004, 205–7 on the importance of recognition and collective identities.

Note. I would like to thank the Commonwealth War Graves Commission and their staff, Roy Hemington and Argyro Francis, at the Archives in Maidenhead, for allowing me access to material on Kenyon and for permission to refer to it in this chapter.

Bibliography

Alexievich, S. 1992. *Zinky Boys: Soviet Voices from a Forgotten War*. London: Chatto & Windus.

Ben-Amos, A. 2000. *Funerals, Politics, and Memory in Modern France, 1789–1996*. Oxford: Oxford University Press.

Becker, A. 1988. *Les monuments aux mort: memoire de la Grande Guerre*. Paris: Errance.

Bennett, G. 2001. *Coronel and the Falklands*. 2nd edn. Edinburgh: Birlinn.

Blight, D. W. 2004. 'Decoration Days: The Origin of Memorial Day in North and South'. In *The Memory of the Civil War in American Culture*, ed. A. Fahs and J. Waugh. Chapel Hill and London: University of North Carolina Press, 94–129.

Blomfield, R. 1932. *Memoirs of an Architect*. London: Macmillan.

Bobu Florescu, F. 1965. *Das Siegesdenkmal von Adamklissi Tropaeum Traiani*. Bucharest: Akademie der Rumänischen Volksrepublik.

Boorman, D. 2005. *A Century of Remembrance: One Hundred Outstanding British War Memorials*. Barnsley: Pen and Sword.

Borg, A. 1991. *War Memorials from Antiquity to the Present*. London: Leo Cooper.

Clairmont, C. W. 1983. *Patrios Nomos: Public Burial in Athens during the Fifth and Fourth Centuries B.C.: The Archaeological, Epigraphic–Literary, and Historical Evidence*. 2 vols. Oxford: BAR.

Curl, J. S. 1980. *A Celebration of Death*. London: Constable.

Daniell, C. 1998. *Death and Burial in Medieval England, 1066–1550*. London: Routledge.

Faust, D. G. 2006. '"Numbers on Top of Numbers": Counting the Civil War Dead.' *Journal of Military History* 70, 995–1009.

——2008. *The Republic of Suffering: Death and the American Civil War*. New York: Knopf.

Galeotti, M. 1995. *Afghanistan: The Soviet Union's Last War*. London: Frank Cass.

Gibson, E. and G. K. Ward. 1989. *Courage Remembered: The Story Behind the Construction and Maintenance of the Commonwealth's Military Cemeteries and Memorials of the Wars of 1914–1918 and 1939–1945*. London: HMSO.

Habicht, C. 1998. *Pausanias' Guide to Ancient Greece*. Revised paperback edn. Berkeley: University of California Press.

Hornblower, S. 1991. *A Commentary on Thucydides*, vol. 1: *Books I–III*. Oxford: Clarendon Press.

Jacoby, F. 1944. '*Patrios Nomos*: State Burial in Athens and the Public Cemetery.' *Journal of Hellenic Studies* 64, 37–66.

Kenyon, F. 1891. *Aristotle on the Constitution of Athens.* 2nd edn. London: Trustees of the British Museum.

——1907. *Aristotle on the Athenian Constitution.* Translated and with notes. London: George Bell.

——1917–18. 'The Position of an Academy in a Civilized State.' *Proceedings of the British Academy*, 37–49.

——1918. *War Graves: How the Cemeteries Abroad Will Be Designed, Report to the Imperial War Graves Commission.* London.

Keren, M. and H. H. Herwig, eds. 2009. *War Memory and Popular Culture: Essays on Modes of Remembrance and Commemoration,* Jefferson, NC: McFarland.

Longworth, P. 1985. *The Unending Vigil: The History of the Commonwealth War Graves Commission.* London: Leo Cooper in association with Secker & Warburg.

Low, P. 2003. 'Remembering War in Fifth-Century Greece: Ideologies, Societies and Commemoration beyond Democratic Athens.' *World Archaeology* 53, 98–111.

Meiggs, R. and D. M. Lewis. 1988. *A Selection of Greek Historical Inscriptions to the End of the Fifth Century BC.* Revised edn. Oxford: Clarendon Press.

Merridale, C. 1999. 'War, Death, and Remembrance in Soviet Russia.' In *War and Remembrance in the Twentieth Century*, ed. J. Winter and E. Sivan. Cambridge: Cambridge University Press, 61–83.

——2000. *Night of Stone: Death and Memory in Russia.* London: Granta Books.

——2005. *Ivan's War: The Red, Army 1939–45.* London: Faber & Faber.

Oliver, G. J. 2000. 'Athenian Funerary Monuments: Style, Grandeur, Cost.' In *The Epigraphy of Death: Studies in the History and Society of Greece and Rome*, ed. G. J. Oliver. Liverpool: Liverpool University Press, 59–80.

Paris, M. 2000. *Warrior Nation: Images of War in British Popular Culture, 1850–2000.* London: Reaktion Books.

Prost, A. and J. Winter. 2004. *Penser la Grande Guerre: un essai d'historiographie.* Paris: Seuil.

Rhodes, P. J. 1984. *The Athenian Constitution.* Harmondsworth: Penguin.

——1993. *A Commentary on the Aristotelian Athenaion Politeia.* Reprint with corrections. Oxford: Clarendon Press.

Ricoeur, P. 2004. *Parcours de la Reconnaissance: trois études.* Paris: Stock.

Rood, T. 2007. 'From Marathon to Waterloo: Byron, Battle Monuments, and the Persian Wars.' In *Cultural Responses to the Persian Wars*, ed. E. Hall, P. J. Rhodes, and E. Bridges. Oxford: Oxford University Press, 267–97.

Scott, D. D. 2010. 'Military Medicine in the Pre-modern Era: Using Forensic Techniques in Archaeological Investigations to Investigate Military Remains.' In *The Historical Archaeology of Military Sites: Method and Topic*, ed. C. R. Geier, L. E. Babits, and D. D. Scott. Austin, TX: A&M Press, 21–9.

Sella, A. 1992. *The Value of Human Life in Soviet Warfare.* London: Routledge.

Sledge, M. 2005. *Soldier Dead: How We Recover, Identify, Bury, and Honor Our Military Fallen.* New York: Columbia University Press.

Stamp, G. 2006. *The Memorial to the Missing of the Somme.* London: Profile Books.

Stow, S. 2007. 'Pericles at Gettysburg and Ground Zero: Tragedy, Patriotism, and Public Mourning.' *American Political Science Review* 101, 195–208.

Strassler, R. B. ed. 1996. *The Landmark Thucydides: A Comprehensive Guide to the Peloponnesian War.* A Newly Revised Edition of the Richard Crawley Translation with Maps, Annotations, Appendices, and Encyclopedic Index. New York: Free Press.

Stray, C. 1998. *Classics Transformed: Schools, Universities, and Society in England, 1830—1960.* Oxford: Oxford University Press.

Ware, F. 1937. *The Immortal Heritage: An Account of the Work and Policy of the Imperial War Graves Commission during Twenty Years, 1917–1937.* Cambridge: Cambridge University Press.

Wills, G. 1992. *Lincoln at Gettysburg: Words that Remade America.* New York: Simon & Schuster.

Winter, J. M. 1995. *Sites of Memory, Sites of Mourning: The Great War in European Cultural History.* Cambridge: Cambridge University Press.

——2006. *Remembering War: The Great War between Memory and History in the Twentieth Century.* New Haven and London: Yale University Press.

——and E. Sivan. eds. 1999. *War and Remembrance in the Twentieth Century.* Cambridge: Cambridge University Press.

7

Cultural Memory and the Great War: Medievalism and Classicism in British and German War Memorials

STEFAN GOEBEL

IN THE AFTERMATH of the first global and mass-industrialized war, contemporary observers coined the term the 'Great War' or *der große Krieg* to suggest a temporal watershed, a departure from the conditions of warfare as they had been known before. The Great War of 1914–18 and its attendant emotional shocks and socio-political upheavals rocked the foundations of all belligerent European societies; there had never been a greater war before. Some survivors, though, set out to redress the fractures of war by asserting historical continuity through monuments and acts of remembrance. The architect Herbert Baker suggested shortly after the Armistice that war memorials should 'express the heritage of unbroken history and the beauty of England which the sacrifices of our soldiers have kept inviolate'.[1]

This chapter explores the kind of temporal anchoring in the wake of the Great War envisaged by Baker, but from a comparative, Anglo-German perspective. In both Great Britain and Germany, there were people whose epochal consciousness was premised on continuity, people who refused to see history as irretrievably past. Looking to a misty past in order to understand the war-torn present, they enveloped recollections of the First World War in an imagery derived from pre-industrial history, particularly the Middle Ages. References to antiquity, by contrast, were less prevalent. Medievalism was the dominant mode of commemoration.[2] It is best understood as a state of mind rather than a state of history, an amalgam of temporal notions rather than a coherent set of intellectual

---

[1] H. Baker, 'War Memorials: The Ideal of Beauty', *The Times*, 41993, 9 January 1919, 9.
[2] Goebel 2007. On classicism and the cultural legacy of the Great War, see Carden-Coyne 2009; Vandiver 2010.

Proceedings of the British Academy, **160**, 135–158. © The British Academy 2012.

propositions. In fact, medievalist narratives also incorporated classical notations as elaborations on the central theme: the theme of historical continuity in the shadow of a human catastrophe.

My approach contrasts with much recent writing on the Great War that discusses to what extent the years 1914–18 marked a cultural disjuncture. What is at issue here is the significance of the war as the incubator of 'modernism', often understood as a new, iconoclastic language of truth-telling about war in art and literature. The controversy was sparked off in 1975 by Paul Fussell's classic book, *The Great War and Modern Memory*. Analysing the writings of (ex-)servicemen and other, non-combatant writers, Fussell comes to the conclusion that the war opened the way to an attitude of ironic scepticism and bitter disillusionment.[3] The feeling of historical dislocation found expression in poems such as 'Dulce Et Decorum Est' by Wilfred Owen. This poem is about a soldier dying horribly from poison gas, but Owen contrasts the circumstances of the soldier's death with the euphemism of Horace's poetry.

Pace Fussell's seminal study of war literature, in the course of this chapter I argue that remembrance activities taking place in the public domain were creative efforts to affirm rather than reject historical continuity: continuity with a remote, pre-industrial past, in particular the Middle Ages. The language of medievalism turned the trauma of war into a coherent narrative. The fallen combatants were meaningfully relocated in pre-industrial history, thereby making the victim visible within a traditional framework. This discourse restored the individual soldier who had perished in the anonymous *Materialschlacht* (battle of material) of the first mass-industrialized war the world had seen (see Figures 7.1a and 7.1b.).

Recovering and Historicizing the Dead

The 1914–18 war triggered an explosion of naming in memorialization. The practice of naming recalled each individual victim, and returned to him an individuated existence against the oblivion to which he had been consigned on the battlefield. Even if the soldiers did not return physically, commemorations gave the pledge that 'Their Name Liveth for Evermore'.[4] At the suggestion of Rudyard Kipling—a man shaken by the fate of his only son who was lost, presumably killed, at Loos—this motto, borrowed

[3] Fussell 1975. See also Hynes 1990.
[4] Mosse 1990, 83. See also Laqueur 1994, 153.

Figure 7.1a *St George* by F. H. Eberhard. Minster church, Weingarten, 1923. (From *Deutscher Ehrenhain für die Helden von 1914/18* [Leipzig: Dehain, 1931], 170–1)

from Ecclesiasticus (xliv.14), was adopted by the Imperial War Graves Commission.

The Commission's Menin Gate memorial to the missing of the Ypres salient, designed by Sir Reginald Blomfield, is a most powerful monument to the eternal perpetuation of soldiers' names.[5] The memorial takes the form of a classical arch on which the names of 54,896 missing dead are recorded. Though a British–Imperial monument, it did not fail to impress German visitors. A journalist from Berlin remarked approvingly: 'It is integrated into the city's former ramparts. In the course of time, the

[5] Longworth 1985, 86–93; Heffernan 1995, 308.

Figure 7.1b   *St Michael* by F. H. Eberhard. Minster church, Weingarten, 1923. (From *Deutscher Ehrenhain für die Helden von 1914/18* [Leipzig: Dehain, 1931], 170–1)

English Gate will grow completely into the surrounding city of Ypres. It will record the names of the Anglo-Saxon auxiliary troops till the far-off days in history.'[6]

The attempt to embed the Menin Gate in history should not be dismissed as journalistic embellishment. Agents of remembrance endeavoured to tie commemoration to history. The names of the fallen soldiers were sacred as such, but history placed the names under eternal guarantee and invested them with meaning. In Halberstadt, in the Prussian province

---

[6] B[undes]Arch[iv], Berlin, R 8034 II/7692, fo. 172, Bährens, 'Endlich deutsches Heldendenkmal von Langemarck', *Berliner Illustrierte Nachtausgabe*, 9 July 1932.

of Saxony, the fourteenth-century chancel of a church founded in the eleventh century was converted into a hall of remembrance. The names of those who had died in the war were listed on the panelling. The plan met with the approval of the local press which emphasized the time-honoured stateliness of the *vielhundertjährige* (many-hundred-years-old) building.[7] Likewise, commemoration of Cambridgeshire's casualties was amalgamated into the fabric of Ely Cathedral, that 'matchless monument of eight hundred years of history'.[8] A side chapel was fitted up as a memorial, decorated with oak panels like shutters on which nearly 6,000 names were inscribed (arranged alphabetically by parish, without rank). A regional newspaper concluded that 'these men who made the greatest sacrifice are part of England, their names, unknown outside their own country, are woven into the texture of her history as the chapel is part of the fabric of the Cathedral'.[9]

The invocation of soldiers' names offered an effective antidote to the 'powerful anxiety of erasure, a distinctly modern sensibility of the absolute pastness of the past', as Thomas Laqueur has pointed out.[10] Naming was crucial to the act of remembrance; precisely this, however, was beyond the bounds of practicality on the level of national commemorations. How could one possibly find space for the plethora of names? Instead, a symbolic language representing more than 720,000 British and 2 million German losses had to be invented.[11] The authorities in charge of the Armistice Day celebrations in London in 1920 formulated an ingenious scheme for recovering the dead: the tomb of the Unknown Warrior.

Following a complicated process of selection, one unidentified corpse, exhumed from one of the major battlefields of the Western Front, was repatriated to Britain where he received a state funeral in Westminster Abbey on 11 November 1920.[12] The ritual of his selection and the choreography of his inauguration guaranteed that the soldier would remain unidentifiable. Hence the Unknown could act as a universal surrogate body. This is a striking case of fictive kinship; the bereaved could imagine him as a lost son, brother, or friend.

---

[7] 'Eine Gedenkhalle in der Paulskirche', *Halberstädter Zeitung und Intelligenzblatt* 99, 27 April 1924, 5.

[8] 'They Died that We Might Live: Cambridgeshire Honours Its Dead', *Cambridge Chronicle and University Journal*, 9041, 17 May 1922, 8.

[9] Ibid. See Inglis 1992, 592–3.

[10] Laqueur 1996, 133. See also Sherman 1999, 65–103.

[11] For full casualty figures, see Winter 1986, 75.

[12] Inglis 1993, 7–31; Cannadine 1981, 219–26. On the aspect of recovering the dead, see Bourke 1996, 210–52.

Even though the French buried a *soldat inconnu* on the same day and other countries followed suit, the semantics of Unknown Warrior are peculiar to the British case.[13] The term both identified ('Unknown') and historicized ('Warrior') the dead. The wording was carefully chosen, partly because it was 'neutral' so as to include army, air force, and navy.[14] The titles 'Unknown Combatant' or 'Unknown Comrade' could have been options, but, as the *British Legion Journal* noted, the 'name Warrior of itself stands for something more than the word Soldier'.[15] By means of 'high diction', the authorities drafted the 'Warrior' posthumously into the armed force of a heroic age. One newspaper even outdid the official rhetoric by dubbing him the 'Unknown Arthur'.[16]

Effectively, the Anglican establishment created a deferential Christian courtier—in stark contrast to Paris's *soldat inconnu* associated with French republicanism. (On his journey through Paris the *inconnu* was accompanied by the heart of Leon Gambetta, hero of French republicanism at the time of the Franco-Prussian war.) Prior to the ceremony in London, the socialist *Daily Herald* exposed the cult of the Unknown Warrior as a political conjuring trick. 'Who have [*sic*] organised the pageant?', the former editor asked in a published letter. He accused clergy, politicians, press, and war profiteers of using the Unknown Warrior as 'emotional doping' to distract people from the fate of the survivors.[17] On the following day, the same newspaper made a volte-face and reported favourably the return of 'this representative of the Common People; the Man Who Won the War; this Unknown British Warrior—to his last resting place among the captains and the kings of long ago'.[18] The burial also had democratic connotations for the liberal *Manchester Guardian*: 'The nave from ancient times was the people's part of a great church.'[19] The left-wing and liberal press was prepared to join in the official rhetoric. More grandiloquent were, of course, accounts printed in the more conservative newspapers.[20]

---

[13] On the French *soldat inconnu*, see Ben-Amos 2000, 215–24, and this volume, pp. 107–8.

[14] P[ublic] R[ecord] O[ffice], The National Archives, CAB 27/99, fo. 57, memorandum summarizing the dean's suggestion, 15 October 1920. See also ibid., fo. 35, secretary's notes of a meeting, 19 October 1920.

[15] Jeans 1929, 118.

[16] Cited in Lloyd 1998, 89. See also Fussell 1975, 175.

[17] F. Meynell, 'The Unknown Warrior', *Daily Herald* 1497, 11 November 1920, 4. See Gregory, 1994, 26.

[18] 'England Honours Its Unknown Dead: The Warrior Laid to Rest', *Daily Herald* 1498, 12 November 1920, 1.

[19] 'A Nation's Remembrance and Devotion: The Nameless Warrior's Abbey Burial', *Manchester Guardian*, 23168, 12 November 1920, 9.

[20] P. Landon, 'Brother of Kings: Unknown Buried in the Abbey', *Daily Telegraph* 20460, 12 November 1920, 13.

It is noteworthy that the Unknown Warrior was interred in Westminster Abbey rather than St Paul's Cathedral, the final resting-place for naval and military heroes like Nelson and Wellington. A memorial chapel holding the graves of Field Marshal Earl Kitchener of Khartoum, secretary of state for war until he was drowned in 1916, and other outstanding generals had been suggested for St Paul's as early as 1915.[21] Eventually, a Kitchener memorial chapel with an empty tomb was consecrated in 1925. St Paul's, it seems, was intended to be reserved for high-ranking officers. Yet, more importantly, the cathedral lacked the abbey's symbolic force. Westminster Abbey established a relationship between the absent dead of 1914–18 and the army of the first battle of the Somme: the men of Agincourt under Henry V. *The Times* saw the historic parallels:

> Fitly is the 'Unknown Warrior' buried in the soil of France [this soil was brought to Britain together with the corpse S. G.], the soil of France henceforth sacred to us as to her own sons, and consecrated for ever by the heroic sacrifices of both in common warfare against the over-weening insolence of armed lawlessness and wrong. Fitly will he rest in French soil, the gift of French hands, beneath the chapel where hang the helmet and the sword of the conqueror of Agincourt. His blood and the blood of his great company, now sleeping in that same soil across the Channel.[22]

The Unknown Warrior, this symbolic gesture of the return of the absent dead granted 'from above', elicited an overwhelming response 'from below'. Millions of mourners paid homage at the tomb in Westminster Abbey during the interwar years, especially on Armistice Day. Ultimately, it was their presence that infused the static signifier with meaning. High politics could prepare the ground for the memorial rite, but it could not endow it with meaning and purpose. Individual and collective pilgrimages to the Unknown Warrior merged public ceremony with private experience, and national (or imperial) history with family history.[23]

This link became visible in the creation of the Empire Field of Remembrance on the old graveyard of St Margaret's Church opposite the abbey.[24] In November 1928 and in subsequent years, the bereaved were invited to plant little crosses or poppies, provided by the British Legion's poppy factory, in remembrance of lost relatives and friends. Like the common act of touching a war memorial, and especially touching names

[21] Guildhall Library, London, Ms 24.468/3, Lord Knutsford to Canon Alexander, 8 March 1915. See also Goebel 2004b, 498.

[22] 'Armistice Day', *The Times* 42565, 11 November 1920, 15. Compare 'The Living and the Dead', *The Times* 42875, 11 November 1921, 11.

[23] In general, see Winter 1999, 42.

[24] Westminster Abbey Muniment Room, Newspaper Cuttings, vol. I, British Legion Poppy Factory, 'The Story of the Empire Field of Remembrance', n.d.

inscribed upon it, putting tokens in the ground of St Margaret's constituted a ritual of mourning and separation.[25] A British Legion pamphlet
noted: 'It is moving and inspiring to see men, women and children plant-
ing their Crosses or Poppies in this hallowed lawn nestling in the shadow
of the historic Abbey.'[26]

Germans, too, felt the need to bring their dead home and put them to
rest, at least symbolically.[27] Edwin Redslob, the Reich art custodian,
brought the idea of an unknown soldier prominently under discussion. In
his capacity as a governmental 'spin doctor' of cultural policies and political aesthetics, the Reich art custodian proposed in an article, published in
a left-liberal newspaper in summer 1925, to inter an 'unknown dead' in
the River Rhine as a memorial to all Germany's fallen. Redslob, himself
a supporter of the avant-garde, found his inspiration in a festival production by the pacifist author Fritz von Unruh, performed as part of the
Rhineland's millennium celebrations of 1925. In his article, Redslob
makes allusions to a Germanic saga: the 'unknown dead' in the River
Rhine, he writes, 'fulfils a fantasy of our people which lives in the legend
of the sunken golden treasure of the Nibelungen'.[28]

The idea of a Nibelungen-style memorial in the Rhine never materialized. In fact, the entire project of a German national or Reich memorial
never got off the ground until after the Nazis' accession to power. In
October 1935, Adolf Hitler personally proclaimed the Tannenberg memorial in East Prussia a Reich memorial (see Figure 7.2).[29] The foundation
stone, however, had been laid by ultra-conservative groups as early as
1924. Built in a style reminiscent of the castles of the Teutonic Order
(which had been defeated in the first battle of Tannenberg in 1410), the
memorial's architecture seemed to protect the grave erected in its centre.
Underneath a huge metal cross, the bodies of twenty unidentified German
soldiers from the Russian front had been entombed.

Tannenberg illustrates a German transformation of the Anglo-French
tradition. The unknown soldier, who originally represented the recovery
and restoration of the individual, had been turned into a symbol of the
völkisch community. A commentary of 1935 explained the ideology behind
the construction of mass graves in Nazi Germany: 'the individual grave

---

[25] Winter 1995, 113.
[26] I[mperial] W[ar] M[useum], Department of Printed Books, Eph. Mem., K 94/113, British
Legion poppy factory, 'The Empire Field of Remembrance', n.d.
[27] Ackermann 1994; Ziemann 2000, 78–88.
[28] BArch, R 43 I/713, fo. 58, Edwin Redslob, 'Das Soldatengrab im Rhein', *Berliner Tageblatt* 362,
28 June 1925.
[29] Tietz 1999.

Figure 7.2 The Tannenberg memorial by Walter and Johannes Krüger. Tannenberg, 1927. *Tannenberg: Deutsches Schicksal – Deutsche Aufgabe* ed. Kuratorium für das Reichsehrenmal Tannenberg [Oldenburg and Berlin: Gerhard Stalling, 1939], fig. 2)

has been subordinated to the idea of community. It is the greater and lasting. Seen over decades and centuries—once the name will have been blown away and faded away—it will merely be crucial to know that those who have been laid to eternal rest here were Germans and soldiers.'[30]

Layers of Commemoration

War commemorations established a striking nexus between the immediate and the remote past, between catastrophe and history. The experience of loss became encoded in a language of historical continuity. Why did people embark upon historicizing or medievalizing the fallen? Medievalism had both a retrospective and a prospective dimension. First of all, it meant a retreat from the uncertainties of the war into the mythologies of an immutable past. In medievalist narratives, the cohesive force of history overshadowed the traumatic watershed for kith and kin of the deceased:

[30] 'Die Bauten des Volksbundes in ihrer geschichtlichen und kulturellen Bedeutung', *Kriegsgräberfürsorge* 15 (2) (1935), 20.

whatever the circumstances of the soldiers' deaths, the mourners could feel assured that the fallen had their place in history.

This assertion materialized in the war monument of Royston, Hertfordshire. It features the bronze figure of a British soldier of the First World War. He is surrounded by a group of pale marble sculptures representing his military predecessors since the Hundred Years War. A journalist reported: 'In the centre is a typical "Tommy" who "did his bit" in the mud of Flanders, accompanied by the shades of those ancestors of Royston, who, in the past, have on the battlefield and elsewhere done their bit.' At the unveiling ceremony the hope was expressed that the memorial will still 'be looked upon reverently by our children and their children's children'.[31]

Like all war memorials, Royston's was designed to mediate between the past (both the immediate and the remote), present, and future. But how could this linkage be maintained? The bereaved sought assurance of the eternal validity of their commemorative efforts. In both Britain and Germany, artistic institutions worked out blueprints for ideal, everlasting memorials. The Royal Academy of Arts regarded the following principle as vital:

> It is essential that memorials within our Churches and Cathedrals, in the close, the public park, or the village green should not clash with the spirit of the past; that, however simple, they should express the emotion of the present and hope of the future without losing touch with the past, and that instead of being a rock of offence to future generations, they should be objects of veneration to those who follow us.[32]

Experts were alarmed by the example of the monumental legacy of the nineteenth century. Built for eternity, by 1918 these works were predominantly deemed to be tasteless and outdated. In Britain, arbiters of taste like Lawrence Weaver criticized the 'exceeding poverty of memorial design' after the Boer War and urged his contemporaries to focus attention on 'sound traditions' in monumental art.[33] Also in Germany, plastered with hideous monuments to the Bismarckian wars, many were embarrassed to witness the 'shelf life' of memory. As a consequence, German central and provincial governments set up special advice centres to improve the artistic quality of memorial projects.[34]

---

[31] 'Royston War Memorial: Unveiling and Dedication Ceremony', *Herts and Cambs Reporter and Royston Crow* 2376, 31 March 1922.
[32] Royal Academy of Arts, 1918, 2; 'The Royal Academy War Memorials Committee', *Architectural Review* 45 (1919), 20.
[33] Weaver 1915, 1–2.
[34] Lurz 1985, 38–9, 46, 64–7; Schneider 1991, 141, 184–8.

The Prussian centre, the Staatliche Beratungsstelle für Kriegereh-rungen, published the 'Ten Commandments' of memorial art, as they were titled. This guideline for memorial committees, drafted by Hermann Hosaeus, was circulated widely in the 1920s. The author, a professor in Berlin and one of the foremost sculptors of the Weimar Republic, recommended war monuments be adapted to their environment and be based upon 'the artistic traditions of our *Altvorderen* [forebears]', and yet avoid slavish copies thereof.[35] The Prussian advice centre as well as Britain's Royal Academy of Arts argued in favour of what might be called contextual memorials. The underlying assumption was that commemorations linked to either or both history and art history would perpetuate memory down through the ages. To put it in the terminology of recent scholarship, the architects of remem-brance intended to contain oblivion through fusing the 'existential memory' of death in war with the 'cultural memory' of the distant past.

It may be helpful to elaborate on the layering of memory on a more theoretical plane. The observations of the Egyptologist Jan Assmann about the workings of commemoration in antiquity have informed a gen-eral discussion, notably in German historiography.[36] Jan Assmann's the-ory (formulated in cooperation with the literary critic Aleida Assmann) combines, in essence, the works of two pioneers of the study of memory, the sociologist Maurice Halbwachs on the one hand and the art historian Aby Warburg on the other. Assmann draws a distinction between two types, communicative and cultural memory. The concept of communica-tive memory, which follows Halbwachs's work on *mémoire collective*, is defined as the memory of everyday life. It is informal, amorphous, barely shaped, and based upon interaction within social groups: 'Every individ-ual memory constitutes itself in communication with others.'[37] Consequently, the duration of communicative memory is the duration of the group producing it. It is bound to die out after three generations— if not transformed into cultural memory.

Cultural memory, this second type, constitutes a community's collec-tive memory materialized in forms and practices and referring to a distant past. Cultural memory has, therefore, to rely upon a system of memory aids like rites, myths, or monuments supervised by specialists. At this point, Assmann reintroduces Warburg's idea of the enduring mnemonic power of cultural artefacts, an aspect neglected by Halbwachs. However,

---

[35] Hosaeus 1920, 8.
[36] J. Assmann 1997; J. Assmann 2000, 11–44; A. Assmann 1993.
[37] J. Assmann 1995, 127.

the notion of a nexus between cultural memory and social framework is Halbwachsian. It is noteworthy that, according to Assmann, the commemoration of the dead represents a special case. The memory of death occupies an intermediate position between spontaneous communicative memory and elaborate cultural memory. 'The commemoration of the dead', Assmann writes, 'is "communicative" in as much as it is a universal human form and it is "cultural" to the extent to which it generates its specific agents, rites and institutions.'[38]

What are the implications of Assmann's theory for the subject of classicism and medievalism in the commemoration of the Great War? I follow Assmann in distinguishing between two intermingled yet distinct layers of memory: first, the *cultural memory* of an idealized remote past, a configuration dating back to the nineteenth century; and, second, the commemoration of the fallen soldiers themselves. The latter I call the *existential memory* of the Great War. In this second point I differ from Assmann who considers the commemoration of the dead, and particularly the war dead, as a means of identity politics, that is 'memory "which establishes community"'.[39]

While Assmann's general treatment of the commemoration of death is not suitable for categorizing the traumatic impact of modern warfare, it rightly highlights its transitory character. In the era of the Great War, the remembrance of the dead soldiers was more sophisticated than communicative memory, but had not yet reached the state of firm cultural memory with an existence of its own. Furthermore, existential memory belonged neither exclusively to the family nor to the public realm, but penetrated both spheres.

Medievalism and Classicism

Medievalism proved a compelling mode of commemoration because the main theatres of battle—northern France, East Prussia, and Palestine— triggered cultural memories of medieval battles and campaigns such as Agincourt, Tannenberg, or the Crusades. Apart from Gallipoli (which conjured up the story of Troy), no battlefield had classical connotations.[40] Even so, allusions to antiquity were not entirely absent from commemorative culture. The work of the sculptor H. C. Fehr is a case in point. His

---

[38] J. Assmann 1997, 61.
[39] J. Assmann 1997, 63.
[40] Macleod 2004, 77–8.

memorial for Leeds, dedicated in October 1922, features bronze ideal figures of peace and war. 'That of Peace', the memorial committee elaborated in a press statement, 'is a beautiful draped female figure, holding aloft a palm branch while on the opposite side, a figure of St. George slaying the Dragon typifies War, and the everlasting struggle of good against evil.'[41] Later, Fehr replaced the palm branch with a dove thus underlining the identity of the figure.

Within a few months of the dedication of the Leeds war memorial, an almost identical group of figures, sculptured by the same artist, was unveiled outside Colchester Castle (see Figures 7.3a and 7.3b). Again, the design amounted to a massive reaffirmation of gender stereotypes. St George as 'symbolical of the chivalry and the manhood of England' contrasted with the figure of peace (with a dove perched on one of her fingers) representing 'the Womanhood of England'.[42] Interestingly, Fehr configured the contrast between manhood and womanhood as one between medievalism and classicism. The female embodiment of peace was classicized in her costume while St George as the male embodiment of war and chivalry was clad in medieval armour.[43]

Many a memorial designer revived commemorative forms of antique origin such as obelisks, arches, and cenotaphs. Notably, Sir Edwin Lutyens, the architect of over ninety war memorials including the Cenotaph in Whitehall in the heart of the national capital, drew on classical examples, but reduced them to simpler, minimalistic outlines. For instance, Lutyens' Stone of Remembrance designed for the Imperial War Graves Commission was based on a complex geometry inspired by Hamlin's study of the Athenian Parthenon.[44]

Lutyens' monument for Leicester takes the form of a triumphal arch, a recurring motif in his oeuvre. Some contemporary viewers compared Leicester's Arch of Remembrance to Roman and Byzantine edifices, the Arc de Triomphe in Paris, and Marble Arch in London.[45] Nonetheless, the memorial committee was anxious to link the arch to the history of Leicester Castle, particularly its connection with Simon de Montfort and

[41] West Yorkshire Archive Service, Leeds, LC/TC/R 17, T. W. Harding, press statement, 26 January 1921; ibid., LC/TC/R 26, 'City of Leeds: Unveiling of the War Memorial', 1922, 2.

[42] Essex Record Office, Colchester, Acc. C3, vol. xvii, 358, 'The Colchester War Memorial', *Essex County Telegraph*, 26 May 1923.

[43] On gendered commemorative forms, see Grayzel 1999, 226–42; Carden-Coyne 2003.

[44] Longworth 1985, 36.

[45] IWM, Eph. Mem., K 3819, 'The Form and Order of the Unveiling Ceremony of the Arch of Remembrance: The Memorial to the City and County of Leicester', 1925, 5; 'Leicester Memorial Arch', *The Times* 44066, 6 July 1925, 11.

Figure 7.3a *St George* by H. C. Fehr. Colchester, 1922. (Photograph by S. Goebel)

Figure 7.3b   *Peace* by H. C. Fehr. Colchester, 1922. (Photograph by S. Goebel)

John of Gaunt. In doing so, the committee hoped to please supporters of
the initial idea to utilize land adjoining the castle as a setting. The unveiling programme suggested

> that in the position finally selected it will still have associations with both these
> Patriots, Soldiers, Statesmen, friends of Freedom and outstanding figures in
> Leicester's and in England's story. Simon de Montford was assuredly in some
> way connected with the land on which the Memorial stands, and in the names
> 'Lancaster Road'—and 'Lancaster Gate', which we understand is to be in the
> name of the new approach to the Arch—we are helping to commemorate one
> whom Shakespeare speaks of as 'Old John of Gaunt, time-honoured
> Lancaster'.[46]

Although the Leicester war memorial was undoubtedly neoclassical in
form, the commentary dwelt on a medievalist theme—a concession to the
popularity of medievalism as a mode of war commemoration.
Iconographic evidence studied in isolation can therefore be misleading. It
is important to examine memorials in both their iconographic and discur-
sive contexts: to pay particular attention to the contexts and processes
that connected objects to words. Memorial designs and inscriptions
needed interpretation, and agents of remembrance were anxious to clear
up any ambiguities in the preliminary discussions, fund-raising campaigns, unveiling and dedication addresses, and newspaper articles.

A discrepancy between iconographical and documentary evidence is
noticeable with regard to German monuments featuring nude warriors.
From an aesthetic point of view, these objects reveal the formative influence of Johann Joachim Winckelmann's teaching on the Greek ideal of
male beauty. Even though the iconography may seem unambiguously
classical, figures of nude soldiers frequently carried multiple meanings.
Three examples will stand for many more. The memorial of the Kaiser
Wilhelm Memorial Church in Berlin by Hermann Hosaeus depicted a
nude warrior storming into a phalanx of lance-bearers: a representation
of Winkelried's kamikaze attack at the battle of Sempach in 1386 (see
Figure 7.4). A memorial in Dortmund, Westphalia, featured a naked rider
armed with a spear, but in a poem the horseman was celebrated as a *deutscher Ritter* (a German knight).[47] Similarly, a *Gymnasium* (Grammar
School) in Zwickau, Kingdom of Saxony, chose a nude warrior as a time-
less and 'eternally valid embodiment of the German fighter spirit'. The
warrior was identified as St George, 'a favourite theme of medieval
German art till Dürer', regardless of his nudity.[48]

[46] IWM, Eph. Mem., K 3819, 4.
[47] Stadtarchiv Dortmund, 502, Postcard 'Ehrenmal Reiter', n.d.
[48] BArch, R 32/352, fo. 214, extract from *Zwickauer Zeitung*, May 1923.

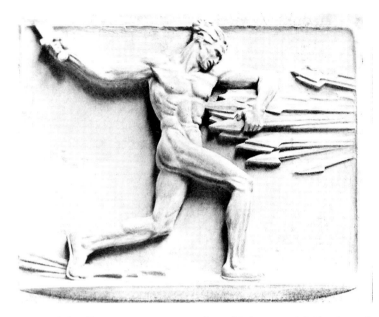

Figure 7.4 *Winkelried* by Hermann Hosaeus. Kaiser Wilhelm Memorial Church, Berlin, 1928. (K. von Seeger, *Denkmal des Weltkrieges* [Stuttgart: Hugo Matthaes, 1930], p. 169)

Classical figures of heroic youth were used for commemorative purposes in Germany, although not as universally as the historian George L. Mosse has claimed.[49] However, Mosse observes correctly that such figures were concentrated in the universities. It is hardly surprising that the principal institutions of the *Bildungsbürgertum* (the educated middle classes)—the university and the *Gymnasium*—would fall back on classical images: they were, after all, the upholders of Latin and Greek.

The war memorial of the University of Munich is a striking example of the invocation of antiquity in commemorative art (see Figure 7.5). The memorial represented a muscular male nude armed with a spear. The figure was a reconstruction of a fifth-century statue by Polykleitos. The dedication accentuated the theme of Greek heroism. It recalled Plutarch's account (*Lycurgus* 21.3) of the antiphonal chanting of the ancient Spartans. The old sing ΑΜΕΣ ΠΟΚ ΗΜΕΣ ΑΛΚΙΜΟΙ ΝΕΑΝΙΑΙ, asserting that they were once young and strong. The young retort that they will grow much stronger than the old had ever been: ΑΜΕΣ ΔΕ Γ ΕΣΣΟΜΕΘΑ ΠΟΛΛΩΙ ΚΑΡΡΟΝΕΣ.[50] In the context of the political culture of the

---

[49] Mosse 1990, 102; see also Mosse 1996. In Berlin, however, figures of nude warriors were exceptionally popular; see Weinland 1990, 108. On Hanover, compare Schneider 1991, 201–3.
[50] Hoffmann-Curtius 1986, 66.

Figure 7.5 *Doryphoros* by Polykleitos. Reconstruction by Georg Römer. University of Munich, 1922. (Photograph by S. Goebel)

Weimar Republic, this inscription had powerful connotations: Germany had been defeated in 1918 and Munich plunged into revolutionary turmoil, but the young generation, the inscription implied, was strong enough to reopen the military campaign, to overthrow the Versailles settlement, and thus to overcome the haunting legacy of defeat. While this was not explicitly stated, few educated observers failed to read between the lines of the Greek inscription.

It was only natural that the intellectual establishment harked back to antique frames of reference; a classical education was an integral part of their class *habitus*. However, academics used classical quotations in order to make thinly veiled calls for remobilization and revenge. Right-wing professors couched revanchist sentiments in classical quotations; Latin and Greek became the language of German revanchism. The University of Berlin, another hotbed of nationalism, also resorted to classical language. *Invictis victi victuri* read the university's commemorative motto. *Invictis* referred to the 'undefeated' war dead; *victi* meant the current generation living in the shadow of a humiliating defeat; and *victuri* suggested the imminence of national regeneration and military victory. The motto was pseudo-classical. It was not borrowed from the corpus of classical literature, but invented by the rector of the university, Reinhold Seeberg.[51] In wartime, Seeberg (as a founder of a right-wing pressure group, the Unabhäniger Ausschuß für einen Deutschen Frieden) had championed expansionist policies; after the war, he was unwilling to concede a humiliating military defeat and to put up with its socio-political consequences.

Seeberg and his successor to the post of rector of the university, the classicist Eduard Meyer, were instrumental in commissioning a monument that translated the dedication *Invictis victi victuri* into memorial art. The design was entrusted to the sculptor Hugo Lederer (the creator of the gigantic memorial to Bismarck in Hamburg), and the architect German Bestelmeyer. Lederer's figure represented a kneeling, nude warrior armed with a round shield. The pose was deliberately ambiguous; the memorial featured a man who had been brought to his knees (analogous to the German nation), but who was in the process of rising to his feet again—a kind of resurrection. The idea for the memorial was inspired by antique sculpture. Lederer was a frequent visitor to the university's archaeological museum: 'I go almost every Sunday ... that is for me like a church service.'[52]

[51] Hoffmann-Curtius 2002.
[52] Cited in ibid., 103.

Notwithstanding the style, at the unveiling ceremony the university memorial was described as a Dürer-like *Ritter* (knight).[53] Representatives of the *Bildungsbürgertum* regarded classicism and medievalism as complementary and not as exclusive modes of commemoration. Consider the memorial of a grammar school in Rheine, Westphalia. It immortalized the names of thirty-five fallen pupils and two trainee teachers who had volunteered between 1914 and 1918—it did not list the names of 113 dead conscripts, who were effaced from memory. The dedication in Latin and German was intended to teach future generations a lesson in selfless service: 'PATRIA VOCAVIT VOS/ WE DIED FOR YOU, DO NOT LAMENT, FIGHT!' Characteristically, the memorial denotes two naked adolescents, a drummer signalling for the attack to begin and a warrior falling under the fatal blow. Regarding the imagery, the school authorities had vacillated between classicism and medievalism. They asked the sculptor to revise his model six times. The first and third proposals showed a medieval knight in armour; the fourth, a nude warrior armed with an antique sword and a medieval shield; the fifth and sixth, nude classical figures. The seventh design was accepted and the memorial unveiled in October 1934.[54]

The naked warrior is practically absent from British memorial art, although educated Britons shared the German *Bildungsbürger*'s adoration of the classics. Inscriptions in Greek or Latin rather than the iconography of public school and 'Oxbridge' war memorials taught the British youth a lesson in antique feats of valour.[55] Take the memorial of the Leys School, Cambridge, a Methodist public school. Horace's motto, 'DULCE ET DECORUM EST PRO PATRIA MORI', is engraved on the monument; this dictum was a popular choice among the British elite despite Wilfred Owen's ironic poem. At the Leys School, the ancient inscription clashes with the medievalist design, for the memorial shows St George as a knight in full armour.[56]

It is not hard to discern a degree of convergence of *habitus* between memory agents of the establishment in Britain and Germany. Yet, in both

[53] Geheimes Staatsarchiv Preußischer Kulturbesitz, I. HA Rep. 76 Va, Sekt. 2 Tit. X Nr. 27 Bd. 6, fo. 151, Friedrich-Wilhelms-Universität zu Berlin, 'Feier bei der Enthüllung des Denkmals für die im Weltkriege gefallenen Studierenden, Dozenten und Beamten der Universität am 10. Juli 1926', 1926; 'Weihe des Ehrenmals der Universität: In Anwesenheit des Reichspräsidenten', *Berliner Lokal-Anzeiger* 322, 10 July 1926.
[54] Dickmänken et al. 1994, 68–77.
[55] See the inventories of Oxford and public school memorials in Utechin 1998; Kernot 1927. See also Jamet-Bellier de la Duboisière 1995.
[56] Hayter Chubb 1925, 32–3. On the Horace quotation, see Koselleck 1998, 34–6.

countries, there were also educated men who objected to this kind of eclecticism. They drew a clear distinction between native and classical, and between Christian and pagan traditions. The British nation's central war monument of 1920, the Cenotaph, was a thorn in the Anglican side. The Cenotaph, literally an 'empty tomb', recalled Greek commemorative forms, without the slightest hint of Christian symbolism.[57] The precariously Established Church responded with the burial of the Unknown Warrior. It was the dean of Westminster who pushed through the tomb in the abbey as a counter-memorial to the Greek 'empty tomb' in Whitehall.

In Germany, too, some people disliked connotations of Greek paganism. In the discussion about a monument at Hagen, Westphalia, Karl Ernst Osthaus tried to exploit popular prejudice to the advantage of his preferred design. Osthaus, a chief patron of modern art in Wilhelmine Germany, agitated against the naturalistic figure of a blacksmith (a symbol of the industrial city at war) by the sculptor Friedrich Bagdons. He denounced the artwork as 'Zeus disguised as a smith' and as a 'showy muscular demigod'.[58] On the other hand, Osthaus endorsed an Expressionist design of a blacksmith by his friend and protégé, Ernst Ludwig Kirchner of the Brücke group. He put Kirchner's figure on a par with one of Germany's finest pieces of medieval sculpture, the statue of St Roland in Bremen of 1404. Osthaus received support from Botho Graef, professor of archaeology and art history at the University of Jena. Graef characterized medieval art as the prime expression of the Nordic–German spirit. The expert certified that the intense artistic quality of medieval German sculpture also pervaded Kirchner's works. Furthermore, Graef echoed Osthaus's disparagement of antiquity. He concluded that Greek gods were alien to German culture: 'We are not Greeks, we do not wish to be and also cannot be Greeks.'[59]

The Great War, the first mass-industrialized war the world had seen, triggered an avalanche of the unmodern. In order to make sense of the carnage of the First World War, the survivors drew on their understanding of a remote yet meaningful past to help people restore and regain control over their lives. The process of joining the existential memory of

---

[57] Lloyd 1998, 87–92; Winter 1995, 102–5. See also Greenberg 1989, 12–20.
[58] K. E. Osthaus, 'Die Kunst und der Eiserne Schmied in Hagen', *Westfälisches Tageblatt*, 214, 13 September 1915; K. E. Osthaus, 'Offener Brief an den Ausschuß zur Errichtung des Eisernen Schmiedes in Hagen', *Westfälisches Tageblatt* 217, 16 September 1915. See Goebel 2004a.
[59] B. Graef, 'Der Eiserne Schmied von Hagen', *Hagener Zeitung* 461, 2 October 1915.

death in war with the cultural memory of the distant past was intended to vindicate memory down the ages. While classicism was by and large confined to academic—and, in Germany, extreme nationalist—circles, medievalism flourished everywhere. Medievalism, this eclectic amalgam of temporal notions, made the catastrophe of war more accessible and enduring.

Instead of saying 'goodbye to all that' and starting afresh, the memorial-makers gazed backwards to misty (medieval) times. Older lines of continuity were reasserted in an effort to turn history into a coherent narrative that overshadowed the rupture of 1914–18. Medievalism (and to a lesser extent classicism) in war remembrance recovered the fallen and the missing soldiers of the First World War and relocated them in the grammar of (medieval) history. It was a search for images and themes that provided historical precedents for an unprecedented human catastrophe. Here was hope of redemption through tradition.

Bibliography

Ackermann, V. 1994. 'La vision allemande du soldat inconnu: débats politiques, réflexion philosophique et artistique.' In *Guerres et cultures, 1914–1918: vers une histoire comparée de la grande guerre,* ed. J.-J. Becker et al. Paris: Armand Colin, 385–96.

Assmann, A. 1993. *Arbeit am nationalen Gedächtnis: eine kurze Geschichte der deutschen Bildungsidee.* Frankfurt am Main and New York: Campus.

Assmann, J. 1995. 'Collective Memory and Cultural Identity.' *New German Critique* 65, 125–33.

——1997. *Das kulturelle Gedächtnis: Schrift, Erinnerung and politische Identität in frühen Hochkulturen.* 2nd edn. Munich: C. H. Beck.

——2000. *Religion und kulturelles Gedächtnis: Zehn Studien.* Munich: C. H. Beck.

Ben-Amos, A. 2000. *Funerals, Politics, and Memory in Modern France, 1789–1996.* Oxford: Oxford University Press.

Bourke, J. 1996. *Dismembering the Male: Men's Bodies, Britain and the Great War.* London: Reaktion.

Cannadine, D. 1981. 'War and Death, Grief and Mourning in Modern Britain.' In *Mirrors of Mortality: Studies in the Social History of Death,* ed. J. Whaley. London: Europa, 187–242.

Carden-Coyne, A. 2003. 'Gendering Death and Renewal: Classical Monuments of the First World War.' *Humanities Research* 10 (2), 40–50.

——2009. *Reconstructing the Body: Classicism, Modernism, and the First World War.* Oxford: Oxford University Press.

Dickmänken, H. et al. 1994. 'Das Langemarck-Denkmal des Gymnasiums Dionysianum in Rheine.' In *Langemarck und ein Denkmal: Nachdenken über unsere Geschichte,* ed. Verein Alter Dionysianer. Berlin: News and Media, 37–100.

Fussell, P. 1975. *The Great War and Modern Memory*. Oxford: Oxford University Press.

Goebel, S. 2004a. 'Forging the Industrial Home Front: Iron-nail Memorials in the Ruhr.' In *Uncovered Fields: Perspectives in First World War Studies*, ed. J. Macleod and P. Purseigle. Leiden and Boston, MA: Brill, 159–78.

——2004b. 'Re-membered and Re-mobilized: The "Sleeping Dead" in Interwar Germany and Britain.' *Journal of Contemporary History* 39, 487–501.

——2007. *The Great War and Medieval Memory: War, Remembrance and Medievalism in Britain and Germany, 1914–1940*. Cambridge: Cambridge University Press.

Grayzel, S. R. 1999. *Women's Identities at War: Gender, Motherhood, and Politics in Britain and France during the First World War*. Chapel Hill and London: University of Northern Carolina Press.

Greenberg, A. 'Lutyens's Cenotaph.' *Journal of the Society of Architectural Historians* 48, 5–23.

Gregory, A. 1994. *The Silence of Memory: Armistice Day 1919–1946*. Oxford and Providence, RI: Berg.

Hayter Chubb, G. 1925. *The Memorial Chapel of the Leys School Cambridge: Its Structure, Windows, Carvings and Memorials*. London: Jenkins.

Heffernan, M. 1995. 'For Ever England: The Western Front and the Politics of Remembrance in Britain.' *Ecumene* 2, 293–323.

Hoffmann-Curtius, K. 1986. 'Der Doryphoros als Kommilitone: Antikenrezeption in München nach der Räterepublik.' In *Arthur Rosenberg zwischen Alter Geschichte und Zeitgeschichte, Politik und politischer Bildung*, ed. R. W. Müller and G. Schäfer. Göttingen and Zürich: Muster-Schmidt, 59–90.

——2002. 'Das Kriegerdenkmal der Berliner Friedrich-Wilhelms-Universität 1919–1926: Siegexegese der Niederlage.' *Jahrbuch für Universitätsgeschichte* 5, 87–116.

Hosaeus, H. 1920. 'Das Denkmal'. In *Vaterländische Bauhütte, Gedenktafeln und andere Kriegerehrenmale: Grundsätze und Ratschläge*, ed. im Auftrage der Staatlichen Beratungsstelle für Kriegerehrungen. Berlin: Deutscher Bund Heimatschutz.

Hynes, S. 1990. *A War Imagined: The First World War and English Culture*. London: Bodley Head.

Inglis, K. S. 1992. 'The Homecoming: The War Memorial Movement in Cambridge, England.' *Journal of Contemporary History* 27, 583–605.

——1993. 'Entombing Unknown Soldiers: From London and Paris to Baghdad.' *History and Memory* 5 (2), 7–31.

Jamet-Bellier de la Duboisière, C. 1995. 'Commemorating "the Lost Generation": First World War Memorials in Cambridge, Oxford and Some English Public Schools.' M.Litt. dissertation, University of Cambridge.

Jeans, H. 1929. 'In Death's Cathedral Palace: The Story of the Unknown Warrior.' *British Legion Journal*, 9 (5), 118.

Kernot, C. F. 1927. *British Public Schools War Memorials*. London: Roberts & Newton.

Koselleck, R. 1998. *Zur politischen Ikonologie des gewaltsamen Todes: ein deutsch-französischer Vergleich*. Basel: Schwabe.

Laqueur, T. W. 1994. 'Memory and Naming in the Great War.' In *Commemorations: The Politics of National Identity*, ed. J. R. Gillis. Princeton, NJ: Princeton University Press, 150–67.

——1996. 'Names, Bodies, and the Anxiety of Erasure.' In *The Social and Political Body*, ed. T. R. Schatzki and W. Natter. New York and London: Guilford, 123–39.

Lloyd, D. 1998. *Battlefield Tourism: Pilgrimage and the Commemoration of the Great War in Great Britain, Australia and Canada, 1919–1939.* Oxford and New York: Berg.

Longworth, P. 1985. *The Unending Vigil: A History of the Commonwealth War Graves Commission 1917–1984.* 2nd edn. London: Leo Cooper.

Lurz, M. 1985. *Kriegerdenkmäler in Deutschland*, vol. 3: *1. Weltkrieg.* Heidelberg: Esprint Verlag.

Macleod, J. 2004. 'The British Heroic–Romantic Myth of Gallipoli.' In *Gallipoli: Making History*, ed. J. Macleod. London and New York: Frank Cass, 73–85.

Mosse, G. L. 1990. *Fallen Soldiers: Reshaping the Memory of the World Wars.* New York: Oxford University Press.

——1996. *The Image of Man: The Creation of Modern Masculinity.* New York: Oxford University Press.

Royal Academy of Arts 1918. *Annual Report 1918.* London: Royal Academy of Arts.

Schneider, G. 1991. *'... nicht umsonst gefallen'? Kriegerdenkmäler und Kriegstotenkult in Hannover.* Hanover: Hahn.

Sherman, D. J. 1999. *The Construction of Memory in Interwar France.* Chicago and London: University of Chicago Press.

Tietz, J. 1999. *Das Tannenberg-Nationaldenkmal: Architektur, Geschichte, Kontext.* Berlin: Bauwesen.

Utechin, P. 1998. *Sons of This Place: Commemoration of the War Dead in Oxford's Colleges and Institutions.* Oxford: Robert Dugdale.

Vandiver, E. 2010. *Stand in the Trench, Achilles: Classical Receptions in British Poetry of the Great War.* Oxford: Oxford University Press.

Weaver, L. 1915. *Memorials & Monuments: Old and New: Two Hundred Subjects Chosen from Seven Centuries.* London: Country Life.

Weinland, M. 1990. *Kriegerdenkmäler in Berlin 1870–1930.* Frankfurt am Main: Lang.

Winter, J. M. 1986. *The Great War and the British People.* Basingstoke and London: Macmillan.

——1995. *Sites of Memory, Sites of Mourning: The Great War in European Cultural History.* Cambridge: Cambridge University Press.

——1999. 'Forms of Kinship and Remembrance in the Aftermath of the Great War.' In *War and Remembrance in the Twentieth Century*, ed. J. Winter and E. Sivan. Cambridge: Cambridge University Press, 40–60.

Ziemann, B. 2000. 'Die deutsche Nation und ihr zentraler Erinnerungsort: Das "Nationaldenkmal für die Gefallenen im Weltkriege" und die Idee des "Unbekannten Soldaten" 1914–1935.' In *Krieg und Erinnerung: Fallstudien zum 19. und 20. Jahrhundert*, ed. H. Berding, K. Heller, and W. Speitkamp. Göttingen: Vandenhoeck & Ruprecht, 67–91.

8

Monument to Defeat:
The Vietnam Veterans Memorial in
American Culture and Society

LAWRENCE A. TRITLE

SOME 58,235 NAMES; 'THE HEALING WALL'; 'the black gash of shame'; the most frequently visited monument managed by the US National Park Service: these are but a few of the many ways the Vietnam Veterans Memorial has been described.[1] It is a place that for me holds personal meaning too: the names of eight classmates from my infantry officers class, a grammar school classmate, and a distant cousin.[2] I have visited the Wall several times, but since the last in 1998 I have avoided going there when visiting Washington. The experience evoked bitter recollection of wasted lives and even antagonism towards those parading through as if on a picnic. My views and reflections about the Wall (as the Memorial will be referred to here for simplicity's sake), and war memorials in general then, are intensely personal. But I hope the perspective brought to this collected study of monuments and memorials, that of a survivor of war and violence, might help shed light on their broader meaning and function in society.

The story of the Wall's construction, and the controversy surrounding its design and its designer, Maya Lin, has been much discussed and a detailed recounting of that story is not attempted here. It should be noted, however, that the Wall's creation and building resulted from a grass-roots campaign initiated by veteran Jan Scruggs, who organized a broad

---

[1] The figure is from Tatum 2003, 4; 'the healing wall', in Shay 2002, 88–9; 'the black gash of shame', in Carhart 1981; 'to heal a nation' is the title of Scruggs and Swerdlow 1985; statistics on visitors in Tritle 2000, 170.

[2] Their names, the importance of which see p. 163 below: Officer Candidate Class 13-69, graduating 12 May 1969, killed and missing were Paul J. Bates Jr, James T. Germain, John J. Kintaro, Warren S. Lawson, Gary R. Mower, William L. Sullivan, Rodney R. Uberman, Morgan W. Weed; grammar school classmate William B. Duncan; cousin Leon P. Tridle.

Proceedings of the British Academy, **160**, 159–179. © The British Academy 2012.

coalition spanning the political spectrum that saw the Wall go up in just two years (1980–82).[3] Scruggs, repelled by the image of American soldiers depicted in Martin Scorsese's film *The Deer Hunter*, vowed to do something to honour and remember those of his friends and all Americans who had died in Vietnam. With a small group of veteran friends and other sympathizers, Scruggs set about forming the Vietnam Veterans Memorial Fund that lobbied Congress for the land on the Capitol Mall and brought in donations from across the country.[4]

Veteran Jan Scruggs's goal was to create a memorial to the men and women who died in Vietnam, to ensure that their names would not be forgotten. While we must accept Scruggs's explanation for his determination to build the Wall and remember the names of the dead, it seems clear that his perspective—that of the veteran and survivor of violence —is but one view of the Wall's meaning. Study of the speeches made by those participating in the various ceremonies held at the Wall (including the statue groups subsequently dedicated) suggests that remembering the dead of Vietnam becomes but part of remembering the Vietnam War itself. This may be seen in the remarks of Presidents Jimmy Carter (1980) and Ronald Reagan (1984), Vice-President (elect) Al Gore (1992), and (then) General Colin Powell (1993). As the dead are recalled, they are recalled in a context that evokes the old imagery of noble sacrifice, of duty, honor, and country.[5] In the same vein, journalist Stanley Karnow explicitly links the War and the Wall, while other visitors, everyday citizens, imagine that the Wall possesses an admonitory power, to make visitors think about entering into a new foreign adventure that sends young Americans overseas into yet new killing zones.[6] For this reason the Wall

---

[3] Among those contributing were entertainer Bob Hope and politician George McGovern, poles apart politically.

[4] See Scruggs and Swerdlow 1985, 7–46.

[5] Carter (1980), 'all of us must be willing to sacrifice to protect freedom and to protect justice'; Reagan (1984), 'you performed with a steadfastness and valor that veterans of other wars salute, and you are forever in the ranks of that special number of Americans in every generation that the Nation records as patriots'; Gore (1992), 'as someone in politics, I believe it's time to put the divisions of the Vietnam War out of our political process'; Powell (1993), 'in fighting for this day [recognition of the nurses who served in Vietnam], you've all performed a tremendous service ... for the women who served with you during the Vietnam years'. For full remarks, see Scruggs 1996, 118–24, 126–32.

[6] Karnow, 'not only does it [i.e. the Wall] recognize the sacrifice of those who died in Southeast Asia, but it also serves as a reminder that the United States can not act as a global policeman ...'; teacher James Miller, 'the Wall honors these brave men and women who died for their country, and forces contemplation of why our country goes to war. Perhaps most importantly, the Wall stands as a constant reminder of that dark era in our nation's history. For if we forget our past mistakes, they will certainly happen again.' See full remarks in Scruggs 1998, 42–4, 69–70.

has to be seen in multiple perspectives: for veterans it is a place where they can see the names of their friends and so remember them. For the non-veteran American population, however, the Wall takes on a more symbolic meaning, that of a monument that commemorates defeat in war, and, for some, a monument that asks visitors to think about the consequences of war.

Building the Wall

No less remarkable than the Wall's rapid building was the identity of the architect, released after the award for the design had been made. Maya Lin was young (only twenty), a woman, and Asian-American—all facts that surprised and angered not a few people, including a number of veterans, for a variety of transparent reasons.[7] The design itself angered some veterans, among them disgruntled competitor Tom Carhart, who infamously dubbed it 'the black gash of shame'—a description that merits a ten-page rebuttal in Jan Scruggs's account of how the Wall came to be built.[8]

As art historian Andrew Butterfield notes, the simplest and oldest form of a monument is a simple stone or pillar known as a megalith, and such monuments date from Neolithic times. These stones are aniconic: that is, they do not depict or symbolise anything. The Wall is such a megalith, a fact revealing perhaps the utter humanity of the design.[9] Many observers and not a few critics of the Wall disparaged it for its apparent V-for-peace shape, but in actuality Maya Lin's intent was to connect the Wall to the Washington and Lincoln memorials at either end of the Mall. As noted in Scruggs's book, the angle formed is 125 degrees, a virtual impossibility for any human hand trying to make a peace sign. The Wall also individualizes the dead by naming them in the order in which they died during the War's course (1959–75). Men are listed with those who died alongside them. For example, the names of the First Cavalry Division's 240 dead from its famous November 1965 battle at the Ia Drang valley are clustered around Panel 3E. Their ranks, meaningless in death, are omitted.

[7] Tritle 2000, 181.
[8] Scruggs and Swerdlow 1985, 80–9.
[9] Butterfield 2003, 28.

In the 1989 film *In Country*, the mother of a dead soldier complains that 'You can't see anything' of the Wall as she and her family arrive for their visit. But as they near, the ground opens up and draws them in until it becomes, as classicist James Tatum notes, 'all-embracing, dwarfing everything in sight once they are at its center'. On leaving the Wall, Tatum goes on to observe, most visitors become aware again of the simplicity of the design, its scale, and its modest low-lying site on the Capitol Mall. This 'telescoping of the mind's eye', as Tatum refers to it, is evoked by the experience of visiting the memorial rather than by its overall dimensions.[10]

Moreover, the highly polished Indian black granite from Bangalore draws you, the viewer, 'in' to the Wall, reflecting you as potentially one of 'them'. The overall design and its startling effect appeared too untraditional and particularly unheroic to critics and some veterans. This impelled additions to the Wall to bring about its 'heroization'. This was accomplished first by the addition to the site in 1984 of three bronze statues cast by sculptor Frederick Hart, another of Maya Lin's critics and unsuccessful competitors. These figures, known to veterans as the 'three dudes', depict a white, black, and nondenominational 'other' soldier. They provide the heroic touch that some veterans want to see whenever they reflect on the Iwo Jima memorial or the heroics of John Wayne and Audie Murphy.[11] In 1994 a second statue group, of two nurses tending to a wounded soldier, was dedicated to the memory of more than 200,000 women who served in Vietnam. Many of these were nurses whose experiences were as horrific as those of combat soldiers. Yet it is my impression that for most visitors to the Wall, who look at and photograph these statues, Maya Lin's design and all the names remain the main attraction.

Naming, Memory, and Mourning

In a May 2004 editorial piece in the *Austin American Statesman*, my classicist friend and commentator Tom Palaima wrote about names and memorials.[12] He mentioned the controversial segment of the ABC evening news programmme *Nightline* in which correspondent Ted Koppel spent

---

[10] Tatum 2003, 3.
[11] It should be emphasized that this is my view, first stated in Tritle 2000, 182. Not all Vietnam veterans would agree, and some would disagree passionately.
[12] Palaima 2004.

nearly an hour reading the names of those American servicemen and women killed during the previous year in Iraq; also noted were the Thiepval memorial at the Somme and, of course, the Wall.[13] Palaima argued that quite simply *this* was the decent thing to do—to remember the names and their number. Such an act of memory is both ancient and most human. Homer's *Iliad* and the Anglo-Saxon epic *Beowulf* are replete with names, and the connection of those names with great deeds is a staple epic theme. The Greek historian Herodotos writes in this same heroic and human tradition, telling of the noble fight and deaths of the 300 Spartans at Thermopylae, and how, in addition to the number, he had learned all the names of the fallen.[14] More recently, in the former Iraqi security prison at Sulaimaniya, a Kurdish prisoner named Ahmed Mohammed wrote on the wall of his cell, 'These were my friends, arrested with me—all were executed'. A simple list of those names followed.[15]

Naming and remembering are acts of decency— these are given substance in Maya Lin's Wall. In reflecting on her design she wrote:

> The use of names was a way to bring back everything someone could remember about a person. The strength in a name is something that has always made me wonder at the 'abstraction' of the design; the ability of a name to bring back every single memory you have of that person is far more realistic and specific and much more comprehensive than a still photograph, which captures a specific moment in time or a single event or a generalized image that may or may not be moving for all who have connections to that time.[16]

Names then preserve memory and memory eases mourning. Remembering the names and perhaps the faces, and for the first time finding peace through this process, is what makes the Wall such a special place for veterans and families alike. But is this memory personal or individual—that is, of the grieving veteran, parent, brother, or sister? Or does the experience of recalling the names take on a larger and collective meaning?[17]

The answer to this last question, at least in the view of Susan Sontag, is no. In her reflective study of images *Regarding the Pain of Others*, she asserts that 'strictly speaking, there is no such thing as collective memory—part of the same family of spurious notions as collective guilt. But

---

[13] The *Nightline* programme was aired on 30 April 2004. Some ABC affiliates chose not to broadcast the programme, claiming that it was purely a political act—apparently insensate to decency and memory.

[14] Herodotus 7.224.1.

[15] Cited in Hedges 2002, 140.

[16] Lin 2000, 9–10.

[17] See, for example, Sturken 1997, 4–7 for a discussion of memory and its varied forms.

there is collective instruction.'[18] She goes on to argue that 'all memory is individual, unreproducible— it dies with each person. What is called collective memory is not a remembering but a stipulating: that *this* is important, and this is the story about how it happened, with the pictures that lock the story in our minds.'[19]

I disagree. First, Sontag ignores that memories can be substantive. One way in which this happens is the role of objects, in which, as Marita Sturken has noted, 'memory is often embodied'.[20] Examples begin with Homer's *Iliad* where the poet records the Cretan hero Meriones wearing a generations-old boar's tusk helmet, one passed on to him by his father but clearly much older.[21] The numerous conflicts of the Greek classical age saw additional examples of objects passed down the generations. One certain example of this occurred after the defeat of the Persians at Plataia (479 BCE). Here the Greek historian Herodotus records how the Greeks found a great mass of loot in the Persian camp. While the Greeks dedicated much of it to the gods (i.e. the sanctuaries at Delphi, Olympia, and Isthmia), as much again made its way into private hands.[22] In this fashion the Persian Wars became substantialized as heirlooms were passed down through the generations just as they have been in many modern American families today.[23] In my own family, for example, there are objects from both World Wars, the Civil War, and even the Napoleonic era. The point here is that such objects become more than interesting curiosities. They become objects that help in fixing or setting memory and bringing a tangible reality to the past.[24]

Objects, however, are not the only way in which a collective memory may be formed or created. It seems that the witnessing of survivors also

[18] Sontag 2003, 85. Note that Sontag does not cite any of the extensive literature that explores the idea of collective memory. See the authors cited in the following note.

[19] Sontag 2003, 86. For a discussion of collective memory (beyond the scope of this essay), the ur-study is that of Halbwachs 1992; other treatments may be found in Crane 1997 and Confino 1997. Both Crane and Confino provide many arguments in support of collective memory's existence *pace* Sontag. See also the discussion of Goebel, Chapter 7, this volume.

[20] Sturken 1997, 19.

[21] Homer, *Iliad* 10.261–70. See also Hainsworth 1993, 179–81, who notes that such helmets were found mostly in the sixteenth and fifteenth centuries BCE, though examples as late as the eighth century BCE are also known.

[22] Herodotus 9.80. Herodotus states that only the Aeginetans bought spoils from the Spartan helots, those charged with collecting the treasure. Much of Herodotus' information, however, comes from anti-Aeginetan sources (particularly the Athenians); moreover, given the great mass of things found it seems unlikely that every item would be tallied for official accounting.

[23] See also Tritle 2000, 171–5, and references to other ancient artefacts and monuments that would have preserved memory of earlier events and persons.

[24] Tritle 2000, 160–1.

serves to preserve, and even push, memory into future generations. This may strike some as debatable. Marita Sturken, for example, has argued that 'survivors of traumatic historical events often relate that as time goes on, they have difficulty distinguishing their personal memories from those of popular culture. For many World War II veterans, Hollywood World War II movies have subsumed their individual memories into a general script.'[25]

I find this assertion questionable, both in terms of my own recollections as well as in what I have seen in my own family. Allow me to explain. During the Second World War my father flew out of a heavy bomber base just outside Norwich (Hethel, home base of the 389th Heavy Bombardment Group). On 5 September 1944, two days before his twentieth birthday, his plane was nearly knocked out of the sky by a flak burst. Picture this: a twenty-ton four-engine bomber knocked upside down and falling like a rock—over 5,000 metres in a matter of a few minutes. Only after his death in 2002 did I learn this story from the plane's pilot, now the only surviving member of the crew.[26] This experience and story will always be that of my father and his crew, but it is one that I can relate to having been in comparable situations. Remembering this story, however, as my students and readers of this chapter do, 'makes it now', observes Vietnam veteran and author Tim O'Brien, and 'sometimes remembering will lead to a story, which makes it forever'.[27]

Memories such as these, I argue, constitute the ingredients of collective memory. This I have also observed in my own teaching of the Vietnam War and how my students learn of the varied experiences and memories of those veterans who speak with them. What they take away with them can only be considered a collective memory. Far from memory dying with each individual, it would seem in reality that memories can and are passed on from one generation to another. Certainly there are differences in the intensity of the memories; that is, in how those memories might be the source of trauma in the person who actually had the experience that created the memory. That said, it remains that another, hearing a father's memories or a teacher's, can make that memory a part of their own memories.

Finally, it must be seen that visiting a monument like the Wall is a personal experience that makes possible a collective one. It is the latter because a tangible object—the Wall—gives substance to collective

---

[25] Sturken 1997, 6, but she offers no evidence in support of her claim.
[26] Recorded in Thomas 1991, 66.
[27] O'Brien 1990, 38.

memories—those of veterans and those with whom they come into contact—that become conscious reality. As Andrew Butterfield argues, 'a
monument is one of the means by which an aggregate of individuals
transforms itself into a community that feels bound together by a common moral experience and a common historical framework. It is proof
that the past is real, that the past is still present.'[28] It should not be thought
that everyone in the community will derive the same experience, or will
have the same emotions and thoughts on any monument like the Wall.
Veterans and civilians will each see something different as each has a different background and range of experiences and these will lead to a variety of reactions and emotions. In essence, the position taken here on what
the Wall represents is similar to what Jay Winter argues for memorials in
Sites of Memory, Sites of Mourning—that they translate individual grief
into public mourning, that there is a universal human desire for psycho-
logical remuneration of loss, in response to the traumatic impact of death
in war.[29]

Veterans and the Wall

Veterans were the prime movers in the building of the Wall. What were
their motivations? The answers to this question are not simple and will
always remain highly individualized, but some of the forces that bring
veterans to the Wall may be noted.

Jan Scruggs reveals one of these in telling of his reaction to seeing *The
Deer Hunter* in 1978, the catalyst in the Wall's creation. Unable to sleep
after seeing the film, Scruggs recalled one terrible night in Vietnam in
which rockets rained down on his base killing and wounding a dozen men,
all his friends. When he came to their aid he found that he had but one
bandage with which to treat them all and did not know where to start—all
he could do was stand there and call for help. The more he thought of this
night, the more he realized that he could not remember the names of the
dead or see their faces. It was this experience that prompted the vow to
make a wall on which to write their names.[30] Beyond recounting this
memory Scruggs does not elaborate. It seems clear, however, that what we

---

[28] Butterfield 2003, 32.
[29] Winter 1995, 223–9; see also Ashplant et al. 2000, 8.
[30] Scruggs and Swerdlow 1985, 7.

see here is simply survivor's guilt, that lingering veteran's burden recounted so often in prose and poetry.[31]

Several paintings commissioned by the Friends of the Vietnam Veterans Memorial confirm the desire of veterans like Scruggs to remember the names and faces of dead friends. In a painting titled *The Grandson He Never Knew*, artist Robert Summers depicts the son of a dead veteran standing before the Wall with his son, who reaches towards the grandfather he never knew, as the grandfather reaches out to him; in the background the grandfather's dead friends hover. In another painting, *Reflections*, Teter depicts a now middle-aged businessman veteran with his hand on the Wall over the names of friends who died: from the Wall, images of those dead friends reach out to him.[32] These and other images of the 'three dudes', in one print looking at the Wall from their vantage point opposite it, demonstrate without question that there is a powerful drive on the part of veterans to remember those who, in the language of Vietnam vets, 'didn't make it back'.

Not long after the Wall's dedication visitors began to leave various objects at the Wall's base. The park rangers in whose care the Wall rests began collecting and storing them as they do today. By 1993, more than 250,000 objects had been left and plans were made to create an exhibit in the Smithsonian Museum where these items could be viewed by the public.[33] Such offerings, as art historian Andrew Butterfield and others including myself have noted, are a basic rite of remembrance, at once acts of love and respect.[34] The objects left include flowers, photographs including those from Vietnam vintage to the present day, medals, including many Purple Hearts suggesting unforgotten acts of self-sacrifice, and even a Harley-Davison motorcycle.[35] The meaning of these is often clear, to establish a connection between the visitor and the dead. At other times the reason for leaving an object—like the Harley!—is more complicated and will always remain known only to the visitor who left it. Again the many things that veterans have left behind confirm that the desire to

---

[31] Examples of this abound, but note the recurrent theme in authors so widely separated in time and place as Homer (*Iliad*), E. M. Remarque (*All Quiet on the Western Front*, *The Road Back*), Robert Graves (*Good-bye to All That*), Larry Heinemann (*Close Quarters*), Bao Ninh (*The Sorrow of War*), and Tim O'Brien (*The Things They Carried*).

[32] A request to Chapter 172 of the Vietnam Veterans of America for permission to reproduce this artwork was apparently denied (as per a telephone conversation of 30 April 2009). I can only surmise that the Chapter's leadership made this decision on the basis of the title of this chapter. So much for people dying in defence of liberty and free speech.

[33] Tritle 2000, 170.

[34] Butterfield 2003, 31; Tritle 2000, 170.

[35] See Allen 1995 for photographs and discussion of the many items left at the Wall.

Figure 8.1   Memorial of the Ia Drang Valley Association, 1st Cavalry Division, at the Vietnam Memorial, Washington DC. (From L. Powell, *Hunger of the Heart: Communion at the Wall* [Dubuque: Islewest, 1995], fig. 89)

remember the names of the dead and to maintain a connection with them is a powerful force in bringing veterans to the Wall (see Figure 8.1).

But what drives so many veterans to make pilgrimage there, to commune with dead friends, and in doing so to remember the trauma of war? Memory and the trauma of war and of loss seem closely connected in the veteran mind, and trips to the Wall, as some letters left there suggest, offer a healing power to old wounds.

Visits to the Wall have actually been incorporated into therapy programmes provided by the Veterans Administration (VA). One such programme, the Veterans Improvement Program (or VIP), at the Boston VA facility, makes an annual trip to Washington and the Wall a formal part of its treatment. Associated with this programme since 1987, Dr Jonathan Shay describes how the visit to the Wall fits into the therapy—required of the veterans are sobriety, self-care, and a commitment to community service—and how the visits are about grieving and healing.[36] Shay observes that the Wall is for these men 'a shrine in the full sense of a sacred precinct, where the power—the fascination and dangerousness—of the holy is present. The living and the dead meet here.'[37] This may sound dramatic, but there is little doubt that for the veteran this is true, and not only the Vietnam veteran. On Memorial Day 2004, the dedication of the World War II Memorial on the Capitol Mall displayed the same intense emotions of veterans now in their seventies and eighties.[38]

The usual routine of the VIP groups is to make the first visit to the Wall at 3 a.m. when the men are literally alone with their memories and each other. Shay has observed how the dynamic at this hour is very different from that when they return in the afternoon. Alone in the dark the experience brings men together, and there is comfort in the company of others who understand the conflicted and conflicting emotions of being there. When they return in the afternoon, there are others—parents and family members of the dead, other veterans not part of their programme, children on school trips, and adult tourists there to see the attraction. Shay has watched the range of reactions:

> Veterans have found great solace in watching groups of school-children, and sometimes speaking with them. The children's 'Thank you' and the poems and stories they leave at the Wall do not provoke any of the bitter reactions that

---

[36] Shay 2002, 169–70.
[37] Shay 2002, 169.
[38] See the account of the dedication, programme, and assembly of veterans and their families by veteran and historian Howard Zinn (2004, 14–15).

the same words from adults sometimes bring: 'Where the fuck were you thirty
years ago'.[39]

There are many things that could be said of these veterans' experiences at
the Wall. Some find in the visit only anger—for something done or not
done, something said or not said. Others feel unworthy of being there in
the company of 'better' men who died—in other words, guilt at having
survived. Again this may sound melodramatic or histrionic, yet in 1918
Wilfred Owen described the same emotions in his poem 'Mental Cases':
'These are men whose minds the Dead have ravished'.[40] Yet that said, for
some veterans the visit or visits often turn into a profoundly healing experience making it possible for them, in a sense, to be made whole again:
that is, to recover their self-esteem and memory, to be able to make sense
of the world around them, to become tolerant of others.[41]

How are such veterans' emotions—especially those of Vietnam veterans—to be explained? While some of it may seem so much narcissism,
there is also the brutal nature of how the war in Vietnam was fought.
While it is a truism that war is brutal or, as Ernest Hemingway put it, a
crime, combat in Vietnam took place in a hostile environment itself.
Moreover, the violence was accompanied by horrific brutalities including
regular summary killing of the wounded and prisoners, extensive killing
of civilians, and mutilation of the dead, all on a scale comparable to that
in the Second World War.[42] This exacted a heavy toll on survivors.

A good example of how survivors responded to the loss of friends is
related by Michael Herr in *Dispatches*—in my view the best work convey-
ing the Vietnam experience. Herr relates the aftermath of the battle fought
in November 1967 at a place called Dak To. Here two battalions of the
173rd Airborne Brigade fought a brutal action with two regiments of the
North Vietnamese Army, and were chewed up in the process.[43] Just to cite
one example, my company commander in Officer Candidate School, CPT
(then LT) Larry Moore, led a platoon of thirty-seven men up the hill:
when he got to the top only seven were left. Herr relates:

[39] Shay 2002, 173.
[40] Owen 1973, 99.
[41] This is an abbreviated list of character improvements cited in Shay 2002, 175.
[42] For the killing of the wounded and mutilations, see Murphy 1993, 83; Tritle 1997, 122–36. For
the killing of civilians, see Sallah and Weiss 2006; Bilton and Sim 1992 (at My Lai). On the
comparable casualty rate of the US Army in Vietnam and the Second World War, see Spector
1993, 317–18.
[43] Murphy 1983, 252–326. The units involved were the 2nd and 4th [Battalions]/503rd Infantry
Regiment, 173rd Airborne Brigade [Separate], versus the 66th and 174th Infantry Regiments of
the North Vietnamese Army. The 173rd's casualties for 19–23 November 1967 totalled 375 killed,
wounded, and missing.

When the 173rd held services for their dead from Dak To the boots of the dead men were arranged in formation on the ground. It was an old paratrooper tradition, but knowing that didn't reduce it or make it any less spooky, a company's worth of jump boots [122] standing empty in the dust taking benediction, while the real substance of the ceremony was being bagged and tagged and shipped back home through what they called the KIA [Killed in Action] Travel Bureau. A lot of people there that day accepted the boots as solemn symbols and went into deep prayer. Others stood around watching with grudging respect, others photographed it and some thought it was a lot of bitter bullshit.[44]

Herr gives one more survivor's comment: 'a dead buddy is some tough shit, but bringing your own ass out alive can sure help you get over it'.[45]

The point here is that grieving did not happen in Vietnam. Lack of time and a military culture that promoted 'payback' as the appropriate response to the deaths of comrades made it impossible for soldiers to indulge their emotions or reflect on the trauma they had experienced and the deaths of friends.[46] They soldiered on and hoped they would survive to the end of their tour of duty, and in doing so shut themselves off emotionally to the terror around them. The catastrophic results of this for the human psyche are plainly evident. The change of character associated with post-traumatic stress disorder (PTSD) that Jonathan Shay describes so eloquently in *Achilles in Vietnam*—the loss of authority over mental functions, particularly memory and trustworthy perception, persistent mobilization of the body for danger, alcohol and drug abuse, and suicidality—are the legacy of combat experience, and not just in Vietnam but anywhere.[47] The sometimes high drama and intense emotions displayed by veterans at the Wall (and elsewhere) then is actually the result of decades-long emotional nihilism finally confronted.

Civilians and the Wall

The powerful drive of veterans to remember their dead friends' names and faces has been noted above. But by far the greater number of visitors to the Wall are not veterans but civilians, often families of the dead but in many more instances visitors who have no personal connection to those remembered. My own and rather cynical view is that most visitors to the

[44] Herr 1977, 23.
[45] Herr 1977, 26.
[46] On this, see the discussion in Shay 1994, 39–68.
[47] See Shay 1994, xx for a full list of the symptoms of PTSD.

Figure 8.2 'Modern day Andromaches mourning'? The Vietnam Memorial, Washington DC. (From L. Powell, *Hunger of the Heart: Communion at the Wall* [Dubuque: Islewest, 1995], fig. 63)

Wall—those with no connection to the dead—go to it as they would any other tourist attraction and walk away with little in the way of understanding of what they have just seen.[48]

Families grieving at the Wall have been caught in photography and depicted in art and film. This is seen in another painting commissioned by the Friends of the Vietnam Veterans Memorial titled *A Touching Moment*, in which an elderly couple see the image of their son and his comrades. My veteran friend and photographer Larry Powell caught an even more moving and tender image of this link, what I have called 'Modern-day Andromaches Mourning'.[49] Here two women sit before the Wall, one supporting the other whose outstretched hand rests on a name (see Figure 8.2). As with the veterans, families too seek to remember the names, the faces, of their loved ones listed on the Wall.

As the veterans are linked to the dead by their offerings at the Wall, so too are the families. Just as it is possible to recognize what a veteran has left behind—medals, 'in country' photographs, and other military-type items—so the families have left appropriately civilian-type objects. These

[48] See Heinemann 2005, 233–8, esp. 237, for similar impressions.
[49] Tritle 2000, 88.

include an unopened package of cookies and Kool-Aid returned to the parents of a soldier killed in action, delivered at last; dolls and teddy bears, and locks of hair left by sisters and daughters of the dead; and, perhaps most haunting, graduation tassels and even diplomas. Other items including Easter baskets and Christmas angels, greetings and holiday cards have also been left by grieving family members.[50]

Among the items left are those from people who have no association with a name. For example, Norman Jewison, who directed the film *In Country* (1989) which concludes with a trip to the Wall by the mother, daughter, and friend of a dead soldier, left some of the movie props. Also left at the Wall was a door on which a Georgia high-school student painted the names of the Vietnam MIAs (missing in action). Such offerings as these have played a part in perpetuating the faith of some Americans who believe, with little or no evidence to support their views, that American POWs continue to be held captive in South East Asia.[51]

How does one explain offerings at the Wall by those who have no connection to any of the dead of Vietnam? Michael Herr closes *Dispatches* with the words, 'Vietnam Vietnam Vietnam, we've all been there'.[52] This is truer in the early twenty-first century than it was in 1977 when Herr wrote these words. Film and other media, the numerous courses that teach 'Vietnam', and the invocation of Vietnam by our politicians—'We've kicked the Vietnam syndrome,' said George Bush in 1991 at the end of the Gulf War— have placed Vietnam in the collective conscience and memory, in spite of Susan Sontag's assertion that there is no such thing. This surely explains why so many unconnected civilians travel to the Wall: it is part of *our* experience as a nation, *our* history as a people.

One Veteran's Observations on the Wall

I would like to close with some personal observations. My first visit to the Wall came in December 1987. On a cold winter's morning I stood there and read the names of my friends—those I had known, the rest friends by association. The experience was not a happy one. It was one filled with anger at the waste and loss, and of guilt at my own survival and escape,

---

[50] Items illustrated, identified, and discussed in Allen 1995.
[51] Allen 1995, 220.
[52] Herr 1977, 260.

though I must confess that I did not know then the reasons for this. That would not come for a decade.

The sense of soldierly camaraderie that made all those named on the Wall my friends and brothers is the bond to those listed on memorials elsewhere. Be it the grave stele of Pollis, a Megarian warrior who fell in the Persian Wars, at the Getty Museum in Los Angeles,[53] the lists of student dead at any of the Oxbridge colleges, or others, including relatives on the *Kriegerdenkmal* in my own ancestral village, there is a link, a sense of identity, with those who died in war. Perhaps most poignantly, this is also about remembering the names of those who have no one else. At home I display the pictures of two great-uncles of my first wife—Robert Oates and Roy Robinson, Canadian soldiers who died in the Great War, aged twenty—who now have no one else to remember them: now you do.

Such identification, in my view, highlights the fundamental difference in how veterans and non-combatants view memorials and those memorialized. This difference is linked to the gulf that separates those who have experienced horrific things and forever remember that experience, and those who have no such experience. I think Siegfried Sassoon put it best in his 1917 statement 'A Soldier's Declaration', in which he protested against the war in the hope that he could 'help to destroy the callous complacency with which the majority of those at home regard the continuance of agonies which they do not share, and which they have not sufficient imagination to realize'.[54]

Many examples of this gulf might be cited. In Larry Heinemann's prizewinning 1986 novel, *Paco's Story*, the sole survivor of a Vietnam battle overhears a young woman reveal her disgust for him, and how she finds not only his scars repulsive, but the very person that he is. Heinemann's tale of survival and the repudiation of the veteran is anticipated by Balzac's *Colonel Chabert*. As James Tatum notes, 'Chabert discovers that, so far as the war dead are concerned, the world would prefer to honor their memory rather than the actual men themselves.' His fate then becomes a *reductio ad absurdum* of the role memory plays in thinking about war.[55]

---

[53] Grossman 2001, 98–100.

[54] Sassoon first published his statement in the *Bradford Pioneer*, the voice of the Bradford Independent Labour Party, Trades Council, and Workers' Municipal Federation; as the accompanying article cited in Graves 1957 [1929], 260 shows, he was critical of the war. For sentiment similar to Sassoon's, see Harrison 2002 [1930], 143–4: to those not participating, 'it's just a war'.

[55] Tatum 2003, 168–9.

The reality of 'Chabert's invisibility' finds its parallel in contemporary American society as seen in the near veneration of the Wall by Americans who visit it in record numbers, and the actual treatment of the veteran population. Visit any large American city and you will notice homeless men—pushing shopping carts containing what passes for all their worldly possessions. The statistics are sobering: veterans constitute 9 per cent of the US population, but 23 per cent of its homeless.[56] According to the US Department of Veteran Affairs, the estimated number of homeless Vietnam veterans is more than twice the number of soldiers—58,000—who died in the war. While most of the homeless veterans are from the Vietnam War, they also include veterans from the Second World War and Korean War, as well as the Gulf War of 1990–91. Even veterans of the current wars in Afghanistan and Iraq may now be found on the streets or coming in for treatment at their local veterans' hospitals.[57] Examples of the former include Vannessa Turner of Boston who returned home injured in the summer of 2003 to life on the street, unable to find a place to live or health care.[58] In fact Americans seem only to notice the veteran twice during the year—on Memorial Day in May and Veterans' Day in November. The rest of the time veterans and their problems are as invisible as Colonel Chabert, and treated little differently. And all the while tourists trudge to the Wall in the nation's capital to read—or gawk in my view—at the names.

Now you may think that the invisibility of the veterans is a social issue, but the treatment of veterans by their own government is not really significantly different or better. This is seen in the continual battle over funding for the Veterans Administration. The budget requested for veterans' care by Congress for the fiscal year 2009 amounted to $93 billion. While this is a great deal of money, much of it in fact goes to the upkeep of the buildings, grounds, and salaries of administrators, with only a small percentage being actually spent on the veteran.[59] Again the contradiction

[56] Information from the National Coalition for Homeless Veterans, www.nchv.org/background. cfm.

[57] In March 2006 it was reported that nearly one-third of troops returning from Iraq sought treatment for their mental health; see Hoge et al. 2006. In October 2006 it was reported that 27 per cent of newly discharged combat veterans filed claims for service-connected permanent disabilities, and some 30,000 Iraq and Afghanistan veterans have sought treatment for PTSD (Shane 2006). At the Los Angeles regional office of the VA, between 12,000 and 15,000 claims for PTSD are filed every month, though many of these will be denied.

[58] Stewart 2004 (also discussing homeless veterans generally).

[59] Of the monies allocated for fiscal year 2007, for example, $38.5 billion included discretionary funding, $42.1 billion entitlements (www.va.gov/budget/summary/index.htm). The VA is the world's greatest buyer of pharmaceuticals and prosthetics and the largest single health-care

between what is done for the living veteran—not much—and the public veneration of the war dead is striking.

Seldom in the USA does the public actually see its survivors of violence. In December 2003, I visited a veteran friend in the Veterans Hospital in Tampa, Florida. Ed Cole had served with the 1st Cavalry Division in Vietnam for what he called a 'cup of coffee'—literally little more than a month. But in that short time he was so badly wounded that he was medevacked to the USA, to the same Bronx VA hospital made famous by Ron Kovic in *Born on the Fourth of July*. In a forty-four-bed ward, Ed was the only man with all four limbs. Thirty-five years later he was being treated for a cancer that was a by-product of exposure to Agent Orange: it claimed his life in the following month. But while walking through the hospital, I found it at once saddening and angering to see other veterans waiting for treatment wearing their tattered old uniforms, men broken in spirit who, though living, remained trapped in the past unable to move forward—in other words the broken remains of the glory of war.[60]

Finally, since the dedication of the Wall a whole generation has grown up and come of age—and learned nothing. In Iraq and Afghanistan in the early twenty-first century the same realities that produced the Wall are being repeated. How many of the young soldiers and marines killed, wounded, and maimed in Fallujah, Baghdad, and countless other places actually visited the Wall? What lessons did they take from it? Not only did these kids not understand why those names were there, but they also fell victim to what Wilfred Owen long ago referred to as the 'Old Lie'—'Dulce et decorum est pro patria mori'.[61] Ernest Hemingway put it a little differently and much harder:

---

system in the world. Modern health care is expensive, but one must wonder if what veterans receive is truly commensurate with their loss and sacrifice.

[60] Since 2003 I have collected many newspaper accounts of US military personnel killed, wounded, and maimed in Iraq and Afghanistan (and stories relating to the Iraqi and Afghani people, who receive comparatively scant notice in US media). Many of these face a life as bleak as those in the Tampa VA hospital, including more than 400 suffering from TBI (traumatic brain injury), the signature wound of the Iraq War (data from Brain Injury Resource Foundation, January 2009). Some of these men and women will require lifelong care. See, for example, Zoroya 2006 and Callaghan 2009.

[61] Owen 1973, 79. The lines are those of the Roman poet Horace, himself a veteran of the Roman civil wars of the late first century BCE (Horace *Odes* 3.2.13–16): 'to die for one's country is seemly and sweet'. Horace repeats the sentiment of the mid-seventh-century BCE Spartan poet Tyrtaeus (10.1–2).

> They wrote in the old days that it is sweet and fitting to die for one's country. But in modern war, there is nothing sweet nor fitting in your dying. You will die like a dog for no good reason.[62]

Instead of glory and honour, what you will find is horror and trauma that will remain part of your life always. Only the dead from today's conflicts can tell what lessons they learned at the Wall. But it seems to me that in honouring and remembering the dead of Vietnam, too little has been done to make visitors aware that war means fighting and fighting means killing—and dying.[63] If more of this could be made evident then perhaps we might see an end to memorials like the Wall.

Note. I would like to express my gratitude and appreciation to Polly Low, Graham Oliver, and P. J. Rhodes, first for their efforts in organizing the July 2004 conference at the British Academy, then editing the conference papers into the present collection. Thanks also to Professor Najwa al-Qattan for several critical readings that improved this chapter. The views and errors are mine alone.

Bibliography

Allen, T. B. 1995. *Offerings at the Wall: Artifacts from the Vietnam Veterans Memorial Collection*. Atlanta, GA: Turner.

Ashplant, T. G., G. Dawson, and M. Roper. eds. 2000. *The Politics of War Memory and Commemoration*. London: Routledge.

Bilton, M. and K. Sim. 1992. *Four Hours in My Lai*. New York: Penguin.

Butterfield, A. 2003. 'Monuments and Memorials: What History Can Teach the Architects at Ground Zero.' *The New Republic*, 3 February, 27–32.

Callaghan, P. M. 2009. 'The Homecoming of José Pequéo.' *The American Legion*, 34–8.

Carhart, T. 1981. 'Insulting Vietnam Vets.' *New York Times*, 24 October, Section 1, 23.

Confino, A. 1997. 'Collective Memory and Cultural History: Problems of Method.' *American Historical Review* 102, 1386–403.

Crane, S. A. 1997. 'Writing the Individual back into Collective Memory.' *American Historical Review* 102, 1372–85.

---

[62] Hemingway 2003, 304, a passage first written in 1935, in 'Notes on the Next War: A Serious Topical Letter'.

[63] Not only this, but no less critical is the failure to remember the other side. It is for this reason that the Turkish memorial at Gallipoli erected by Kemal Ataturk (1934) is so strikingly human. Cf. the closing two sentences of his remembrance: 'You, the mothers who sent your sons from far away countries, wipe away your tears, your sons are lying in our bosom and are in peace. After having lost their lives on this land they became our sons as well.'

Graves, R. [1929] 1957. *Good-bye to All That*. Revised 2nd edn. New York: Doubleday.

Grossman, J. B. 2001. *Greek Funerary Sculpture: Catalogue of the Collections at the Getty Villa*. Los Angeles: J. Paul Getty Museum.

Hainsworth, J. B. 1993. *The Iliad: A Commentary*, vol. 3: *Books 9–12*. Cambridge: Cambridge University Press.

Halbwachs, M. 1992. *On Collective Memory*. Edited, translated, and with introduction by L. A. Coser. Chicago: University of Chicago Press.

Harrison, C. Y. [1930] 2002. *Generals Die in Bed*. Toronto: Annick.

Hedges, C. 2002. *War is a Force That Gives Us Meaning*. New York: Public Affairs.

Heinemann, L. 2005. *Black Virgin Mountain: A Return to Vietnam*. New York: Doubleday

Hemingway, E. 2003. *Hemingway on War*. Edited with introduction by S. Hemingway. New York: Scriber.

Herr, M. 1977. *Dispatches*. New York: Knopf.

Hoge, C., J. L. Auchterlonie, and C. S. Milliken. 2006. 'Mental Health Problems, Use of Mental Health Services, and Attrition from Military Service after Returning from Deployment to Iraq or Afghanistan.' *Journal of the American Medical Association* 295, 1023–32.

Lin, M. 2000. *Boundaries*. New York: Simon & Schuster.

Murphy, E. F. 1993. *Dak To: America's Sky Soldiers in South Vietnam's Central Highlands*. Novato, CA: Presidio.

O'Brien, T. 1990. *The Things They Carried*. Boston, MA: Houghton Mifflin.

Owen, W. 1973. *War Poems and Others*. Edited with introduction and notes by D. Hibberd. London: Chatto & Windus.

Palaima, T. 2004. 'In the Name of Decency, Let Us Acknowledge How Many Are Dying for Us and Who They Are.' *Austin American-Statesman*, 4 May, A11.

Sallah, M. and M. Weiss. 2006. *Tiger Force: A True Story of Men and War*. New York: Little, Brown.

Scruggs, J. C. ed. 1996. *Why Vietnam Still Matters: The War and the Wall*. Washington, DC: Vietnam Veterans Memorial Fund.

——ed. 1998. *Voices From the Wall*. Washington, DC: Vietnam Veterans Memorial Fund.

——and J. L. Swerdlow. 1985. *To Heal a Nation: The Vietnam Veterans Memorial*. Introduction by H. K. Smith. New York: HarperPerennial.

Shane, S. 2006. 'Data Suggests Vast Costs Loom in Disability Claims.' *New York Times*, 11 October, www.nytimes.com/2006/10/11/washington/11veterans.html.

Shay, J. 1994. *Achilles in Vietnam: Combat Trauma and the Undoing of Character*. New York: Atheneum.

——2002. *Odysseus in America: Combat Trauma and the Trials of Homecoming*. New York: Scribner.

Sontag, S. 2003. *Regarding the Pain of Others*. New York: Farrar, Straus & Giroux.

Spector, R. H. 1993. *After Tet: The Bloodiest Year in Vietnam*. New York: Free Press.

Stewart, J. Y. 2004. 'From the Ranks to the Streets.' *Los Angeles Times*, 29 May, A1, A32

Sturken, M. 1997. *Tangled Memories: The Vietnam War, the Aids Epidemic, and the Politics of Remembering*. Berkeley: University of California Press.

Tatum, J. 2003. *The Mourner's Song: War and Remembrance from the Iliad to Vietnam*. Chicago: University of Chicago Press.

Thomas, R. J. 1991. *Haven, Heaven, and Hell: The United States Army Air Force Aircraft and Airmen Interned in Switzerland during World War II*. Monroe, WI: Puka Press.

Tritle, L. A. 1997. 'Mutilation of the Dead in Ancient Greece and Vietnam.' *Ancient History Bulletin* 11, 123–36.

——2000. *From Melos to My Lai: War and Survival*. London and New York: Routledge.

Winter, J. M. 1995. *Sites of Memory, Sites of Mourning: The Great War in European Cultural History*. Cambridge: Cambridge University Press.

Zinn, H. 2004. 'Dissent at the War Memorial.' *The Progressive* 68, 14–15.

Zoroya, G. 2006. 'Slow to Heal.' *Army Times*, 16 October, 20–1.

General Index

The General Index presents names, people, and places as well as selected subjects and themes. The *Index locorum* provides the references to ancient epigraphical and then literary sources mentioned in the book.

Academy (Athens, Greece), 29 fig. 2.7, 30–1
Acropolis (Athens), 58, 147
Adamclissi (Romania), 67–71, 79–86
Aegina, 28 n. 43, 164
Aetolian League, 56–7
Afghan War, 129–30
Agathe Tyche, 45 n. 16
agency, state and individual, 8, 15–16, 115, 123–5
Agent Orange, 176
Agincourt, 141, 146
Agonothetes, 58
Agora (Athens, Greece), 25 n. 36
Agoranomos, 54
Airborne Brigade (167th), 170
Akraiphia (Boiotia, Greece), 41
Alalkomenios (Boiotian month), 49
Alexandria, 47
All Saints' Day, 114
Allia, River (battle), 83
allies, 17
allocation of roles, 91–3
alphabet: *see* lettering
Alsace, 104, 108 n. 37
altars:
  at Adamclissi, 67–71, 85
  of Homonoia (concord), 59
  of Zeus Eleutherios, 48, 59
Amazons, 46, 58
ambassadors: *see* envoys
Amnesty International, 1
Amphictyony, 56
ancien régime, 94, 101
anger, 170, 173–4
Angers, David d' (sculptor), 102
Angoulême, Duc d' (Louis-Philippe de Bourbon), 99
anniversary, commemorative, 44 n. 14, 46, 51, 58–9
  Bastille Day, 107
  of battles, 47
  of battle of Austerlitz, 103
  of battle of Cannae, 85

of battle of Marathon, 47, 50
of battle of Plataia, 47–8, 49
of battle of Salamis, 47, 50
of D-Day, 55
of death, 43
of defeat at River Allia (= dies Alliensis), 83–4, 85
of First Republic (France), 106
of Persian wars, 59
of Victor Hugo's birth, 106
Antigonos Gonatas (King of Macedonians), 46, 57–8
Antigonos Monophthalmos, 45 n. 16
Antonius, Marcus, 64–7, 85
Antony, Mark: *see* Antonius, Marcus
Aphrodisias (Caria, Asia Minor), 54
Apollo, 56–7
  Pythios, 56–7
  Soterios, 56
Apollonios (commander of troops of Metropolis, 133 BCE), 42
Arausio (Orange, France), defeat at, 84
Arc de Triomphe (Paris), 91, 93, 95, 97–9, 102–3, 104–10, 128, 147
arch, 75
  Marble Arch (London), 147
  Menin Gate (Ypres, Belgium), 137
  of Peace (Paris), 98
  of Remembrance (Leicester), 147
  of Titus (Rome), 98
  see also Arc de Triomphe; triumphal arch; Germanicus,
archers, 16
architects, 93, 97, 98–9, 123, 135, 147, 153, 161
architecture:
  neoclassical, 93, 116 n. 11, 137, 150
Argive lettering, 18, 18 n. 20
Argos, 17, 18, 35
Argout, Comte d' (French politician), 99
aristocracy, 92
Aristogeiton (Athenian tyrant-slayer), 24 fig. 2.4

Index locorum